The
Templar
and the
Ark of the Covenant

Also by Graham Phillips

Atlantis and the Ten Plagues of Egypt:
The Secret History Hidden in the Valley of the Kings

The Chalice of Magdalene:
The Search for the Cup That Held the Blood of Christ

The
Templars
and the
Ark of the
Covenant

THE DISCOVERY OF THE
TREASURE OF SOLOMON

Graham Phillips

Bear & Company
Rochester, Vermont

To Yvan

Thanks for your unstinting help

Bear & Company
One Park Street
Rochester, Vermont 05767
www.InnerTraditions.com

Bear & Company is a division of Inner Traditions International

Library of Congress Cataloging-in-Publication Data
Phillips, Graham.
   The Templars and the Ark of the Covenant : the discovery of the treasure of Solomon / Graham Phillips.
      p. cm.
   Includes bibliographical references and index.
   ISBN 1-59143-039-9
   1. Ark of the Covenant. 2. Templars. I. Title.

BM657.A8P45 2004
296.4'93—dc22
                                                        2004012910

Printed and bound in the United States at Lake Book Manufacturing, Inc.

10 9 8 7 6 5 4 3 2 1

Text design and layout by Priscilla Baker
This book was typeset in Sabon, with Baskerville as the display typeface

Contents

Acknowledgments

The author would like to thank the following people for their invaluable help:

Yvan Cartwright for compiling the index, for preparing the illustrations, and for fantastic IT support. Debbie Benstead, without whose help this book would not have been possible. Jane Taylor for permission to use her truly spectacular photographs of Petra. My historical researchers Louise Simkiss and Kellie Knights. Gila Kalimi for Hebrew translations and as advisor on modern Judaism. To all who helped me in Israel and Jordan, especially David Deissmann, Dr. Otto Griver, and Jonathan Warren. To the modest copyeditor who wishes to remain anonymous. To all at Inner Traditions: Vickie Trihy, Jeanie Levitan, Jon Graham, Jamaica Burns, Kelly Bowen, Patricia Rydle, Rob Meadows, and Cynthia Coad. Dr. James Mellor for his scientific analysis and advice, and David Baylis for providing important help into the mystery of Jacob Cove-Jones. Andrew Collins for photography and for invaluable background research, and Sue Collins for extra support and insight. And a very special thanks to Graham and Jodi Russell, without whom the final discoveries would never have been made.

For more information about Graham Phillips, his books,
and his research, please visit his Web site at
grahamphillips.net

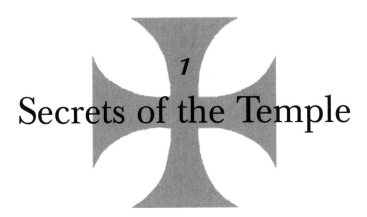

Secrets of the Temple

And there was seen in his temple the ark of his testament:
and there were lightnings, and voices, and thunderings,
and an earthquake, and great hail.

THE BOOK OF REVELATION 11:19

If it existed as it is portrayed in the Bible, the Ark of the Covenant would have to be one of the most extraordinary artifacts in history. It could summon storms, radiate divine fire, level city walls, smash chariots, and destroy entire armies. Moreover, it could summon angels and even manifest the voice and presence of God.

According to the Bible's Old Testament, the Ark was made by the ancient Israelites while they were at Mount Sinai—a sacred mountain in the Sinai Desert—following their escape from slavery in Egypt somewhere around three and a half thousand years ago. It was made on God's instructions given to Moses, the Israelite prophet and leader. It is described in detail as an ornate chest, approximately four feet long, two and a half feet wide, and two and a half feet high, made of wood overlaid with gold. A decorated golden rim ran around the top, and on the sides of the Ark there were rings through which poles could be passed so that it could be carried. On the lid, facing each other, were two golden cherubim, or angels, with their wings outstretched. The most sacred part of the Ark was something that modern English translations of the Bible

1

term a "mercy seat." What exactly this was we are not told, merely that it was located on the lid of the Ark between the wings of the angels.

The Old Testament tells us that the Ark contained the two stone tablets inscribed with the Ten Commandments that were cut by Moses from the living rock at the summit of Mount Sinai. However, protecting the tablets that detail the covenant between the Israelites and Yahweh was not the primary purpose of the Ark—it was used to commune with God. The term *Ark of the Covenant,* by which the artifact is commonly known, is not the name by which it is referred to throughout most of the Bible. Rather, it is usually described as the Ark of Testimony or Testament. In other words, it is a vessel through which testimony or religious instruction is given. According to the Old Testament book of Exodus, when the Israelites are instructed to make the Ark, God tells them:

> I will meet with thee and will commune with thee from above the mercy seat, from between the two cherubim which are upon the ark of the testimony. (Ex 25:22)*

Elsewhere in the Bible, the voice of God is said to come from the mercy seat. For example, in the book of Numbers we are told that Moses "heard the voice of one speaking unto him from off the mercy seat that was upon the ark of testimony" (Nm 7:89). Not only is God heard, he is also seen. In an account in Leviticus, God actually promises to appear: "For I will appear in the cloud upon the mercy seat" (Lv 16:2). In what form God appeared to the Israelites is not clear, but usually the appearance is described as "the glory of the Lord." Leviticus 9:23, for instance, describes how "the glory of the Lord appeared unto all the people." The presence of God also manifests from the Ark as a miraculous cloud or as divine fire. Indeed, from the biblical descriptions, it seems that God is even thought to dwell within the Ark.

The Ark is not only a means of talking to and apparently seeing God, it is also portrayed as the protector of the Israelites in their

---

*All scriptural citations refer to the King James I English Bible.

journeys through the wilderness and as a holy weapon to be used in defeating the Israelites' enemies. Numbers 10:35–36 alludes to the Ark's power as it presides over the Exodus:

> And it came to pass, when the ark set forward, that Moses said, Rise up, Lord and let thine enemies be scattered; and let them that hate thee flee before thee. And when it rested, he said, Return, O Lord, unto the many thousands of Israel.

In the book of Joshua we are told more explicitly that the power of the Ark is even able to bring down the mighty walls of the ancient city of Jericho:

> And Joshua the son of Nun called the priests, and said unto them, Take up the ark of the covenant, and let seven priests bear seven trumpets of rams' horns before the ark of the Lord. And he said unto the people, Pass on, and compass the city, and let him that is armed pass on before the ark of the Lord . . . So the ark of the Lord compassed the city . . . and it came to pass, when the people heard the sound of the trumpet, and the people shouted with a great shout that the wall fell down flat, so that the people went up into the city, every man straight before him, and they took the city. (Jo 6:6–20)

In this account, when the Ark is carried around the city walls, something happens that makes them collapse. We are not told specifically what causes such devastation, but another passage in the Old Testament does describe a destructive power actually emanating from the Ark. According to Leviticus 9:24, "there came a fire out . . . and consumed upon the altar the burnt offerings" that the Israelites had offered to God.

If the Bible is right, the Ark of the Covenant was an object like no other—it was said to be the dwelling place of God and could be used as a dreadsome weapon. However, the Bible fails to reveal what ultimately happened to this, the Israelites' most sacred possession. We are told that the great King Solomon built a fabulous temple especially to house it and at some unspecified time it was removed— but to what location, no one knows. In the Middle Ages the crusader

Knights Templar spent years in the quest to rediscover it, and some legends say that they found it. Until this day, however, the true fate of the Ark of the Covenant remains completely unknown. No wonder, then, that so many biblical scholars, archaeologists, and adventurers alike have spent so much time, effort, and expense trying to find it. Until now, however, its secret hiding place has remained one of history's most enduring mysteries.

This book is an account of my personal quest to solve the secrets of the lost Ark. Did it really exist? If it did, did it have the powers the Bible says? And the greatest enigma of all—what became of it?

It all began during a visit to Jerusalem when I was researching for an altogether different book about the early Christian Church. I had arranged to meet with David Deissmann, an archaeologist from Israel's Hebrew University. David had been involved in excavations around the famous Wailing Wall, and he had offered to take me on a guided tour of the dig, which had, among other things, uncovered a building that may have been used by some of the very first Christians. It was during this tour that my interest in the Ark of the Covenant was first aroused.

Standing on the plaza at the foot of the Wailing Wall waiting for David, I was flanked on each side by dozens of Jewish worshipers rocking rhythmically and reverently before the ancient, weathered stones. Bowing repeatedly, they dutifully recited from prayer books that were cupped devoutly in their hands. Others came and bowed just once or twice before slipping a piece of paper, a written prayer, into cracks in the crumbling facade. This 1,600-foot-long rampart, some 60 feet high, is a place of pilgrimage for Jews from around the world. Also known as the Western Wall, it is all that remains of what had once been Judaism's holiest shrine—the Temple of Jerusalem, originally built by the ancient Israelites to house the Ark of the Covenant.

According to the Bible, the ancient Israelites, also called the Hebrews, were twelve nomadic tribes who conquered and settled in the land of Canaan—what is now Israel, Palestine, and part of

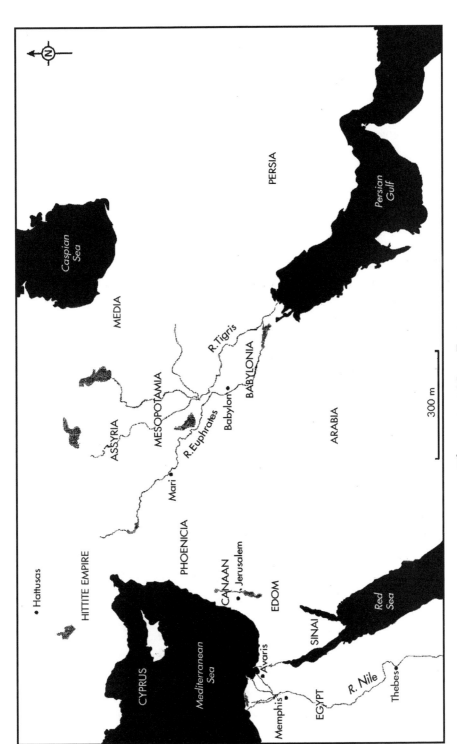

The ancient Near East

Jordan—over three thousand years ago. The invasion culminated with the conquest of the city of Jerusalem by the Israelite king David around 995 B.C. According to the Old Testament second book of Chronicles, David's son and successor, Solomon, built the first temple in Jerusalem so that the Ark had a permanent resting place. As Solomon relates in his own words:

> The Lord therefore hath performed his word that he hath spoken: for I am risen up in the room of David my father, and am set on the throne of Israel, as the Lord promised, and have built the house for the name of the Lord God of Israel. And in it have I put the ark, wherein is the covenant of the Lord, that he made with the children of Israel. (2 Chr 6:10–11)

Built on what is now called the Temple Mount or Mount Zion, a flat-topped hill at the edge of the city, the Jerusalem Temple became the focal point of the Hebrew religion. It has since become the most fought-over patch of land in the world. In ancient times the Egyptians, Babylonians, Persians, Greeks, Romans, and Jews all fought and died for control of it. In medieval times Arabs and Crusaders shed their blood to take, hold, lose, and retake the sacred mount. And today hundreds of Palestinians and Israelis lose their lives each year as both believe that the holy city of Jerusalem is theirs by right. Before Solomon built his Temple here, Jerusalem was just a typical fortified citadel, one of dozens in what was then the land of Canaan. After, it became the center of the world.

When Solomon died around 925 B.C., the largest of the Israelite tribes, the tribe of Judah, split from the other tribes and founded its own independent kingdom and made Jerusalem its capital. Roughly encompassing the area that is now southern Israel, this kingdom was known as Judah—later to be called Judea by the Romans—and its people became known as the Jews. It was the people of Judah who were to develop the early Hebrew religion into what became Judaism and made the Jerusalem Temple into the holiest shrine of the Jewish religion for over three hundred years—until the city was invaded by the Babylonians. At that time thousands of Jews were enslaved and carted off to exile in the city of Babylon (near modern Baghdad), and in 597 B.C. the Babylonian king Nebuchadnezzar ordered the Temple sacked and destroyed. However, in 539 B.C., when the Persians, from what is now Iran, defeated the Babylonians, the Jews were allowed to return to Jerusalem. Soon after, the Temple was rebuilt on a smaller scale, but by the time the Romans took over the city in 63 B.C. the shrine was in an advanced state of disrepair. Paradoxically, the Roman occupation of Judah actually brought greater prosperity to the area than it had known for centuries. When the Jewish aristocrat Herod was installed by the Romans as puppet king, he used this newfound wealth to reconstruct the Temple on an even grander scale than the original. Work began about 19 B.C., and by the time it was completed in A.D. 64, the new Temple was one of the largest and most impressive structures in the entire Roman Empire and had earned its patron the title Herod the Great.

The Jewish historian Josephus, writing around A.D. 90, tells of the astonishing magnitude of the project. The outer walls' dimensions measured approximately 800 by 3,300 feet, creating an incredible outside perimeter of one and a half miles. The walls were almost 100 feet high in places and made from stones, many weighing as much as fifty tons. At the grand entrance to the south end of the town-sized complex, broad flights of steps led upward to the gateways of the Royal Portico—a great columned hall, opening onto the vast outer courtyard. According to Josephus, the massive pillars that supported the portico roof were so huge that it took four men standing with arms outstretched to encircle them. The outer courtyard was large enough to fit thirteen modern football fields and was surrounded on all sides by colonnades. Beneath these covered walkways, which provided shade from the blistering sun, visitors could meet and teachers and students could debate religious issues. Glistening in the middle of the courtyard was the inner Temple complex, built on top of a gigantic stone platform almost 4 feet high. Its walls measured some 500 by 1,000 feet and were about 100 feet in height with defensive turrets at strategic points. At various intervals steps led up the platform to eight huge doors covered with gold and silver plating. The main entrance, the Corinthian Gate, was on the eastern side. Over 50 feet high, its double bronze doors were so heavy, Josephus tells us, that twenty men were needed to push them shut.

Anyone could enter the Royal Portico and the outer courtyard but only Jews were allowed inside the central complex. Notices written in Greek and Latin warned everyone who was not Jewish to keep out under penalty of death. Through the Corinthian Gate, worshipers entered an outer court, some 220 feet square, again surrounded by covered walkways. This was known as the Women's Court, as beyond this court women could not venture. Only men were allowed to climb a further flight of steps and pass through a final gate and stand in the inner court before the Temple itself—an exact reconstruction of Solomon's original Temple as described in the ancient scriptures.

Solomon's Temple had been around 160 feet high and some 1,000 feet square, its walls flanked by columns and its roof surrounded by gilded spikes to prevent birds from perching along its edge. Inside the Temple proper, there was an outer sanctuary, housing braziers for the animal sacrifices required by contemporary religious law, and the high altar, bearing the menorah, the golden seven-branched candlestick that symbolized the presence of God. Finally, beyond this, was the innermost sanctuary called the Holy of Holies: a dark, windowless chamber built to contain the sacred relic that the entire Temple was erected to house—the Ark of the Covenant.

Unfortunately, Herod's new Temple survived for less than a century. According to the New Testament, its destruction was foretold by Jesus during his ministry around A.D. 30. During Jesus's time, shortly after Herod's Temple had been partially completed, religious law impelled every Jew to pay a tax toward the Temple's upkeep once a year, and it could only be paid in silver shekels. For this and other reasons money changers were stationed in the Royal Portico to exchange travelers' coins. In fact, the portico was a hive of industry, as there were also lines of stalls selling sacrificial animals, such as birds, sheep, and goats. Many of the traders charged extortionate commissions and unfairly high prices, taking advantage of the pilgrims, many of whom had spent their savings traveling from far away to worship at the Temple. The traders had to pay for permission to have their stalls in this area and the priesthood was growing rich off the profits. It was thus that matters stood when, according to Saint Mark's gospel, Jesus went into the temple. Finding the entire procedure abhorrent, he "began to cast out them that sold and bought in the temple, and overthrew the tables of the moneychangers, and the seats of them that sold doves" (Mk 11:15). Jesus was so appalled at the corruption of the Temple that he even foretold its destruction: "Seest thou these great buildings? There shall not be left one stone upon another that shall not be thrown down" (Mk 13:2).

About forty years later, Jesus's prediction came true when the Jews revolted against Roman rule and the Romans retaliated. In A.D. 70 the magnificent Temple was reduced to rubble when the Romans looted it of its treasures and burned it to the ground. The Roman emperor even ordered the entire complex to be demolished stone by stone. Only the Wailing Wall still remains. The several courses of stones that now rise above the modern pavement of Old Jerusalem were once part of the western wall of the Royal Portico.

When David arrived, we began the tour of the network of underground tunnels he had helped excavate. Now open to the public, they are entered off to the south of the plaza and skirt the western side of the wall, running for almost a quarter of a mile to the exit on the Via Dolorosa at the northern end of the Temple Mount. Discovered in 1967 by engineers laying water pipes, they turned out to be a complex of passageways and artificial caverns built over eight hundred years ago.

We began by entering an underground vault about forty feet square, which David explained was just one of a series of chambers connected by the stone-clad passageways. They date from the 1180s when the Arab leader Saladin defeated the European Crusaders who had occupied Jerusalem for years. For centuries Jerusalem had been a holy city for Moslems as well as Jews, as the prophet Mohamed was said to have ascended to heaven from the site where the temples of Solomon and Herod once stood. In the seventh century, long after the Romans had brought the last Jewish Temple to ruin, a mosque had been built here, which became one of Islam's most holy shrines. As this shrine had been in its turn desecrated and vandalized by the Crusaders, Saladin ordered it to be lavishly rebuilt, and today it is still the site of the gold-leafed Dome of the Rock mosque. It was during the rebuilding that Saladin decided to completely restructure the surrounding area, which he did by raising the level of the land to accommodate new buildings to be erected around the mosque. This feat was achieved by the construction of a series of vaulted chambers that not only acted as a mean of support but were also used for storage and to house essential water cisterns.

Leaving the vault through a narrow doorway, David led me into a dimly lit tunnel. The temperature dropped sharply and the musty smell of mold and ancient, crumbling brickwork hung in the air. The network of tunnels led from vault to vault until we reached a much larger and differently designed chamber. The others were plain and clearly functional constructions, whereas this was far more decorative, its roof supported by ornamental columns and its walls adorned with dressed stonework of classical design. Known as the Hall of the Hasmoneans, it is much older than the medieval passageways and dates from before the time of Herod the Great. David explained that this had once been a structure at ground level that had been filled in and buried during Saladin's reconstruction of the city. After archaeologists had excavated the building, they concluded that it had originally been a public hall just outside the Temple complex where Jewish pilgrims could rest, eat, and generally prepare for worship. This was the building David had wanted to show me because there was evidence that first-century Christians may also have used it as a meeting place, as early Christian graffiti had been found inscribed on the walls.

David pointed to a pile of large round rocks, stacked in the corner of the chamber. They were *ballisticae*, he told me—stones uses as missiles that were flung from catapults by the Romans when they stormed Jerusalem after the Jewish Revolt in A.D. 70. Being found in the rubble during the excavations, they revealed that the building had been attacked. Perhaps families of ordinary Christians as well as Jews had sought sanctuary here when the legions looted, pillaged, and sacked the city after the ill-fated rebellion. These terrible Roman reprisals not only resulted in the annihilation of the first Christian Church in Jerusalem, David explained, but some scholars believe they were also responsible for the loss of the sacred Ark.

Despite this apparent evidence to the contrary, the Romans were generally tolerant of other religions and allowed conquered nations to continue with their religious practices so long as they paid tribute to the gods of Rome. Elsewhere, this created few problems, as the occupied peoples simply venerated the Roman gods alongside their own. The Greeks, for example, were permitted to continue worshiping their fertility goddess, Artemis, as long as they also consecrated Artemis's temple in Ephesus to the Roman fertility goddess, Diana. The Greeks agreed, and Diana and Artemis were thereafter considered merely different names for the same deity. Such compromise, however, was completely alien to Jewish thought. The Jews could begrudgingly live with Roman administration, but Roman gods were heresy. Despite this, when the Romans annexed Judah in 63 B.C., they not only tolerated Judaism, they even allowed the Sanhedrin—the priesthood of the Jerusalem Temple—to retain considerable political power. They also appointed a Jewish king, Herod, to rule on their behalf and even granted Herod permission to rebuild the dilapidated Jerusalem Temple as one of the grandest structures in the entire Roman world.

Unfortunately, this amicable relationship began to erode a few years after Herod's death when Rome replaced Herod's incompetent successor with a Roman governor. This meant that a Gentile, a non-Jew, was directly ruling Judah—now called Judea—and the holy city of Jerusalem. Anti-Roman sentiments grew over the ensuing decades, and Jewish rebellion finally erupted during the despotic rule of the Emperor Nero in A.D. 66. For four years, rebels managed to hold the city of Jerusalem, but it was retaken by Titus with ruthless efficiency in A.D. 70; thousands of innocent men, women, and children were butchered in the streets. (Subsequent repression resulted in the death of an estimated half million Jews and the dispersal of the Jewish people around the world for almost two millennia. Even the name Judah was erased from contemporary Roman maps, and Jerusalem became part of the Roman province of Palaestina, from which we get the name Palestine.) As part of the reprisals against the rebels, Titus ordered Herod's magnificent new Temple reduced to rubble and its precious treasures carted off to Rome. Some scholars, David explained, believe that the Ark of the Covenant was among them, whereas others believe that it had been safely hidden in a secret chamber deep beneath the Temple Mount long before the Romans descended.

Moving further into the labyrinth of passageways, David and I arrived at yet another chamber, one that seemed to be at the deepest point in the tunnel complex. Here, a simple table strewn with prayer books was illuminated by candles and a dozen or so people were bowing in silent prayer.

"We are now closest to what many Jews believe to be the most holy place on earth," whispered David. He pointed to what appeared to be a bricked-up archway. Somewhere beyond, he told me, was the spot where the Holy of Holies is thought to have been— the sacred chamber directly underneath where the Ark of the Covenant was thought to have been kept.

"Why hasn't it been opened up?" I asked when we moved on. David explained that in the 1980s an influential rabbi organized a dig through the bricked-up archway and into what appeared to be a filled-in passageway behind it. The rabbi was convinced that somewhere below what had once been the Holy of Holies there had been a secret chamber where the Ark was hidden. Once the Temple was destroyed, the hundreds of tons of rubble covering it made it inaccessible for almost two thousand years. Whether or not the rabbi was right and the Ark of the Covenant really was hidden here, he was never to know. Arab protests brought the excavation to a halt. The rabbi's dig was heading right beneath the Dome of the Rock, sacred ground to Moslems, and Jerusalem's Arab population believed that the project was a plot to undermine the mosque's foundations. When they learned of the search, the rabbi was attacked and there was rioting in the streets in which eight people died. The Israeli government decided to order the work to cease and to avoid further trouble sealed the rabbi's excavation with tons of cement.

"I thought the Romans seized all the Temple treasures," I said, wondering why the rabbi should have thought the Ark was still here. I explained that I remembered seeing a scene carved on the Arch of Titus in Rome, a monument erected by that same Titus who demolished the Temple when he succeeded his father as emperor in A.D. 79. The arch shows the menorah and other Temple vessels being carried triumphantly through the streets of Rome during a victory parade after Jerusalem was retaken in A.D. 70. According to some historical sources, these golden artifacts were melted down, sold off, and used to fund the building of the Colosseum.

"Yes, but the scene does not show the Ark," said David. Although, like the rabbi, David thought it unlikely that the Romans took the Ark of the Covenant, he doubted it was still in Jerusalem when the Temple was sacked.

"Some historians have speculated that the Ark was hidden by the priesthood shortly before the sacking of the Temple—perhaps in a cave in the Judean Wilderness to the east of Jerusalem," he said. "This was where some of the Dead Sea Scrolls were hidden around the same time."

Nevertheless, David considered this scenario to be equally unlikely. The Jewish historian Josephus, who lived at this very time, left a detailed description of the Temple rebuilt by Herod, but nowhere does he refer to the Ark. In fact, Josephus states categorically that the Holy of Holies was left empty. It was David's belief that the Ark had already been lost to the Jews well before Herod's time.

"Another popular theory is that the Ark was lost when the Greek king Antiochus IV plundered the Temple in 169 B.C.," said David.

During much of the time of the Second Temple—which began when the Persians allowed the Jewish exiles to return from Babylon in 539 B.C. and ended when the Romans captured Jerusalem in 63 B.C.—the Jews experienced a period of religious autonomy despite Judah's political identity first as a subdistrict of the Persians, then of the Greeks. However, fearing the spread of Judaism, the Seleucid king Antiochus IV reversed this trend and imposed Greek culture on the people of Judah. Jewish practices were forbidden and scriptures were destroyed. Worst of all, in 169 B.C. Antiochus plundered the Jerusalem Temple and erected a giant statue of the Greek god Zeus over the high altar. This so angered the Jews that in 167 B.C. Judas Maccabaeus, the son of the Temple's high priest, led a mass uprising against Seleucid rule. Although the revolt forced Antiochus's successor to reverse the repressive policies and establish a new and tolerant administration in Judah, many of the Temple treasures had been irretrievably lost—including, some believe, the sacred Ark.

As we continued through the seemingly endless maze of passageways, David told me of other theories alleging that the Ark had already been lost centuries earlier. I was becoming so intrigued by the mystery of the lost Ark that I was forgetting my original purpose for the visit.

I was surprised to learn that there were even those who claimed that the Ark that Solomon built the Temple to house was a fake, created to replace the original made at the time of Moses. According to Ethiopian church tradition, Solomon's son Menelik secretly switched the Ark for a replica and took the real one to Ethiopia. The people of the Ethiopian town of Axum believe that it is still housed in their local chapel, although it has never been seen by anyone from the outside world. Unfortunately, as the Axum religious authorities refuse to let anyone inside the inner sanctum of their church, the claim cannot be put to the test.

The most well known theory concerning the whereabouts of the Ark, made famous by the movie *Raiders of the Lost Ark*, places it in the ruins of the ancient city of Tanis in Egypt. This theory proposes that the Ark was plundered by the Egyptians shortly after Solomon's death. According to the Old Testament, the pharaoh Sheshonq I of Egypt attacked Jerusalem, raided the Temple, and plundered its treasures (1 Kgs 14:26). Sheshonq I established Tanis as the new Egyptian capital, and so it is here that Indiana Jones discovers the lost Ark in Steven Spielberg's movie.

This attack on Jerusalem was a historical event recorded by the Egyptians around 914 B.C. However, whatever happened during the raid, the Old Testament writers themselves claimed the Jews still had the Ark after it was over. In fact, 2 Chronicles 35:1–3 makes reference to the Ark still being in the Jerusalem Temple at Passover during the reign of the Jewish king Josiah, three centuries later, around 622 B.C. This, however, is the last Old Testament reference to the Ark of the Covenant in the Jerusalem Temple, and no other contemporary source makes mention of it.

"It's possible that the Ark was removed from the Temple about twenty-five years after Josiah's time," David concluded.

He explained that in 597 B.C. the Jerusalem Temple was looted of its treasures when it was pillaged by Babylonians. Two Old Testament passages, 2 Kings 25:13–15 and Jeremiah 52:17–22, refer to the Babylonians taking away all the sacred vessels that were in the Temple. Nevertheless, if the Old Testament is right, then all the stolen items were eventually returned to the Temple around seventy years later, after Babylon fell to the Persian Empire. The Old Testament book of Ezra refers to the Persian king Cyrus (who was sympathetic to the Jews) seizing the Temple vessels plundered by the Babylonians so that they could be returned to Jerusalem.

"The seized vessels are listed in full in the book of Ezra," said David. "However, there is no reference to the Ark. If the Ark was in the Temple during Josiah's reign, around 622 B.C., then it must have been removed before the Babylonian invasion. There is certainly no reliable record of it ever being seen again."

Finally, we reached the end of the passageways and emerged into the daylight, to be met by two Israeli soldiers armed with Uzi submachine guns. We were now in the Arab Quarter of Old Jerusalem, and all visitors to the tunnels had to be escorted back to the Jewish area of the city. Tensions between Arabs and Jews were running high. Indeed, the present troubles originally began with the rabbi's excavations of the tunnel beneath the Dome of the Rock to search for the Ark. However, fighting in Jerusalem was nothing new. I wondered whether the city would ever have become so contentious had the Temple never been built. Regardless of whatever power the Ark really had, it seems to have shaped the course of history.

"I have no idea whether the Ark was lost, stolen, destroyed, or hidden," said David, when we returned to the Wailing Wall. "All I know is that if it does survive and is ever found, it would be one of the most important archaeological discoveries in history."

David's informative tour had left me fascinated by the Ark of the Covenant. As I looked around me at the worshipers at the wall, at the armed soldiers stationed all around the plaza and heard the call to prayer echoing from the Dome of the Rock mosque, I decided there and then that I would temporarily abandon my other project and try to discover more about the lost Ark. I could never have imagined where the investigation would take me and what it would ultimately lead me to discover.

2
The Ark and Scripture

𝕬 search for the lost Ark was an exciting idea: a lost treasure of immeasurable historical and religious—not to mention monetary—value, credited with spectacular power. First, however, I needed to determine if it really existed. There was no point in looking for an artifact that was only a myth. The awesome events said to have surrounded the Ark of the Covenant certainly seemed mythological. Nevertheless, it did not necessarily follow that the artifact itself was fictitious—perhaps only the accounts of the Ark's power were. Maybe these were religious allegories or legends added on to reliable ancient accounts over the course of time. What I needed to determine—at least to my own satisfaction—was if there was a realistic possibility that this fabulous golden chest was a genuine, historical relic that once stood in the Temple of Jerusalem.

I decided that the best place to examine the surviving historical references to the Ark was at the National Library of Israel in West Jerusalem. Unlike the Old City around the Temple Mount with its ancient monuments, western Jerusalem is a modern city with extruded office buildings and high-rise apartment blocks. At the far southwest corner of the New City is the Valley of the Cross, so named because early Christians believed that this is where the tree grew that provided the wood for the cross of Jesus's crucifixion. Here, beside luxuriant rose gardens filled with outdoor sculptures, is Israel's National Library.

After consulting just a few books, it quickly became apparent

17

that nearly everything that is known about the Ark of the Covenant comes from what Christians call the Old Testament of the Bible. The Bible, as we know it today, is a collection of religious and historical texts compiled into one volume by the Christian Church in the fourth century A.D. Coming from the Greek word *biblia*, meaning "books," it is divided into two sections, the Old and the New Testaments. The New Testament is a purely Christian collection of manuscripts, written in the mid-to-late first century, which record the life and teachings of Jesus and his immediate successors. The Old Testament, however, is taken from a much older collection of Jewish manuscripts known as the Tanak. Early copies of the Tanak vary somewhat in size but include various separate texts, referred to as books—which were originally scrolls—that first came together in one collection around 400 B.C. Written by different scribes and in different periods, these Hebrew manuscripts outline the history of the ancient Israelites and the Jews, concentrating on their faith and relationship with God. Many of the Tanak books were translated into Greek in the third century B.C., and it is from these and fresh Hebrew translations that the Latin Old Testament was compiled by the Roman Catholic Church. This, in turn, was later translated into the worldwide languages of the modern Bible. Today, the most widely used English version of the Bible is the King James translation, which was made for the British king James I in the early 1600s and which includes thirty-nine of the original Tanak books. Luckily, the National Library had a copy on computer, so I was able to quickly look up all references to the Ark and read in detail its extraordinary story.

Precisely when many of the events described in the Old Testament occurred is notoriously difficult to determine as no specific dates are given (the authors rely on internal reference points to show the passage of years). However, the events begin with the creation of the world and end with the Persian occupation of Judah, known from other sources to have occurred during the sixth century B.C. The first book of the Old Testament, the book of Genesis, explains the origin of the Israelites. Most modern historians, however, consider its content to be mainly mythological or religious allegory. Few would accept as historical the Genesis accounts of how God created the world in six days, how the first man and woman were Adam and Eve, or how the whole earth was flooded at the time of Noah. Many would also doubt that the entire Israelite nation descended from one man. (According to Genesis, the twelve Israelite tribes were all descended from the twelve sons of Jacob. Jacob's sacred Hebrew name was Israel—meaning "God saves"—and it is said to have been after him that his descendants were called the Israelites, or "Children of Israel.") However, Genesis does provide some more verifiable data, telling us that Jacob was a Semite, from what is now northern Israel, and that he and his sons settled in Egypt sometime between 1800 and 1700 B.C. From this point on, the Old Testament takes a more historical stance.

The second book, the book of Exodus, recounts the Israelites' slavery in and flight from Egypt. According to Exodus, some three centuries after Jacob's time, an unnamed pharaoh enslaved thousands of Israelites in Egypt because he feared their growing numbers. About a hundred or so years after that—somewhere between 1400 and 1300 B.C.—the Israelite leader Moses was inspired by God to lead his people to freedom. This he did when Egypt was thrown into turmoil by a series of terrible disasters and plagues that allowed the Israelites to flee into the Sinai Wilderness, a huge desert region to the east of the Red Sea. This flight from Egypt is known, not coincidentally, as the Exodus. According to the book of Exodus, the Israelites remained in the Sinai Wilderness for the next forty years, leading a nomadic existence while Moses revealed to them God's laws and founded the Hebrew religion. It is during this period in the wilderness that the Ark is said to have been made. Exodus describes its design in considerable detail, but what the Ark actually did isn't revealed until the next three books of the Old Testament (Leviticus, Numbers, and Deuteronomy), which all cover the forty-year period the Israelites remain in the wilderness.

Deuteronomy describes how, after the Ark was made at Mount Sinai and the two stone tablets inscribed with the Ten Commandments were placed inside, men of the Israelite tribe of Levi (the Levites) were chosen as its priestly guardians. Leviticus describes

God's appearance in a cloud above the Ark, and Numbers describes God speaking from it and the "cloud of the Lord" hovering above it to protect the Israelites when it was carried through the wilderness. It is in Numbers that the Ark is first described being used as a holy weapon to destroy the Israelites' enemies.

In Joshua, the next book of the Old Testament, the Ark enables the Israelites to conquer the Promised Land. The events cover the period immediately after the forty years in the wilderness when the Israelites moved north into Canaan. According to Joshua, the Ark was used to miraculously part the waters of the River Jordan so that the 40,000-strong Israelite army could cross into Canaan and begin their conquest of the region. At the time, many tribes occupied the area, which formed a kind of no-man's-land between the Egyptians' empire to the south and the Hittites' empire to the north. The book of Joshua refers to these tribes—such as the Amorites, the Perizzites, and the Jebusites—occupying strongholds it calls cities, although archaeology has shown that these cities were in fact fortified settlements from which the occupants could control small areas of fertile land in an otherwise inhospitable region.

The first city to be conquered was Jericho, about thirteen miles northeast of Jerusalem. Here the Ark was deployed with devastating results to bring down Jericho's impregnable walls. Repeatedly, the Ark is used as a weapon to destroy enemy armies, not only of the small local tribes but also of the mighty Hittites who occupied the north of Canaan. Originating from what is now Turkey, the Hittites were the strongest military force in the world apart from the Egyptians. The final Israelite victory referred to in Joshua is at Hazor, in the extreme north of what is now Israel, where chariots were burned to ashes and the combined armies of an alliance of tribes were completely wiped out. Following this, the city of Hazor was utterly destroyed and reduced to rubble. We are not told specifically how the Ark defeated these people, but it is clear that its power was catastrophic. According to Joshua, God told the Israelites to remain at least two thousand cubits from it when it is deployed as a weapon. In modern measurement that is almost three and a half thousand feet—well over half a mile.

The next book of the Old Testament is the book of Judges, named after a series of Israelite leaders referred to as judges. It covers a period of some ten generations, in which the twelve tribes of Israel lived a precarious existence in Canaan, surrounded by a number of hostile peoples. According to Judges, during this time the Ark was kept in a temple in the city of Mizpeh, in territory occupied by the tribe of Judah in the south of Canaan. It is only referred to as being used once during this period, again as a weapon, but this time in a civil conflict against the Israelite tribe of Benjamin.

The Ark is next mentioned in the two books of Samuel, which are named after the prophet Samuel, God's chosen spokesman who brings the quarreling tribes of Israel together under one monarchy. The first book of Samuel describes how God spoke to Samuel from the Ark—which was housed in a temple in Shiloh, about twenty miles north of Jerusalem—and appointed him the chief prophet of the Israelites. At this time the main Israelite enemy was the Philistines, whose kingdom of Philistia was along the Mediterranean coast around what is now Gaza. According to 1 Samuel, the Ark failed to work against the Philistines because God was apparently dissatisfied with the Israelites' internal squabbles. The battle was lost, and the Philistines captured the Ark and took it back to their capital city of Ashod. However, when it was put on display in the temple of their god Dagon, the power of the Ark was unleashed, destroying the temple and inflicting on the people of the city a plague of boils that claimed hundreds of lives.

Seeing what the Ark could do, the Philistines decided to try to use it themselves as a weapon against rebellious forces in their city of Ekron. However, although the mighty power of the Ark was unleashed, it was out of control and killed not only the rebels but the Philistines as well. Terrified by the Ark's power, the Philistine king ordered it returned to the Israelites, and it was left in Bethshemesh, a town in the land occupied by the tribe of Judah. Unaware of the danger, some curious locals decided to open it up, resulting in the deaths of over 50,000 people. A party of Levite priests then came to collect the sacred relic, and it was taken to Kirjathjearim, another town in Judean territory. Here it was secretly kept for twenty years, in the hilltop house of a holy man named Eleazar, while Samuel attempted to unify the Israelites. Eventually, Samuel appointed a warrior named Saul as the first king of the united kingdom of Israel, and the Ark was taken from its hiding place and brought to the Judean city of Gibeah.

According to 2 Samuel, after Saul's death, Samuel proclaimed Saul's son-in-law, David, king in Hebron in the south of Israel, whereas Saul's son Eshbaal declared himself king in the city of Mahanaim in the north of the country. The two rival kings' forces met in battle about halfway between the two cities, at a place described as the pool of Gibeon, and here Eshbaal's army was decisively beaten. Now that Israel was united again, as undisputed king, David was able to defeat the Philistines. We are not told whether or not David used the Ark during the civil war or against the Philistines, but after the conflicts were over a victory celebration of dancing and feasting was held before it. During the festivities, a man called Uzzah attempted to steady the Ark when it tipped, and died instantly. After this, for safety, David ordered the Ark to be kept in the house of the Levite priest Obed-edom, where it remained for three months.

One last stronghold was still occupied by foreign forces, right in the middle of Israelite-held territory—the Jebusite city of Jerusalem. It was, however, well defended by massive walls. On this occasion using the power of the Ark was not an option, as David wanted to capture the city intact. Nonetheless, by good fortune and stealth, the Israelites managed to take the city, which David proclaimed the new capital of Israel. The Ark was brought to the city in triumph. On Mount Zion, later to be called the Temple Mount, David erected a tabernacle, or sacred tent, to house the Ark, and the land was consecrated. Here, God spoke to David and told him that he must build a permanent temple for the Ark, but it was left to his son and successor Solomon to carry out the work.

After the books of Samuel come the two books of Kings. They are so called because they deal with the succession of Hebrew kings from David's son Solomon until their eventual destruction by the Babylonians. The second book of Kings doesn't mention the Ark, but 1 Kings describes how Solomon built the Temple specially to house it. When it is placed in the Temple's Holy of Holies, Solomon ordered it opened, and inside he found the two stone tablets inscribed with the Ten Commandments. A miraculous cloud filled the Temple and something described as "the glory of the Lord"— seemingly divine fire—appeared above the Ark.

The remaining books of the Old Testament tell us little more about the Ark, other than recounting what has already been said. As there is no further mention of it being used again, either as a weapon or for communing with God, the general inference among biblical scholars is that its power was lost when the Israelites displeased God by dividing into two separate kingdoms after Solomon's death: the tribe of Judah in the south and the other tribes (still calling their kingdom Israel) in the north. All we can really tell from the Old Testament is that, following the building of the Temple, the Ark remained untouched in the Holy of Holies for some unspecified period of time.

As day's light faded outside the windows of the National Library, I realized that I had no way of knowing whether the ancient Israelites really had possessed what Spielberg's *Indiana Jones* movie refers to as "a radio for talking to God" or whether they had created some kind of futuristic weapon of mass destruction. However, I could at least attempt to determine the historical feasibility of the more likely possibility—namely, that the ancient Israelites fashioned a splendid golden chest as a portable altar to God, the Jerusalem Temple was ultimately built to house it, and over the years myths and legends arose concerning its purported power. The first thing I needed to do was to discover just how accurate the Old Testament is as a historical text. If its account of early Israelite times conflicted with known history or archaeological evidence, then there would be little reason to give much credence to its story of the sacred Ark.

Beginning in the sixth century B.C., various non-Hebrew cultures— the Babylonians, Persians, Greeks, and Romans—recorded what was going on in the area once called Canaan. However, before this time, there is almost no mention of the Israelites by foreigners, such as the Egyptians or Hittites, and nearly all the Jews' own historical records were destroyed by the Romans following the Jewish Revolt in A.D. 66. In fact, the Old Testament is virtually the only pre-Roman history of the ancient Israelites to survive. Although it purports to explain the Israelites' origins and to outline their history for a period of well over a thousand years before Roman times, the narrative is also filled with religious annotations that are, by their very nature, far from objective. Needless to say, it also contains numerous accounts of miraculous episodes that hardly seem credible to the modern mind.

Perhaps the most important question to address concerning the books of the Hebrew Tanak that make up the Old Testament is, When and by whom were they written? As many are named after leading historical religious figures, the impression the reader has is that they were compiled by eyewitnesses to the events over many centuries. Traditionally, the first five books were written by Moses himself and the rest by a variety of Hebrew scribes and prophets. However, although many of the books of the Old Testament refer to a time many centuries earlier, most biblical scholars now believe that they were not committed to writing in their present form until the sixth century B.C.—half a millennium after the Ark is said to have been placed in the Temple of Jerusalem.

Comparative studies of other ancient civilizations suggest that many episodes in the Old Testament could not have been written during the period in which the events are set, as the text contains anachronisms. In the 1970s, for example, archaeologist and scholar Donald Redford drew attention to numerous Egyptian terms and references found throughout the Old Testament that did not exist until 650 B.C. at the earliest. There are many, for instance, in the story of Jacob and his family settling in Egypt, which may have occurred as early as 1800 to 1700 B.C. According to Genesis 37:25, Joseph and his brothers encounter traders, "who came from Gilead with their camels bearing spicery and balm and myrrh, going to carry it down to Egypt." The Egyptians depicted every type of animal in their art, but never once show camels as a means of transport until the mid-seventh century B.C.; instead they show asses being used to carry goods. The oldest literary reference to domesticated camels comes from Arabs around 850 B.C., and not for another two centuries do the Egyptians record their use. Other anachronisms abound. Money in the form of coins is referenced repeatedly, although the oldest known form of coinage was that used by the Lydians, from what is now Turkey, around 650 B.C. On linguistic grounds too, many of the Old Testament texts show evidence of having been composed long after the events they portray. In fact, none of them could have been committed to writing in their present form until at least the eleventh century B.C. as there was no written Hebrew before this time.

From such assorted evidence, most historians now consider the books of the Old Testament to have been written sometime between 650 and 500 B.C. by a variety of Jewish scholars. Although there may have been earlier written or oral accounts from which these texts were transcribed, in the form in which they now survive they are not thought to be a historically accurate record of the early Israelites. Moreover, as they were written for religious purposes, it has even been suggested that the Tanak scripts were allegories and were never intended to be read as a record of real events. Indeed, considering the miraculous episodes the Old Testament portrays, the skeptic can be forgiven for thinking that the entire narrative is no more historical than the mythologies of ancient Greece or Rome. Miracles aside, even the purely practical and military episodes appear highly improbable: It scarcely seems credible that a poorly armed alliance of nomadic Hebrew tribes could have conquered the land of Canaan as the Bible asserts. Surprisingly, however, modern archaeology has shown that a number of principal battles in the Old Testament's account of the Israelite conquest of Canaan were indeed historical events.

According to the Bible, the conquest of Canaan began with the fall of Jericho and its capture by Joshua. Although the story of the miraculous fall of the city walls may have been an exaggeration of events, there is considerable archaeological and scientific evidence that Jericho was destroyed by foreign invaders at the time and in much the way the Bible describes. In 1952 the British archaeologist Kathleen Kenyon excavated a Bronze Age fortification at Tell-es-Sultan near the Dead Sea, thought to be the site of ancient Jericho.

She concluded that from about 1900 B.C. the city was a prosperous walled town, just as the Bible describes, until it was destroyed by fire around 1500 B.C. Remarkably, the city walls did appear to have been leveled flat by some unknown catastrophe. Although Kenyon decided that this was probably an earthquake, it may have been a fortuitous event for the Israelites that inspired a later legend of the Ark's power.

Until recently, few archaeologists saw Kenyon's findings as evidence of the destruction of the city by Joshua and the Israelites, as the Old Testament narrative seems to place the invasion of Canaan at least two centuries later than she had dated the carnage. However, in 1996 radiocarbon tests, at the Center for Isotope Research at Groningen University in Holland, determined a much later date for the destruction of the city. Six separate samples of ancient cereal grains found in the burned layer of the citadel excavation were tested, providing a reliable central date of around 1320 B.C., which did fall well within the period the Bible seems to place Joshua's capture of the city. This, though, is not the only biblical account of a battle of the Israelites' Canaan campaign to have been supported by archaeology.

According to the Old Testament, after the conquest of Jericho there followed a series of battles in which, one by one, the cities of Canaan were taken by the Israelites, ending with the sacking of the city of Hazor, during which its pagan inhabitants were mercilessly slaughtered by Joshua's troops:

> And they smote all the souls that were therein with the edge of the sword, utterly destroying them; there were not any left to breath, and he burned Hazor with fire. (Jo 11:11)

This final stage of Joshua's conquest of Canaan as described in the Bible was not only verified but also dated in the 1950s.

Beginning in 1955, Israeli archaeologist Yigael Yadin began excavating the site of ancient Hazor, modern Tell-el-Qedah, some nine miles north of the Sea of Galilee. Here Yadin unearthed the remains of a huge fortified palace that had been destroyed by fire sometime around 1300 B.C. The dating was made possible by broken Mycenaean (early Greek) pottery found lying in the level of destruction. Such ceramics were popular throughout the Near East during the thirteenth century B.C. but ceased to be imported into Canaan by the twelfth. The destruction of the city had almost certainly been the work of an enemy, rather than accidental, as statues and temple decorations had been deliberately defaced. As the stratum directly atop this one revealed a combination of the remains of hearths, tent bases, and hut footings with a characteristic desert-style pottery, archaeologists concluded that the city was occupied by tent dwellers—a previously nomadic people—after its destruction. Part of the area was rebuilt again as a fortified city in the tenth century B.C., and distinctive artifacts, such as beads, show this to have been the work of the Israelites.

Yadin was satisfied that the discoveries at Hazor matched the biblical account of Joshua's conquest in a number of ways. The conquerors had razed the city just as the Bible says, they had attempted to destroy the cultic practices of the Canaanites as we are told God charged the Israelites to do, and they had been a nomadic people just as the Israelites had recently been. Dr. Yadin was certain that the Israelites had occupied the area from the time of the burning, but had not had the power or motivation to rebuild the city until the creation of the unified kingdom after the time of David.

It seems then, based on archaeological evidence, that the Israelites did conquer Canaan in much the way the Bible relates, sometime during the late fourteenth or early thirteenth century B.C. What, however, of the period when the Hebrew tribes were said to have been united into the kingdom of Israel by David, somewhere around 995 B.C.? As there are very few known non-Hebrew historical texts mentioning the kingdom of Israel at this time, and there is no contemporary reference to King David, many scholars have doubted the existence of either. Perhaps David and the unified kingdom of Israel were simply later legends of a mythical golden age that the Israelites had never really enjoyed. David Deissmann, however, assured me that he could show me physical evidence that went a long way toward proving that King David's campaigns had really occurred.

From my own research into the history of the Ark, I knew that when Saul died, his son Eshbaal became king at the capital of Mahanaim in northern Israel. However, the powerful tribe of Judah anointed David king at the city of Hebron in the south of the country. David's army, led by his commander Joab, marched north and met with the forces of Eshbaal, led by his commander Abner, about halfway between the two capitals. The place where the two armies converged is described as the pool of Gibeon. The two leaders at first agreed to a conference and, together with their officers, they met "at the pool of Gibeon; and they sat down, the one on the one side of the pool, and the other on the other side of the pool" (2 Sm 2:13). However, the conference ended in disarray and a battle ensued: "And there was a very sore battle that day; and Abner was beaten, and the men of Israel, before the servants of David" (2 Sm 2:17).

Although the war continued for some time, the death of Abner and the defeat of his army ultimately resulted in the collapse of the Saul dynasty, and Eshbaal was murdered by two of his officers. With the death of Eshbaal, David was accepted as king of all Israel.

Consequently, the pool of Gibeon is where the fate of Israel is said to have been decided. If the account is true, then it is one of the most important military sites in the biblical Middle East. From the description in 2 Samuel, the pool of Gibeon was situated where the Arab village of el-Jib now stands, some seven and a half miles north of Jerusalem. However, for many years historians seriously doubted the story because there was no evidence that the place had ever been called Gibeon; for their part, archaeologists doubted the account because geological surveys indicated that there could not have been a pool in the area of sufficient size to be noted as a prominent landmark. That was until the 1950s when the site was excavated by the American archaeologist James Pritchard. He astounded all the critics when he uncovered what could well have been described as a pool—a great stone water shaft sunk into the bedrock, some forty feet in diameter and thirty-seven feet deep. It was actually part of an elaborate system to supply water to an adjoining vineyard. It had a spiral stone stairway winding down to the bottom, where a tunnel continued another fifty feet down to a natural reservoir that lay ninety feet below the surface. Furthermore, radiocarbon tests later conducted on organic deposits found during excavations of the adjacent wine cellars dated the site to as early as 1000 B.C., the time of King David. That something that could be described as a pool—and dated to precisely the right period—was found at the site convinced some biblical scholars of the historicity of the Old Testament account. However, skeptics still doubted that it gave credence to the story, as there was no evidence that the site had ever been called Gibeon.

The day after I visited the National Library, David Deissmann took me to Israel's National Museum, which is also situated in the Valley of the Cross. Here he showed me what seemed to be an unimpressive piece of pottery housed in a glass display cabinet along with other dull-looking ceramic artifacts. He explained that the item had been found during a later dig in the area of the water shaft and that it revealed the ancient name of the place. It was a simple clay jar handle, inscribed with the Hebrew words "Vineyard of Gibeon."

"For an archaeologist to find the name of an ancient site at the site itself is almost too good to be true," David explained. "At first, the archaeologist who found it was accused of a hoax. Later, however, no fewer than fifty-six of these inscribed jar handles were found, all marked in the same way. The pool of Gibeon had been buried for centuries before the Samuel text was written, so it must have been composed based on a much earlier account. Strong evidence, in my opinion, that the battle was a historical rather than legendary event."

David had yet another piece of evidence to support the historicity of the Old Testament account of King David's campaign. We left the museum and took a taxi back to East Jerusalem, where David led me to Kidron Valley—to the bottom of Ophel Hill in the southeastern quarter of the Old City. Here, on the dusty escarpment, there was a tiny brick shrine where a line of enthusiastic tourists had formed. The structure was the entrance to a cave that contained a subterranean pool, known by Jews as the spring of Gihon and by Christians as the Virgin's Spring because early Christian legend held that the Virgin Mary washed the swaddling clothes of the infant Jesus here. While we waited our turn to go inside, David told me the Old Testament story of King David's capture of Jerusalem.

According to the account that appears in both 2 Samuel and

1 Chronicles, when David became king, the Jebusite stronghold of Jerusalem still remained, right in the middle of Israelite-held territory. As noted earlier, David was determined to take it and make it the capital of Israel because it was such an easily defended and prosperous city. According to the account, David discovered a secret method of entry into the walled city—through a water shaft or underground gutter that the Jebusites had dug from inside their city down to a spring outside the defensive walls. David offered a big reward to any men who could climb up this shaft and lead an attack on the Jebusite defenders from the inside. This, according to 2 Samuel 5:6–8, is how the city was taken.

"This is another episode in the biblical story of the establishment of the kingdom of Israel that was once considered fanciful," said David.

Once inside the shrine, we made our way along a narrow rock-cut passage that led down to the clear freshwater spring. David pointed to an opening in the roof of the tiny cavern, around which stalactites of green algae hung like Christmas decorations. He explained that in 1876, the British engineer Charles Warren visited the spring and noticed the hole that led up into darkness. As it was large enough for a man to climb into, he decided to investigate. He returned the next day with climbing tackle and made his way up into the opening. It took him a long time to worm his way up a vertical forty-foot shaft, in places barely wide enough to squeeze though, which eventually widened into a sloping passage that ascended a further hundred feet. Finally, he struggled through a narrow crevice that brought him out into daylight at the bottom of a sixteen-foot, brick-lined shaft, overgrown and forgotten, halfway up the hill above the spring.

Immediately, his discovery caused a sensation among biblical scholars of the day. Was this the gutter that David's troops had used to capture the city? There could be little doubt that some ancient inhabitants had gone to considerable effort to dig down through solid rock to connect a shaft to the spring waters at the bottom of the hill. However, there was a serious flaw in this theory as it stood. The walls of ancient Jerusalem were over a hundred feet further up the hillside. The shaft would have been useless to King David, it seemed, as it would not have allowed his men to get inside the city.

However, in 1961 the British archaeologist Kathleen Kenyon was the first to properly excavate the remains of the walls on the crest of the hill. To her surprise, she discovered that they only dated from around 600 B.C. and were probably built in an attempt to defend the city against the Babylonians. Determined to discover the course of the original walls, Kenyon dug at various locations on Ophel Hill. At first she discovered the foundations of a wall some sixty-five feet down the escarpment that had been built around 850 B.C., probably to defend the city against the Syrians. Eventually, a hundred feet further down the hill, she unearthed the foundations of a thick city wall that did date from the eleventh century B.C. She had, she concluded, found the line of the eastern wall of the Jebusite city. Incredibly, it was sixty-five feet below the entrance to the shaft but above the Gihon Spring. This prompted her to excavate the brick-lined shaft that led down into the gutter passage. It was, she discovered, contemporary with the Jebusite wall.

"The shaft existed just as the Samuel account describes. The fact that it would not have led inside the city walls after the ninth century, when the new walls were built, means that the story must have been a contemporary, or near contemporary account. Pretty persuasive evidence that the story is true," David concluded.

I was satisfied that there was no serious reason to doubt that the Israelite conquest of Canaan and the establishment of the kingdom of Israel by King David had occurred basically as the Old Testament described. However, was the Ark of the Covenant equally historical? Regardless of whether or not it did have miraculous powers, had the ancient Israelites really made a splendid golden artifact that they believed harnessed the power of God? Unfortunately, there was no archaeological or historical evidence from the time of the Israelite conquest of Canaan to shed any light on the enigma one way or the other. I needed to look further back—back to the time when the Ark is said to have been made. Was there any historical evidence from the time that Moses is said to have lived to show that the Ark was a historical artifact?

3

Hellfire and Brimstone

According to the Bible, the man divinely inspired to make the Ark of the Covenant was Moses, the prophet who led the Israelites during their escape from slavery in Egypt. Before beginning any search for clues as to the origins, or even the existence, of the Ark at this time, I first needed to ascertain not only when but whether the events of the Exodus occurred at all. The main problem facing any historian is that the period in which the events are set is difficult to determine from Old Testament evidence, and outside textual and archaeological evidence regarding Moses or the Israelites' existence at this early time remains elusive. All we learn from the Bible is that the Israelites had settled in Egypt, in an area called Goshen in the northeast Nile Delta, some four hundred years before the time of the Exodus. For generations they had lived in peace with the Egyptians until an unnamed pharaoh enslaved them. One generation or so later—during the time of another unnamed pharaoh—the events of the Exodus are said to occur. So when exactly was this supposed to have been?

Historically, the Israelites were part of a group of peoples called the Semites who originated in Canaan some four thousand years ago. Both archaeology and Egyptian records have shown that large numbers of Semites did settle in northeast Egypt over a number of centuries until around 1500 B.C., when the Egyptians became embroiled in a series of campaigns against the Semites in Canaan. At this time the pharaoh Tuthmosis III regarded the Semites who remained in Egypt as enemy aliens and many were enslaved and conscripted into work gangs. There is no specific reference to Israelites in Egyptian records, but there are repeated references at this time to a group of foreign workers called Habiru, possibly an Egyptian rendering of the word *Hebrew*. It seems, then, that the Israelite captivity, as described in the Bible, was a realistic historical possibility. What, however, of the Exodus itself?

Biblical scholars once tended to place the Exodus during the reign of the pharaoh Ramesses the Great because the Bible refers to the Israelite slaves being used during building projects in a city it calls Ramesses. The city, previously called Avaris, was rebuilt by Ramesses and renamed after him around 1290 B.C., so at first glance dating the Exodus to Ramesses' reign seems to make sense. However, the Old Testament account was not committed to writing until many centuries later, and the Bible contains many anachronistic place-names. Indeed, the Old Testament book of Genesis refers to Avaris as Ramesses some five hundred years before it could have been so named (Gn 47:11). We know for certain, therefore, that the city was at least once referred to in the Old Testament by the name it only later acquired. The same could equally be the case in the Exodus account. In other words, the fact that the city where the Israelites toiled is referred to as Ramesses does not necessarily mean that the events occurred during the rebuilding of the city under Ramesses II.

Archaeology has now provided evidence that the Exodus story was actually set sometime before the reign of Ramesses the Great. According to the Bible, forty years after the Israelites escaped captivity and left Egypt, they conquered the city of Jericho. The Groningen University radiocarbon dating of the organic remains found there in 1996 dates the Israelite conquest of the city to around 1320 B.C.—over thirty years before Ramesses' reign is known to have begun. If the Bible is right about the fall of Jericho occurring forty years after the Exodus from Egypt, then the Exodus itself must have taken place about 1360 B.C.—around the end of the reign of the pharaoh Amonhotep III. Amonhotep was a powerful king of Egypt who did instigate a massive new building project in Avaris, just where the Bible says the Israelites were forced to work. This, then, would appear to be the period of time the Old Testament authors had in mind for the Exodus story. However, the big question was, Is there any real evidence that the story of Moses and the Israelite Exodus from Egypt really occurred? Many historians have considered it little more than a myth or religious allegory tagged onto history by later generations. If this was indeed a myth, then so, presumably, was the making of the Ark.

At one time I tended to agree with the popular consensus that much of early Old Testament history was little more than mythology—for instance, the plagues of fire from the sky, darkness in daytime, and water turning to blood that are said to have made the Exodus possible. That was until I examined the biblical account in more detail. In the mid-1990s I was working on a book that concerned the 3,000-year-old mystery of an Egyptian tomb. The era of Egyptian history I was investigating included the period in which the Exodus story seems to have been set. To my astonishment, I discovered that a natural catastrophe occurred in Egypt some 2,500 years ago that closely matched the plagues of the Exodus as described in the Old Testament.

According to the Old Testament book of Exodus, God spoke to Moses and told him to lead the enslaved Israelites to freedom. Moses obeyed and confronted the Egyptian pharaoh and demanded that he set the Israelites free. When the pharaoh refused Moses's demands, God is said to have punished Egypt by a series of what the Bible calls plagues: darkness over the land, the Nile turning to blood, fiery hailstorms, cattle deaths, a plague of boils, and infestations of frogs, lice, flies, and locusts. To the modern mind it all sounds very much like myth and legend. However, such events could have been the result of a natural catastrophe such as the gigantic volcanic eruption my research had revealed.

First came the plague of darkness, which might have been the result of a massive cloud of fallout ash. One of the largest eruptions in recent years was the Mount Saint Helens eruption in Washington State in 1980. After the eruption the sun was obscured for hours five hundred miles from the volcano, and after the even larger eruption on the island of Krakatau near Sumatra in 1883, the skies were darkened to a much greater distance—it was actually as dark as

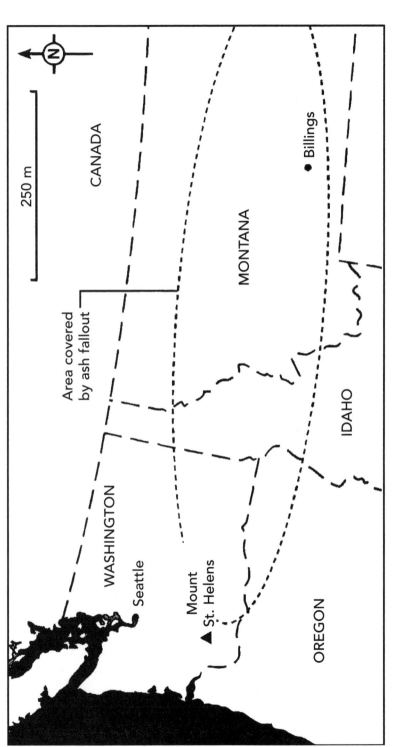

Volcanic fallout from the Mount Saint Helens eruption

night for days on end almost a thousand miles away. According to Exodus 10:21–23:

> And the Lord said unto Moses, Stretch out thine hand towards heaven, that there may be darkness over the land of Egypt, even darkness that may be felt. And Moses stretched forth his hand towards heaven; and there was thick darkness in all the land of Egypt three days: They saw not one another, neither rose any from his place for three days: but all the children of Israel had light in their dwellings.

If just one of the ten plagues matched the effects of a volcanic eruption, it would have been interesting enough; the fact is that they all do. In Exodus 9:23–26, we are told that Egypt was afflicted by a terrible fiery hailstorm:

> And Moses stretched forth his rod toward heaven: and the Lord sent thunder and hail, and fire ran along upon the ground; and the Lord rained hail upon the land of Egypt. So there was hail and fire mingled with the hail, very grievous, such as there was none like it in all the land of Egypt since it became a nation. And the hail smote all throughout the land of Egypt, all that was in the field, both man and beast, and brake every tree in the field.

This, too, could be an accurate description of the dreadful ordeal suffered by the people on the Sumatra coast after the eruption of Krakatau in 1883—pellet-sized volcanic debris falling like hail; fiery pumice setting fires on the ground and destroying trees and houses; lightning flashing around, generated by the tremendous turbulence inside the volcanic cloud. Even after the lesser eruption of Mount Saint Helens in 1980, volcanic debris fell like hailstones, flattening crops hundreds of miles away.

The Exodus account of yet another of the plagues could easily be a report given by someone living in the states of Washington, Idaho, and Montana, over which the volcanic fallout was blown after the Mount Saint Helens eruption: "And it shall become small dust in all the land of Egypt, and shall be a boil breaking forth with blains upon man, and upon beast" (Ex 9:9).

Fine dust causing boils and blains! Hundreds of people were taken to hospital with skin sores and rashes after the Mount Saint Helens eruption, due to exposure to the acidic fallout, and livestock perished or had to be destroyed, due to prolonged inhalation of the volcanic dust. According to Exodus 9:6, "all the cattle of Egypt died."

After the Mount Saint Helens eruption fish also died and were found floating on the surface of hundreds of miles of waterways. The pungent odor of pumice permeated everything, and water supplies had to be cut off until the impurities could be filtered from reservoirs. According to Exodus 7:21:

> And the fish that was in the river died: and the river stank, and the Egyptians could not drink of the river, and there was blood throughout all the land of Egypt.

As well as the gray pumice ash volcanoes blast skyward, many volcanoes, such as Krakatau, have another, more corrosive toxin in their bedrock—iron oxide. (This is the same red material that covers the surface of Mars.) At Krakatau thousands of tons of iron oxide were discharged, killing fish for miles around. It would certainly explain the Exodus reference to the Nile turning to blood, as iron oxide would turn the river red: "And all the waters that were in the river turned to blood" (Ex 7:20).

The remaining plagues do not immediately suggest themselves as having anything to do with a volcanic eruption—frogs, flies, lice, and locusts. However, they can be just as linked with volcanic activity as the fallout cloud itself. Those who have not suffered the dreadful effects of a volcanic eruption might imagine that once the eruption has subsided, the dead have been buried, the injured tended, and the immediate damage repaired, the survivors can begin the task of putting their lives back together, free from further volcanic horrors. This is very often far from true, as the entire ecosystem has been affected. Most forms of life suffer from volcanic devastation but, remarkably, some actually thrive.

When volcanoes blanket the countryside with fallout ash, crawling invertebrates and insects in their larval, chrysalis, or egg stage can remain safe underground, as can burrowing snakes and rodents and frog-spawn, protected under submerged ledges. Insects have a short life cycle and accordingly reproduce at a frightening rate. After such a cataclysm, they have plenty of opportunity to establish a head start on larger predators and competitors. Moreover, compared to bigger animals, they reproduce in vast numbers. Swarming insects are therefore commonly associated with the aftermath of volcanic eruptions. Having survived the calamity, the ashfall forces them to seek out new habitations and food supplies—and heaven help anyone who gets in the way!

An excellent example is the flesh-crawling aftermath of the Mount Pelee eruption on the Caribbean island of Martinique in 1902. Volcanic debris covered the nearby port of Saint Pierre, killing over 30,000 people, but the horrors did not end there. The survivors endured a terrifying episode when huge swarms of flying ants descended upon the sugar plantations and attacked the workers. As people fled for their lives, the vicious creatures seared their flesh with dreadful acid stings. It was no fluke that the insect assaults had followed the eruption; the creatures had attacked before when Mount Pelee had erupted in 1851. On this occasion they not only drove away workers and devoured entire plantations, they were even reported to have attacked and killed defenseless babies while they were still in their cots.

Exodus recounts three types of insects infesting Egypt: lice, flies, and locusts. First there were lice:

> Aaron stretched out his hand with his rod, and smote the dust of the earth, and it became lice in man, and in beast; all the dust of the land became lice throughout all of the land of Egypt. (Ex 8:17)

Then came the flies, as God instructed Moses to tell the pharaoh:

> Behold I will send swarms of flies upon thee, and upon thy servants, and upon thy people, and into thy houses: and the houses of the Egyptians shall be full of swarms of flies, and also the ground whereon they are . . . And the Lord did so and there came a grievous swarm of flies . . . and the land was corrupted by reason of the swarm of flies. (Ex 8:21–24)

Finally, the locusts descended:

> The locusts went up over all the land of Egypt, and rested in all the coasts of Egypt: very grievous were they; before them there were no such locusts as they, neither after them shall be such. For they covered the face of the whole earth, so that the land was darkened; and they did eat every herb of the land and all the fruit of the trees which the hail had left: and there remained not any green thing in the trees, or in the herbs of the field, through all the land of Egypt. (Ex 10:14–15)

Frogs are perhaps the best prepared of all the vertebrates for such cataclysms: Like insects, they produce vast numbers of offspring. Each frog lays literally thousands of eggs. Under normal conditions, this is a biological necessity, as the tiny tadpoles emerge from the eggs almost completely defenseless. When frog-spawn hatches, the local fish are in for a banquet and only one or two of the tadpoles ever survive to become frogs. The only chance the species has for survival is in numbers. However, after the Mount Saint Helens eruption the predatory fish were decimated. The tiny eggs, on the other hand, survived the fallout. By the time they emerged, the hazardous chemicals had washed away down river, but the fish had not yet returned. The result was a plague of frogs throughout much of Washington State. In the thousands, they littered the countryside—there were so many squashed on the roads that they made driving conditions hazardous: They clogged waterways, covered gardens, and infested houses. According to Exodus 8:2–8, this is exactly what happened to the ancient Egyptians:

> [God said,] Behold, I will smite all thy borders with frogs. And the river shall bring forth frogs abundantly, which shall come up and come into thine house, and into thy bedchamber, and upon thy bed, and into the house of thy servants, and upon thy people, and into thine ovens, and into thy kneading troughs [bowls for making bread] . . . And Aaron stretched out his hand over the waters of Egypt; and the frogs came up, and covered the land of Egypt.

Over the years, various scholars have individually attributed the plagues of the Exodus to different natural phenomena. The darkness could have been due to a particularly violent sandstorm, the hail the result of freak weather conditions. The boils could have been caused by an epidemic, and the bloodied river may have been the result of some seismic activity far to the south, near the Nile's source. Swarms of locusts, flies, and infestation of lice would not have been that uncommon. However, the likelihood of them all happening at the same time seems just too remote. A volcanic eruption, however, would account for them all.

The only real problem with attributing the plagues of the Exodus to a volcanic eruption is that Exodus does not present them in the order in which they would naturally have occurred. The darkness and fiery hail should come first, followed by the sores, the bloodied river, the dead cattle and fish, and some time later the frogs and insects. In Exodus they appear in a different order: blood, fish, frogs, lice, flies, cattle deaths, boils, hail, locusts, and darkness. However, the book of Exodus seems to have been written many centuries after the events being described. The account of the plagues might have been handed down orally for many generations and certain details could easily have been shuffled.

When we realize just how similar the plagues of Egypt are to the terrible effects of a volcanic eruption, then these particular episodes of the Exodus account no longer seems so implausible. However, there still remains a big question mark. Did a volcanic eruption actually affect Egypt sometime around 1360 B.C., when the story of the Exodus appears to be set? In a word, yes. While there have been no known volcanoes in Egypt in recent geological times, an eruption large enough to have afflicted the country did occur on the Mediterranean island of Thera sometime around the period in question.

Thera was the southernmost of the Greek Cyclades islands, and in the fifteenth century B.C. it had supported an important trading port of the Minoan civilization, centered on the nearby island of Crete. Today Thera is a crescent-shaped island, now called Santorini, forming a bay over six miles wide. The cliffs surrounding it are ribbed with layers of volcanic debris and once-molten rock, testifying to the island's violent past. The bay itself is actually a crater formed by the ancient eruption, and it is so deep that it is said that no ship's anchor reaches the bottom. In the 1930s, the Greek archaeologist Spyridon Marinatos was the first to propose that at some point toward the end of the Minoan period a gigantic volcanic eruption had all but destroyed the island. In 1956 two geologists, Dragoslav Ninkovich and Bruce Heezen, conducted a survey of the seabed to try to determine precisely how large the eruption had been. From their survey ship, the *Vema*, they were able to ascertain the exact size of the volcanic crater—thirty square miles—and from this they estimate the incredible magnitude of the event.

There are various types of volcanic eruptions: Some spew forth rivers of molten lava, others produce searing mud slides, but by far the most devastating are those in which the pressure of the magma causes the volcano to literally blow its top. Based on the island's crater size, that is what happened at Thera almost three and a half thousand years ago. It was, in fact, the kind of eruption produced by Mount Saint Helens that blasted away the mountainside with the power of a fifty-megaton bomb.

In an instant, on the morning of May 18, 1980, a mass of searing volcanic material blasted outward, killing every living thing within 150 square miles. Thousands of acres of forest were flattened, and molten debris covered everything like the surface of the moon. What had once been a bustling tourist resort over ten miles from the Mount Saint Helens volcano was now covered entirely by pumice. Within a few hours, a cloud of ash some five miles high, containing billions of tons of volcanic material, had rolled five hundred miles east. In three states—Washington, Idaho, and Montana—the massive volcanic cloud covered the sky and day was turned to night. Throughout the whole area ash fell like rain, clogging motor engines, halting trains, and blocking roads. Seven million hectares of lush farmland looked like a gray desert, and millions of dollars worth of crops were flattened and destroyed. Hundreds of people, as far away as Billings in Montana, six hundred miles from the volcano, were taken to the hospital with sore eyes and skin rashes caused by exposure to corrosive fallout. For weeks afterward, fish in hundreds of miles of rivers were found floating on the surface, killed by chemical pollutants in the water.

Mount Saint Helens was one of the most destructive volcanic eruptions in recent years, yet compared with the explosion of Thera, it was tiny. When Ninkovich and Heezen published their findings regarding the Thera eruption, they used the Krakatau eruption as a comparison. In August 1883 when Krakatau exploded with a force twenty times that of Mount Saint Helens, the eruption was heard over three thousand miles away in Melbourne, southern Australia; a volcanic cloud rose fifty miles into the air, and fallout ash covered thousands of square miles. Over 36,000 people perished! It has been estimated by the size of the resultant crater that six cubic miles of volcanic material blasted skyward from Krakatau—yet Thera's crater is almost six times bigger. Accordingly, the explosion would have been heard halfway around the world, volcanic debris would have been hurled over a hundred miles high, and the ash fallout would have covered well over a million square miles.

To get a sense of just how massive this explosion was, consider the last nuclear weapon mankind used in warfare: the atom bomb that totally destroyed half the Japanese city of Nagasaki in 1945. It was a 20-kiloton explosion. Mount Saint Helens exploded with a far greater force of 50,000 kilotons; Krakatau reached an incredible 1,000,000 kilotons; yet Thera dwarfs them all with a staggering 6,000,000 kilotons. It would take six thousand of the most destructive modern nuclear warheads—each with the power to wipe out an entire city—to equal the explosive magnitude of Thera. It is estimated, by comparing the dimensions of the original volcano with the size of the crater, that seventy cubic miles of debris was ejected skyward. Most important, it would have formed a massive fallout cloud that was blown in the direction of Egypt.

The *Vema* survey showed that pumice and volcanic debris from the Thera eruption covered the seabed only to the southeast of the volcano, showing that the prevailing wind had carried the fallout cloud right in the direction of Egypt, some five hundred miles away. Judging by the effects of the smaller Mount Saint Helens and Krakatau eruptions, it is certain that the land of Egypt would have suffered the full horrors of the fallout cloud. The Israelites may well

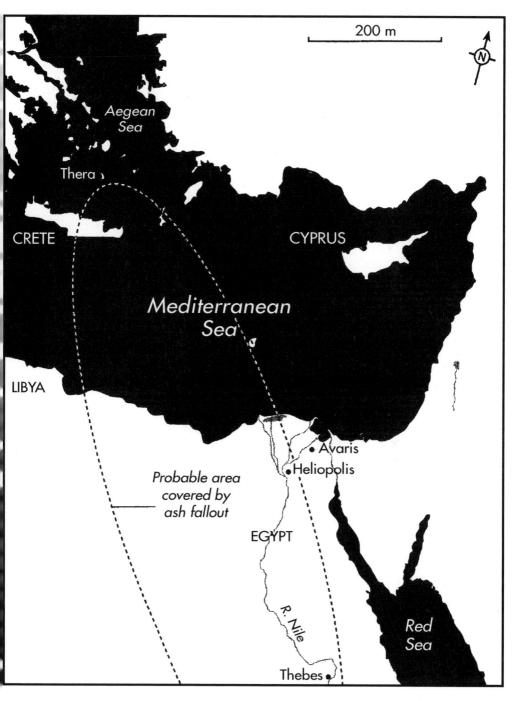

Volcanic fallout from the Thera eruption

have interpreted the event as divine intervention by God, as the chaos caused by the calamity could well have enabled the Hebrew slaves to escape Egypt in pretty much the way the Bible describes.

So it seems that the story of the Exodus from Egypt is nowhere near as fanciful as it was once thought. Indeed, the similarity between the effects of the Thera eruption and the plagues of the Exodus are extraordinary. Nevertheless, the ultimate proof that they were one and the same would come if the eruption could be shown to have occurred at the same time that the Exodus story is set—around 1360 B.C.

Over the years the Thera eruption has been variously dated between 1600 and 1300 B.C. Compelling scientific evidence for a more precise dating, however, appeared in the 1970s with—believe it or not—ice-core samples from Greenland. Every winter a fresh layer of ice forms on the Greenland icecap, creating clearly defined strata, one for each year. Every layer contains trapped air, holding a sample of the earth's atmosphere as it was when the ice formed. In the 1970s, Danish scientists began taking core samples many feet down into the ice to recover a year-by-year record of the earth's atmospheric conditions going back some 100,000 years. The team, led by C. U. Clausen, H. B. Hammer, and W. Dansgard, soon observed that samples from years when there had been major volcanic eruptions, such as the one that destroyed Roman Pompeii in A.D. 79, evidenced high levels of acidity. In an article in *Nature* magazine in November 1980, the team reported that there had been a massive eruption somewhere in the world around 1390 B.C., with a margin of error of some fifty years either way—in other words, sometime between 1240 and 1340 B.C. The only eruption large enough to have resulted in the atmospheric conditions recorded by the Danes, and known by geologists to have occurred within two hundred years either side of this period, was the Thera eruption. This means that Thera could well have erupted at the time the Exodus story appears to be set. Nevertheless, some scholars still opted for a date in the earlier hundred-year-period in which the ice-core findings showed the eruption occurred.

However, archaeological evidence that the eruption had in fact occurred in the second half of this hundred-year period (during the fourteenth century B.C.) had actually been discovered as long ago as the 1930s, but it remained stored away in the vaults of the National Archaeological Museum of Athens, Greece, for almost seventy years. The discovery had been made on the island of Crete.

In the early fourteenth century B.C., Crete was the heart of the Minoan civilization, a race of master shipbuilders that had dominated the Aegean for centuries. Through trade, rather than conquest, the Minoans had become one of the wealthiest powers in the entire Mediterranean. Crete is only seventy miles south of Thera and so would have suffered the effects of the eruption on a far greater scale than Egypt. In fact, archaeological evidence has shown that the eruption so destroyed the infrastructure of the civilization that it totally collapsed. The Thera firestorm may have devastated life on Crete, but the fallout was not the only peril. During the eruption on the island of Krakatau in 1883, a gigantic tsunami—a tidal wave almost a hundred feet high—swept away 165 villages on the Sumatran coast, between twenty and fifty miles from the volcano, and 35,000 people died as a result. Based on the Krakatau event, it has been estimated that a similar tsunami would have thrashed the coast of Crete after the eruption of Thera. The towering wall of water would have lashed the densely populated north coast, sweeping through its ports, pulverizing towns and villages. In the 1930s the Greek archaeologist Spyridon Marinatos found evidence of just such an occurrence. Excavating the site of Amnisos, once the harbor town for the Minoan capital of Knossos, he uncovered a villa whose walls had been strained outward in a curious way. Large upright stones seemed to have been prized out of position as if by some huge external force, suggesting that they had been hit by the backwash of an enormous tidal wave. It seemed that the harbor town had been drowned by a towering wall of water that might well have been the result of the Thera eruption. Moreover, an Egyptian artifact found here by Marinatos suggests strongly that the Thera eruption could not have taken place until at least the reign of the Egyptian pharaoh Amonhotep III who ruled from circa 1385 to 1360 B.C.

Beginning in the seventeenth century B.C., close commercial

contact existed between the Minoans and Egypt. Egyptian pottery turns up frequently in excavations of Minoan sites dating over the next three centuries, and by the fourteenth century B.C., the two cultures had forged strong diplomatic ties. One example of an exchange of goods between the two nations was found by Marinatos in the ruins of Amnisos beneath the fallen walls of the villa—the broken fragments of an Egyptian alabaster jar. It has been housed in the National Archaeological Museum of Athens since the 1930s. However, it was not until 1999 that Greek archaeologist Kristos Vlachos examined the artifact and realized its implications. If Amnisos was destroyed in the Thera event, then as the artifact was found beneath its fallen walls, the eruption could not have taken place until after the jar was made. It was decorated with a hieroglyphic inscription that made reference to the thirty-third year of the reign of Amonhotep's father, Tuthmosis IV. Inscriptions in Tuthmosis IV's tomb in Egypt's Valley of the Kings reveal that this was the last year of his reign, which many Egyptologists date around 1400 B.C., which means that the Thera eruption must have occurred after this date.

So the Thera eruption seems to have occurred during the latter part of the hundred-year dating from the ice-core samples. This means that the volcano erupted between 1385 and 1340 B.C., and the date of the Exodus—1360 B.C.—falls almost in the middle of this forty-five-year period. Considering that ancient Egyptian history spanned over 3,500 years, this match is pretty persuasive evidence that the effects of the Thera eruption and the plagues of the Exodus were one and the same. There is, in fact, one final piece of evidence that places the eruption more precisely in the year 1360 B.C.

Most historians who doubt the Exodus story as a historical event point to the fact that there is no historical mention of it in the records of ancient Egypt. Surely, they argue, such monumental events would have been recorded. However, most Egyptian writings that survive are inscriptions on stone monuments and tombs. These were almost exclusively of a religious nature or were written to commemorate the accomplishments of the pharaohs: battles won, captives taken, and possessions acquired. Day-to-day records that might have included historical reference to the Thera eruption would have been on perishable papyrus (an early form of paper) and few of these have survived. There is, however, indirect contemporary evidence that an unprecedented catastrophe did occur during the last year of the reign of Amonhotep III, in 1360 B.C.

In the last year of his reign, Amonhotep III erected literally hundreds of statues to honor the goddess Sekhmet. At Asher, just to the south of the contemporary Egyptian capital of Thebes, Amonhotep was in the process of rebuilding a temple to the chief goddess Mut, when he suddenly reconsecrated it as a temple to Sekhmet. Furthermore, inscriptions reveal that he decreed that Sekhmet should replace Mut as the principal goddess. He also ordered the erection of literally hundreds of statues to the goddess. So many statues of Sekhmet did he erect, here and elsewhere, that nearly every Egyptological collection in the world can boast at least one example. The British Museum has the largest number: over thirty specimens in various states of preservation. Hundreds still remain in situ in Egypt, the majority being at the temple of Luxor in southern Egypt. It has been estimated that there were originally around seven hundred here alone. In fact, as the Egyptologist Cyril Aldred pointed out in 1988, no other deity of ancient Egypt is represented by so many large-scale statues—and nearly all of them were erected by order of Amonhotep III. These statues of Sekhmet are a clear indication that, despite the apparent stability and wealth of the country, something was wrong. Sekhmet was the goddess of devastation!

Why these monumental statues of the goddess exist in such unrivaled numbers has never been satisfactorily explained. The fact that Amonhotep erected more statues to her—by far—than he did to the chief god Amun, suggests that something had occurred to make him question the power of the principal deity. Sekhmet was represented as a lioness or a woman with a lion's head. In Egyptian mythology she was the daughter of the sun god Ra and she had once almost annihilated mankind. According to the myth she had obscured the sun and rained down fire from heaven, and humanity was only saved through Ra's personal intervention. Sekhmet's mythical vengeance is markedly similar to the calamity that would have been caused by the Thera eruption. Believing her responsible for the catastrophe, Amonhotep may well have erected the statues in an attempt to appease the goddess. We now know for certain that the eruption happened sometime between 1385 and 1340 B.C., and we know for certain that it would have devastated Egypt. Given other clues that the eruption happened during Amonhotep's reign, the fact that he erected hundreds of statues to the goddess of devastation in the year 1360 is compelling evidence that this is precisely when the event actually occurred.

I was convinced that the story of the Exodus was based on real, historical events that occurred around 1360 B.C. The Old Testament story of the Israelite invasion of Canaan a few years later seemed equally historical, as was the establishment of the kingdom of Israel under King David three centuries after that. There could be little doubt that the historical backdrop to the biblical events in which the Ark plays a central role was real enough. In its own right, this gave greater credence to the Ark as a historical artifact. However, it still did not prove that the Ark existed. I needed to examine in more detail the man at the very heart of the Ark mystery—Moses himself. Did *he* really exist? Or was he simply a legend—the personification of a religious system that actually developed many years later? Furthermore, if he did exist, was there any historical precedent for his seemingly unique creation, the Ark of the Covenant?

4

Moses and Yahweh

efore I could reach an informed opinion about whether the Ark of the Covenant was a historical artifact or a fabulous legend, I had to try to answer two last, crucial questions. First, did Moses, the man who is said to have inspired its making, really exist; and second, was the Hebrew religion, for which it was said to have been the holiest relic, really in existence at the time the Exodus seems to have occurred? If the answer to these questions, particularly the second one, was no, then it would seem most unlikely that the Ark was real. It would have served no purpose. It would be like the Vatican existing without Jesus or the Christian Church he founded.

According to the Bible, Moses was the prophet who first revealed God's holy laws for the Hebrew religion while the Israelites were wandering in the wilderness for forty years after they escaped captivity in Egypt. In effect, he was the founder of what became Judaism. Most archaeologists and historians, however, consider Moses to have been the mythical founder of a religion that developed over time. Not only do they doubt that Moses was a historical figure, they seriously question whether organized Israelite religion could have begun anywhere near so early. Were they right? I needed to reflect on all I had learned about Moses.

According to the Old Testament book of Exodus, Moses was born in Egypt into a family of Israelite slaves. During a purge, when the pharaoh orders the terrible slaughter of Israelite babies, Moses's mother saves her infant son by placing him in a little boat made

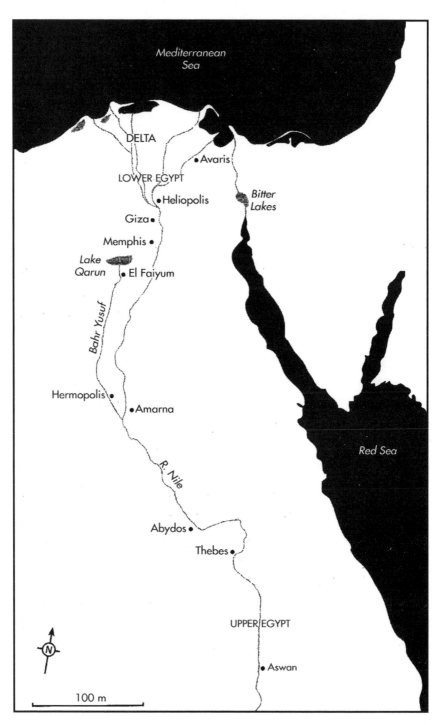

Ancient Egypt

from bulrushes and hiding him in the reeds that grow along the banks of the River Nile. The pharaoh's daughter finds the baby Moses and, sympathetic to the plight of the Israelites, adopts him and raises him as her own child. It seems that everyone at court remains unaware of the boy's true identity, and the pharaoh accepts him as his grandson. According to Exodus 2:14, Moses even becomes an Egyptian prince. The reason many historians doubt that Moses was a historical figure is that they expect such a royal person to be found somewhere in Egyptian records. While it is true that day-to-day records may have perished, as they were written on papyrus, thousands of inscriptions from monuments and tombs throughout ancient Egypt's long history survive to reveal the names of Egyptian kings and princes. Among these, there is no record of a Moses during the reign of Amonhotep III—or indeed of any Egyptian pharaoh of any time.

The name Moses, however, may be misleading. It may not have been the man's true name. The modern translations of the Old Testament took the name Moses from the Greek translation of the Bible, where it is rendered as *Mosis*. This, in turn, was taken from the books of the Hebrew Tanak, where it appears in its original form as *Mose*. Exodus 2:10 tells us that the pharaoh's daughter decided to name him this "because I drew him out of the water." It is generally assumed that the Exodus author is referring to the similarity between the name Mose and the Hebrew word *masa*, which means "to draw forth." In 1906 the German historian Eduard Meyer contended that this passage was inserted by a later Old Testament copyist to provide a Hebrew origin for what was really an Egyptian name. The episode, he argued, makes no sense in the context of the narrative as it now survives. If the princess wished to keep Moses's nationality a secret from the court—which she must have done, since Moses survived the pharaoh's order to kill the Hebrew babies—then she would not have given her adopted son a Hebrew name. As Meyer's contemporary, the famous British Egyptologist Flinders Petrie, pointed out, *mose* is an Egyptian word meaning "son." It is a common suffix in many Egyptian names. It is found, for example, in the name of the Egyptian pharaoh Ahmose, a name that means "son of the moon."

In 1995 the Israeli historian David Ullian speculated that Mose may have been a title rather than a personal name, just as the term Christ—"the anointed one"—later became the epithet for Jesus. He suggested that it might have been the shortening of the title "Son of God." In later times the kings and prophets of Judah were often described as the "sons of God." It is possible, then, if such a figure did lead the Israelites to freedom, that he appears in Egyptian record under another name. Is there anyone, that is, of any name, at the court of Amonhotep III who fits the Moses profile?

To start with, it is doubtful that we are in fact looking for an adopted Israelite. The entire story of Moses's Hebrew origins seems to have been a later interpolation into the Exodus account for two crucial reasons. First, the boat of bulrushes story appears to be taken from Babylonian legend. In Exodus 2:3 we are told how Moses's mother hides him:

> And when she could no longer hide him, she took for him an ark
> of bulrushes, and daubed it with slime and with pitch, and put the
> child therein; and she laid it in the flags of the river brink.

The Icelandic author and literary historian Magnus Magnusson, in his book *BC: The Archaeology of the Bible Land,* draws attention to a Mesopotamian myth concerning King Sargon I of Akkad, dating from around 2350 B.C. Here, the king too is floated on a river in a basket of bulrushes when his mother tries to hide him. Like Moses, he is found and adopted by someone else:

> My changeling mother conceived me, in secret she bore me. She set
> me in a basket of rushes, with bitumen she sealed my lid. She cast
> me in the river which rose not over me.

Second, and more significant, the story of Moses's adoption fails to withstand historical scrutiny. The Exodus account says that the pharaoh's daughter adopted Moses and that he was raised as a prince. In ancient Egypt the bloodline of the royal family was strictly controlled and manipulated. The pharaohs were considered gods, and their daughters could only conceive children with someone of the king's choice—very often the king himself. Adoption was completely out of the question. It is inconceivable that a pharaoh's daughter would have been allowed to adopt a son.

If Moses really was a prince at the Egyptian court, as the Bible says, then he is far more likely to have been a native Egyptian. Interestingly, there is one Egyptian prince from Amonhotep's reign who has much in common with Moses—his name was Prince Tuthmose.

Not much is known about Tuthmose, but enough Egyptian inscriptions have survived to provide a brief outline of his life. He was Amonhotep's eldest son and heir to the throne. As a young man, he acted as governor of Memphis in northern Egypt before being appointed commander of the king's chariot forces and seeing active service against the Ethiopians. After a successful campaign, he turned to the religious life and was installed as high priest at the Temple of the god Ra in Heliopolis, also in northern Egypt. In the twenty-third year of Amonhotep's reign he suddenly, and for no given reason, resigned his position as high priest and mysteriously disappeared. Two years later, when Amonhotep's reign ended, it was his younger brother Akhenaten who ascended to the throne.

Prince Tuthmose fits the Moses profile in a number of ways. First, he commanded the army during an Ethiopian campaign. So also, it seems, did Moses. Although the Bible tells us next to nothing about Moses's time as an Egyptian prince, the first-century Jewish historian Josephus provides an entire chapter on the subject in his *Jewish Antiquities*. In what seems to have been the accepted version of events around two thousand years ago, we are told that the pharaoh appointed Moses commander of an army he sent to fight the Ethiopians, and it was his success in the campaign that led to his exile. Jealous of Moses's popularity among the soldiers, the pharaoh eventually orders his arrest but, forewarned, Moses escapes the country. The Josephus account seems to have greater historical validity than the biblical narrative regarding the reason for Moses's exile. In Exodus we are told simply that Moses is forced to flee Egypt after he saves the life of an Israelite by killing a vicious slave driver. In reality, an Egyptian prince could order a common slave driver executed on the spot if he so desired. This was probably another episode that was added to make Moses an Israelite.

The second similarity between Moses and Prince Tuthmose is that for a time Tuthmose was a high priest at the Temple of Ra in Heliopolis. So also, it seems, was Moses. According to an account Josephus found in the work of an Egyptian historian named Manetho, who wrote in the fourth century B.C., a revolt took place among the Semite slaves during the reign of Amonhotep III. Interestingly, the revolt is said to have taken place in Avaris, the very place where the Israelites seem to have been enslaved. According to Manetho, Amonhotep was advised by one of his officials to purge the country of "undesirables" and set them to work in the stone quarries of Avaris. For many years they were forced to work as slaves until they were joined by a priest from the temple of the god Ra in Heliopolis. Evidently, the priest had abandoned the gods of Egypt and had been condemned to bondage. He had, Manetho says, once been a soldier, and during his captivity he trained the "undesirables" to fight. When he ultimately led them in rebellion, thousands managed to escape and return to their homeland. The "undesirables" are not named, nor is their homeland, and the priest is simply referred to as Osarseph, which means "leader." Josephus, however, was in no doubt that the "undesirables" were the Israelites and that Osarseph was Moses. If Moses was the priest who appears in Manetho's work, then Tuthmose does indeed fit the profile. Manetho tells us that the priest was a servitor at the temple of Ra in Heliopolis before he abandoned the Egyptian gods. This was precisely the position held by Prince Tuthmose before he disappeared.

The third similarity between the two figures is that, like Moses, Tuthmose may have been driven into exile. The reason for this assumption is that his tomb was never used. The Italian explorer Giovanni Belzoni discovered Tuthmose's tomb in the early nineteenth century at the far end of Egypt's Valley of the Kings, and it immediately posed an enigma. Royal tombs were prepared while the owner was still alive; only the final funerary decorations were added after death. This tomb, however, was finished, but the usual illustrations depicting the owner's funeral and mummification were absent. This meant that the tomb was empty not because it had been robbed but because it had never been used. Why not?

It is possible that Tuthmose had commissioned another tomb, although this seems most unlikely. Tombs were expensive and time-consuming projects. It took years to cut out the hundreds of square feet of solid rock to create the burial and treasury chambers deep underground. Coupled with his sudden and unexplained disappearance from the temple of Ra, and the lack of any memorials or obituaries, the empty tomb suggests that Tuthmose had been disgraced in some way and had either been executed or driven into exile.

The only major difference between Tuthmose and Moses is their supposed ages. The Exodus seems to have occurred at the end of Amonhotep's reign when Tuthmose would have been no older than thirty-five. According to the Exodus account, however, it is many years after Moses's exile that he returns to lead the Israelites to freedom, by which time he is eighty. And here we would do well to remember that we have to treat biblical ages with caution. We often read of people living to more than a century when forty or fifty was considered a good life span.

If the Exodus took place during the reign of Amonhotep III, then Prince Tuthmose is the best candidate by far for the historical Moses. His background uniquely matches Moses in a number of ways: He was commander of the army in Ethiopia, a priest at the temple of Ra, and he was disgraced or exiled. Even his name is intriguing: Tuthmose means "son of [the god] Thoth." If Tuthmose had abandoned the old gods and decided to drop the divine *Tuth*—Thoth—from his name, then he would actually have been called Mose, the original rendering of the name Moses.

Although none of this is absolute proof that Tuthmose was the historical Moses, he does fit Moses's profile and he does live in the right place and at the right time. It is, however, clear why the ancient Israelites might have needed to concoct an alternate story of Moses's origins. Israelite nationalists would have found it hard to accept that their great lawgiver, who established the covenant with God and protected it in the Ark, was actually an Egyptian prince.

Evidence that the Israelite religion was in existence at the time of the Exodus is yet more persuasive than that connecting Moses to Tuthmose. Indication that the Israelite slaves were already practicing monotheism—a single-god religion—by Amonhotep III's reign is found, indirectly, in Egyptian sources. It seems that Hebrew religious ideas had influenced an Egyptian sect. Known as Atenism, this sect worshiped a single, universal deity and denied the existence of all other gods. The Atenist sect seems to have come into existence very quickly around the end of Amonhotep's reign, and by the time Amonhotep's son Akhenaten came to the throne, around 1360 B.C., Atenism had grown so influential that the new pharaoh even adopted it as Egypt's state religion for a while. Its practices are so similar to the Hebrew religion that biblical commentators and Egyptologists alike have seen a connection. Some have even suggested that Atenism was directly inspired by the religion of the Israelite slaves, in a manner similar to the way early Christianity inspired the religion of Imperial Rome.

The correlation between the two religions does seem too close to be coincidental. Apart from the fact that they both believe in a single, universal god and deny the existence of all others—a concept unknown anywhere else in the world at the time—they share a number of other unique themes. First, both venerate a nameless god that is only referred to by titles. The name Jehovah, the name for God familiar to Christians today, is actually a Greek rendering of the Hebrew *Yhvh* or *Yahweh*, which actually means "the Lord." The God of Israel has no name. Neither does the god of the Atenists. No matter how reverently, in Egypt gods were usually addressed directly and by name. Indeed, the name of the god was thought to invoke its presence. However, the god of the Atenists was a unique exception. The common name used by Egyptologists for the Atenist god is "the Aten." However, this was not actually the god's name but the name for the glyph, or symbol, that represented it. A direct transliteration of the word *Aten* is "giver of life." Aten was not the name of the Atenists' deity; it was merely a description. Its other titles and forms of address are in fact identical to those used for the Hebrew god. This is known from a chance discovery made at Thebes, the ancient capital in southern Egypt.

In the first years of his reign, Akhenaten erected a new temple to the Aten at Karnak in Thebes. However, shortly after his reign, when Egypt abandoned Atenism and reverted to the pantheon of traditional gods, the temple was torn down. By chance, many of the sculptured blocks that decorated the temple were preserved inside two giant gate towers that were erected in front of the nearby temple of the god Amun. In the 1930s, when these towers were dismantled for structural repairs, over 40,000 of these sculptured blocks were found inside, having been used as fill over three thousand years ago. Now called the Karnak *talatat*, from an Arabic work for brickwork, many are inscribed with Atenist prayers that bear striking resemblance to Hebrew texts.

In the biblical account, Moses is first spoken to by God at Mount Sinai when he appears in a miraculous burning bush. Unaware of which god is speaking, Moses asks God to reveal his name, and God replies: "I am who I am" (Ex 3:14). He was simply God—the only God. The Hebrew word for "god" was *El*. This had various forms such as *Elyon*, "god most high," and *Elohim*, "your god," or *El Shaddai*, "god Almighty." The word *Yahweh*, "the Lord," is used often, as in *Yahweh-tsidkenu*, the "Lord of Hosts." (The Hebrew word *tsidkenu*, which modern translations render as "hosts," actually refers to armies, such as the hosts of Judah, the hosts of Israel, or hosts of angels.) However, because the Israelites even considered *Yahweh* too personal, the word *Adonai*—"my Lord"—was substituted in prayer.

In the *talatat* inscriptions we find the Aten addressed in an almost identical fashion. One reference is highly reminiscent of the "I am who I am" in the burning bush episode: "Thou art what thou art, radiant and high over every land." Others refer to the Aten, just as the Bible repeatedly refers to God, as God almighty and God most high. For example: "O great Aten, god almighty, who furnishest man's sustenance" and "O great Aten, god most high, who drivest away the dark." The Aten is even referred to as lord of armies, just as the god of Israel is called the Lord of Hosts: "Thou who art Lord over all of the armies of the world." Most frequently, however, the Aten is addressed in a similar fashion to the way God is addressed as *Adonai,* using the word *Neb,* the Egyptian word for "Lord."

It is not only the forms of address that are so alike but the very way the two religions perceive their deities. A lengthy prayer to the Aten survives in a number of inscriptions in the ruined city of Amarna in central Egypt. Known as "The Hymn to the Aten," it was seen by the American Egyptologist James Henry Breasted, as early as 1909, to bear a striking similarity to Psalm 104 in the Old Testament. Both prayers describe in identical terms how God and the Aten are respectively seen as creators, nurturers, and prime movers of all phenomena on earth.

Another unique correlation between the God of Israel and the Aten is that neither deity was permitted to be represented by images. According to the Bible, although the early Israelites did make icons to represent aspects of God's power, Israelite religion proscribed the making of effigies of God himself. In Egypt, an effigy or statue of a god was traditionally an essential part of cultic practice. The Egyptians believed that deities actually inhabited such images and the making of them was described in ancient texts. In all of Egypt, only Atenism diverged from this practice. The Atenists forbade the making of any idols and effigies of the Aten. According to one of the *talatat,* "No form in all the earth may reflect thy glory."

Both religions managed to get around the problems that such a doctrine created by employing a symbol to represent the deity's presence. When they eventually settled in Canaan, the Israelites used the menorah, a holy seven-branched candelabrum, to represent God's light and presence in the temple. The practice still survives in modern synagogues and Jewish homes. As noted above, the Atenists also used a symbol of light to represent the Aten. It was a glyph: a disc with arms extending downward to end in hands holding the ankh, the symbol for life. It actually depicted the sun with its rays bringing life-giving sunlight to the earth. Early Egyptologists inferred this to be evidence of sun worship. However, as more archaeological finds were made during the twentieth century, it became clear that the glyph represented sunlight and not the sun itself. (The sun was actually portrayed as a winged disc.) Atenism forbade the representation of its god in any other form. It is now clear that sunshine—

which brings warmth, light, and life, yet cannot be seen in its own right—was the way the sect conveyed the idea of an invisible, omnipresent, all-providing god.

The only exception the Atenists made to the prohibition against making images is exactly the same exception the early Israelites seem to have made: the image of a sacred bull. Even after Akhenaten abandoned all the traditional deities and everything associated with them, he gave specific instructions for the Mnevis bull, an animal sacred to the sun god Ra, to be brought to his new capital at Amarna and buried in a special tomb in the nearby hills. The Mnevis bull, or Nemur, was a living animal worshiped at the temple of Heliopolis that, when dead, was buried with great pomp and ceremony and replaced by a new bull located in the wild according to prescribed portents. A number of hand-size figures of such bulls, in both stone and bronze, have been discovered at the ruins of Amarna.

The early Israelites also continued to venerate a sacred bull, much to the annoyance of Moses, as can be seen in the biblical story of the golden calf. According to Exodus, when Moses was absent communing with God on Mount Sinai, his people, fearing some ill had befallen him, asked his deputy Aaron to make sacred images to protect them. Agreeing, Aaron collected golden jewelry from the people and made a "molten calf." In fact, contrary to the popular Hollywood image, it is not one calf they made but many, as the others are said to follow Aaron's lead. Aaron declared that these calves were "thy gods, O Israel, which brought thee up out of the land of Egypt" (Ex 32:4). Furthermore, they do not seem to have been life-size representations either. We are not told how big they are, but the inference is that, like the Egyptian bull effigies, they are small enough to be held in the hands. When the people gave Aaron their gold to make the idol, "he received them at their hand and fashioned it with a graving tool" (Ex 32:4).

Moses may have objected to the practice of bull worship, but it seems that it continued for eight centuries. The Old Testament book of Jeremiah concerns events immediately preceding the Babylonian invasion of Judah in 597 B.C., and in it there is reference to twelve bronze bull statues actually adorning the Jerusalem Temple.

According to Jeremiah 52:20, when the Babylonians looted the Temple they made off with the "twelve brazen bulls" that stood at the bases of the Temple pillars. On linguistic grounds, the book of Jeremiah is dated to around 550 B.C.—near enough to the sacking of the Temple that it is doubtful that this detail was invented. If the author himself had not witnessed the event, many people still alive would have. There can be little doubt, therefore, that the veneration of bull effigies was a part of early Hebrew religion.

That the early Israelites did venerate such idols is also supported by archaeological evidence. A number of hand-size bull effigies have been found at early sites throughout Israel and Palestine. Perhaps the most interesting is a bronze bull, some eight inches long, found at the site of Shechem and now in the possession of the Israeli archaeologist Amihay Mazor, of the Hebrew University, Jerusalem. It dates from the twelfth century B.C., a time well after the period of Moses and consequently a time when the Hebrew faith was apparently fully established. According to the Old Testament, Shechem was one of the holiest sites in ancient Israel. The bronze bull, coming from this highly revered site, is clear evidence of the continued veneration of the bull, certainly by some Israelites, well after they had invaded Canaan. Of all the hundreds of religious practices that there were in the world, that both the Atenist and Hebrew religions should seemingly have retained an earlier pagan one that is exactly the same is surely more than a coincidence.

Perhaps the most compelling evidence that Atenism and the religion of the Israelites were related came with an astonishing archaeological discovery made in 1989. In that year the French archaeologist Alain Zivie discovered a rock-cut tomb at Sakkara, near Cairo. Amazingly, the man interred in the tomb was a priest of both the Aten and the Hebrew God. Inscriptions revealed that the mummy had been an important Egyptian official from the reign of Akhenaten named Aper-el. In fact, he was one of the most important figures in Akhenaten's government. He was a grand vizier, the chief minister of northern Egypt. Surprisingly, DNA testing revealed that Aper-el was not a native Egyptian but a Semite, which in itself would have been unusual enough. More remarkable, however, he

seems to have been an Israelite. His name, Aper-el, Alain Zivie realized with surprise, appeared to have been a title. Translated, it
means literally "Servitor of [the god] El." *El,* of course, was the
Hebrew word for God. His name clearly implied that Aper-el was a
chief practitioner of the Israelite religion during Akhenaten's reign.
The most astonishing discovery, however, was the tomb illustrations
revealing that Aper-el was also the high priest of the Atenist temple
in the city of Memphis. Here we not only have evidence of a shared
link between the Hebrew religion and Atenism, but an example of
someone who seems to have been a priest of both religions and saw
no contradiction. The only conclusion that can be drawn is that the
religions of the Israelites and the Atenists were very closely related.

We have only the books of the Old Testament as evidence of the
Hebrew religion in the 1300s B.C.—books that were not written
until many centuries later. However, what is known of Atenism is
based on contemporary finds. These prove beyond any doubt that a
religion in many ways identical to the Hebrew religion came into
existence for a short time in Egypt at exactly the time that Moses
seemed to have lived and the Exodus appears to have occurred. In
fact, no other people anywhere else in the world are known to have
established a monotheistic religion before, and would not again—
apart from the Israelites—for a further thousand years. It seems
most improbable, therefore, that the two religions could be anything
other than related. Whether Atenism sprang from the religion of the
Israelites or the other way around may never be known. What was
important for my own current research was that there was ample
evidence that the Hebrew religion, in some form or other, did exist
at the time the Ark of the Covenant is said to have been made. There
was, however, not only evidence from Egyptian sources of early
monotheism around the time the Exodus story is set; there was also
evidence of a sacred vessel almost identical to the Ark.

In Egypt a god's presence was believed to reside within a specially made image, usually a statue or figurine. During Amonhotep
III's reign, a statue of the chief Egyptian deity Amun stood in a dark
inner sanctum at the temple of Karnak. Just like the chamber where
the Ark of the Covenant later stood in the Jerusalem Temple, this

sanctum was called the Holy of Holies. In some way that is now unclear, the god was believed to reveal its instructions to the priesthood. Only on special occasions would the statue ever be moved, and then it was carried in a sacred container that, like the Ark, was made of gilded wood and carried by poles inserted into rings on either side. A further similarity between this sacred container and the Ark of the Covenant is its name. An inscription on a scene depicting the god statue being carried in this container on a wall relief at the temple of Medinet Habu in Thebes reads: "The divine Amun is carried on the sacred Bark."

The words *ark* and *bark* have a common origin in the word *Ak*, an Egyptian word meaning a sacred container or vessel. The word found its way into later Latin where it became *barca*, a royal boat. Eventually, this Roman word came into common usage as the word for any small boat; in modern English the word is *barge*. The original word *Ak*, however, did not only refer to an inanimate object; it could also apply to a person through whom a god spoke, such as in the title of the Egyptian pharaoh Akhenaten that meant "vessel of the Aten." So the Egyptian Bark and the Hebrew Ark were both vessels for containing their respective gods or something that channeled the deities' power.

It stands to reason that the early Hebrew religion would have been influenced by the religious practices in Egypt, as Egypt is where the Israelites had been living for some four hundred years before the Exodus. Although none of my investigation actually proved that the Ark of the Covenant existed, it did place the biblical relic within a realistic historical context. As a people forced to live a nomadic existence in the Sinai Wilderness for many years after their escape from Egypt, it makes perfect sense for the Israelites to have made their own version of an Egyptian bark. It enabled them to transport their most sacred possessions, in particular the enigmatic item through which God is said to have manifested—namely, the mysterious mercy seat.

Like the Egyptian statue of the chief god Amun, the mercy seat somehow revealed God's instructions. The term *mercy seat* is an English translation of the Hebrew *kiseh chesed,* where the word for mercy, *chesed*, also means wisdom, and the word for seat, *kiseh*, also means a place of judgment, such as a king's "seat" of power. In 1 Chronicles 28:11, the throne room of King Solomon is also referred to by the term *mercy seat*. It seems, therefore, that it was not necessarily a chair, but a site from which wisdom is dispensed, judgments made, and power wielded. The nearest equivalent English word is actually *oracle*. As Hebrew tradition forbade the making of images of God, this oracle is unlikely to have been a statue or figurine. The book of Exodus gives the only description of the mercy seat: "And he made the mercy seat of pure gold: two cubits and a half was the length thereof, and one cubit and a half the breadth thereof" (Ex 37:6).

This is not much to go on, but judging by the fact that the dimensions given are the same as those of the Ark, it appears to have been its lid. Whatever it was, the mercy seat was the oracle of God, just as the Amun statue was the oracle of the chief Egyptian deity. A portable golden bark for carrying an oracle of the Egyptian god, and a portable golden ark for carrying an oracle of the Hebrew God—surely the one must have inspired the other.

So there was historical evidence of a figure matching the Moses profile, there was archaeological evidence for the existence of the Hebrew religion, and the Ark fitted into a historical context. I was now in a position to make an informed speculation about the historical reality of the lost relic.

5

Into the Wilderness

It seemed that the biblical events during the period from when the Ark was supposedly made until it was apparently installed permanently in the Jerusalem Temple were historical enough—at least in general terms. Although many scholars long considered the Bible's account of this era of Israelite history to be mythological, there was now plenty of evidence to show that it was far more accurate than once thought. Evidence from the Thera eruption corroborated the Bible's account of the plagues that afflicted Egypt and the Israelites' subsequent Exodus, and archaeology had revealed that some forty years later the Israelites did capture Jericho and a couple of decades after that sacked Hazor. David's unification of Israel into a single kingdom with Jerusalem as its capital was also equally likely to be historical, as indicated by the existence of the pool of Gibeon and the shaft into the spring of Gihon.

As for the Ark itself, many historians doubted its existence for two principal reasons. First, there appeared to be no historical evidence for the existence of the Hebrew religion at the time the Ark is said to have been made, and second there seemed to be no historical context or precedent for such a relic. However, both of these assumptions could be seriously questioned. According to the Bible, the Ark was made shortly after the Israelites escaped captivity in Egypt, an event for which a fairly precise date could be determined from a number of different perspectives. The radiocarbon dating of the cereal grains found in the ruins of Jericho dated the fall of the city to approximately 1320 B.C., and adding forty years—the period the Israelites spent in the wilderness—a date of around 1360 B.C. could be arrived at for the Exodus. The Thera eruption could also be dated to around this year from three completely separate pieces of evidence: the ice-core samples, the alabaster jar found at Amnisos, and the Sekhmet statues erected by Amonhotep III. There was evidence that at the same time—for the first time anywhere in the world—a monotheistic religion came into existence in Egypt that was extraordinarily similar to the religion of the Israelites as described in the Old Testament. Furthermore, at this very time in Egypt, a religious vessel was used as a portable altar to carry a god image, just as the Ark was used by the Israelites as a portable oracle of God. Even the names of the two vessels were remarkably similar. Although the story of the Ark of the Covenant may initially have seemed removed from history, it now appeared to fit neatly into a historical context. Although I had no absolute proof that the Ark existed, it seemed to me to be a safe bet that it probably did—at least as a historical relic, if not as a supernatural weapon or "radio for talking to God." Enough evidence existed for me to spend time trying to discover what might have become of it.

Further investigation at the Shrine of the Book revealed that there are five main episodes in ancient Hebrew history during which various scholars believe the Ark may have been lost: two from the period of the united kingdom of Israel and three from later Jewish times. The early theories concern the period immediately after the Jerusalem Temple was built, either when Solomon's son is said to have stolen it and taken it to Ethiopia around 950 B.C. or when the Egyptians raided Jerusalem some thirty-five years later. The later theories concern the occasions when the Temple was plundered: by the Babylonians in 597 B.C., the Greeks in 169 B.C. and the Romans in A.D. 70. By the time of these later invasions, beginning some three centuries after Solomon's death, the northern tribes of Israel had been wiped out by the Assyrians from the north of Iraq. Of the original Israelites, only the Judeans—the Jews—and their kingdom of Judah survived. Accordingly, those who subscribe to the early period theories concerning the Ark's disappearance have been referred to as the "Israelite camp" and those who subscribe to the later theories as the "Judean camp."

Israelite camp scholars point out that there are almost two hundred references to the Ark of the Covenant in the Old Testament, nearly all concerning the period between the Exodus and the building of the Temple. None of the few later references, they contend, mention the Ark being used in any way whatsoever. If the Israelites still had the Ark, they argue, then why did they not use it? Judean camp scholars, on the other hand, draw attention to the fact that the Ark appears to have still been in the Jerusalem Temple at a Passover festival during the reign of the Judean king Josiah, over three centuries after Solomon's time. According to 2 Chronicles:

> Moreover Josiah kept a passover unto the Lord in Jerusalem: and they killed the passover [lamb] on the fourteenth day of the first month. And he set the priests in their charges, and encouraged them to the service of the house of the Lord. And said unto the Levites that taught all Israel, which were holy unto the Lord, "Put the holy ark in the house which Solomon the son of David king of Israel did build." (2 Chr 35:1–3)

It is clear that the writer of this particular passage was in no doubt that the Jews still had the Ark at this time. Later in the same chapter we are even told precisely when this was:

> In the eighteenth year of the reign of Josiah was this passover kept. After all this, when Josiah had prepared the temple, Necho king of Egypt came up to fight against Carchemish by Euphrates: and Josiah went out against him. (2 Chr 35:19–20)

Egyptian records of Necho's campaigns date this event to around 622 B.C. On linguistic grounds, biblical scholars consider this part of 2 Chronicles to have been written between 600 and 550 B.C., so it may actually have been a close contemporary account. Even if it was written as late as 550 B.C., it could still have been composed by a scribe who consulted eyewitnesses to the events. On balance, as the later period seemed a more likely option for the Ark's disappearance from history, I decided to join the

Judean camp. However, this still left me with three possibilities.

The very last mention of the Ark in the Old Testament is in the book of Jeremiah and concerns the period just before the Babylonians sacked the Temple in 597 B.C. Purporting to be the words of Jeremiah, the chief Jewish prophet at the time, this passage reads:

> And it shall come to pass, when ye be multiplied and increased in the land, in those days, saith the Lord, they shall say no more, The ark of the covenant of the Lord: neither shall it come to mind: neither shall they remember it; neither shall they visit it. (Jer 3:16)

Jeremiah is referring to the words of God, but whether these were meant to be God's past or present words is unclear. Had the Ark already been lost, or was Jeremiah predicting that it would be lost some time in the future? From this passage alone, it is impossible to say whether the Jews still possessed the Ark by the time the Babylonians sacked the Temple. Nevertheless, most Jewish commentators whose work survives from Roman times accepted that the Ark was still in the Temple immediately before the Babylonians invaded.

Of the three possible times the Ark may have been lost during the Judean period, the Roman plundering of the Temple seemed most unlikely, as the Jewish historian Josephus, who lived when the event occurred, states categorically that the Holy of Holies had been left empty in Herod's new Temple. This left me with two possibilities, which seemed to be equally feasible. The first option, the sacking of the Temple by the Babylonians, is included in two Old Testament accounts that refer to the Babylonians taking away all the sacred articles that were in the Temple (2 Kgs 25:13–15 and Jer 52:17–22). If the Old Testament is right, then all the stolen items were eventually returned to the Temple about seventy years later, after Babylon fell to the Persian Empire. These are listed in Ezra 1:7–11, but there is no mention of the Ark. However, this does not necessarily mean that the relic was permanently lost to the Jews at the time of the Babylonian invasion. It may have been hidden from the Babylonians and later recovered.

After the Persians defeated the Babylonians, the Jerusalem

Temple was rebuilt, but whether the Ark was eventually returned to it cannot be learned from the Old Testament, as the narrative ends at this time. From sources such as Greek and Roman records and the work of Josephus, however, we know that the Greek Seleucids plundered the Jerusalem Temple in 169 B.C. No inventory survives regarding what was taken; neither does any record of what items survived after a full-scale Jewish revolt ensured that the stolen Temple treasures were returned. I decided that my best course of action was to first examine the Greek plundering of the Temple, as there were more historical sources surviving from this time than the earlier Babylonian period. Perhaps, somewhere, there was evidence from which to determine whether or not the Ark was still in the Jerusalem Temple by the time it was sacked by the Greeks.

When I next spoke to David Deissmann, he put me in touch with a man who was a leading exponent of the theory that the Ark was removed from Jerusalem at the time the Greeks plundered the Temple. His name was Dr. Otto Griver, and he was a retired Israeli linguist from the Hebrew University who had spent years searching for the Ark in the Judean Wilderness. This inhospitable, craggy, and mountainous territory—some twelve miles wide and forty-five miles long—lies ten miles east of Jerusalem on the western side of the Dead Sea. Like a Swiss cheese, the area is pitted with hundreds of caves, niches, and caverns, some of which were used as hiding places for the famous Dead Sea Scrolls. If these ancient scrolls could remain here undiscovered for almost two thousand years, Dr. Griver proposed, then why not the Ark? Since the first scrolls were discovered in the 1940s, a number of expeditions have also scoured the Judean Wilderness looking for the Ark of the Covenant, and the most sophisticated of these had been led by Dr. Griver. David assured me that he was one of the world's leading authorities on ancient Hebrew mysticism and probably knew as much about the Ark as anyone alive. As it turned out, he was more than happy to meet with me.

"I doubt if he'll tell you where he thinks it's hidden," David told me. "But I'm sure he'll share his thoughts concerning his general theories about the Ark."

Dr. Griver had been one of the experts who helped translate the

Dead Sea Scrolls in the 1980s, and his work led him to some unique and controversial theories about the Ark. It was his opinion that the relic had been in the custody of a Jewish sect called the Essenes. The first-century historian Josephus describes how the Essenes had been a part of the Jerusalem Temple priesthood who broke away to form an ascetic monastic community in the Judean Wilderness at the time of the Greek plundering of the Temple in the mid-second century B.C. Based at Qumran, at the northwestern end of the Dead Sea, the Essenes survived in virtual isolation for two centuries until they were slaughtered by the Romans during the Jewish Revolt in 68 B.C. Little was known about their beliefs until the discovery of the Dead Sea Scrolls, which turned out to be a complete library of sacred Essene texts that had been hidden before the Roman massacre.

The first of the Dead Sea Scrolls were found in 1947, discovered by accident in a cave about half a mile north of Qumran by Bedouin shepherd boys. They had apparently wandered into the cave looking for a lost goat when they noticed a number of half-buried ceramic storage jars that turned out to contain seven of the scrolls. Written in Hebrew and Aramaic (a local dialect), these were found to be commentaries on the books of the Old Testament and other Jewish scriptures, together with religious teaching specific to the Essene sect. All have been translated and are now on public display in the Shrine of the Book at Jerusalem's Israel Museum. However, these were only the first of dozens of such scrolls discovered in other caves in the area over the following decade. Only one of these further scrolls was put on display; the others remain stored in the Rockefeller Museum building in Jerusalem, the premises of the Israel Antiquities Authority. Translation of these scrolls has been going on for years, and only some of them have ever been published. In fact, many of them are still being translated, as modern science has only recently been able to render the faded ink legible.

At the same time as the scrolls were being found, the remains of the Essene monastery at Qumran were also discovered. On a rock-strewn terrace between the rugged cliffs beside the Dead Sea, a labyrinth of foundation stones, some 350 feet square, was all that remained of the once-thriving community. I had visited the site on a previous trip to Israel and, walking through the ruins, I found it hard to believe that anyone could have lived here. The sun beat down mercilessly, and the ground was so hot that the soles of my boots actually began to smell of smoldering rubber every time I stood on bare rock for more than a few seconds. Yet despite the burning, arid conditions, despite the fact that less than two inches of rain falls in any year, the community that lived here two thousand years ago had all the fresh water it needed. When the site was excavated by the French archaeologist Roland de Vaux in the mid-1950s, his team discovered that an elaborate series of aqueducts, lined with an ingenious ceramic coating to prevent leakage, supplied the community with abundant water from springs in the surrounding hills. The water not only provided for the necessities of life, it was essential for the religious practices of the monastery. Large rectangular depressions were found at the dig, which are the remnants of huge communal baths in which the inhabitants regularly immersed themselves for ritual cleansing. The main feature of the site had been a three-story tower that overlooked a central courtyard, surrounded on all sides by buildings of considerable size: workshops where everyday utensils were made, a long hall where the community gathered for meetings and communal meals, and a scriptorium where the Essenes' sacred manuscripts—the Dead Sea Scrolls—were written. This last could be determined because pottery found here was identical to the vessels containing the scrolls.

It had been Dr. Griver's study of one of the scrolls that led him to conclude that the Essenes had been the guardians of the Ark and had taken it from the Temple when it was sacked by the Greeks. He also believed that the Ark was never returned to the Temple after the troubles with the Greeks were over because it was no longer considered a safe place to keep the holy relic. Dr. Griver offered to pick me up from my hotel in Jerusalem and drive me out to show me the cave where the scroll was found, and on the way he explained some of the ancient Hebrew beliefs regarding the Ark. He was quite happy to talk openly about his theories, and he didn't even have a problem with my taping our conversation.

Dr. Griver explained that the Israelites apparently needed twelve sacred stones to use the Ark. According to the Old Testament, God told Moses how to make the Ark and gave him instructions for its use. First, it could only be carried by members of the priesthood— the Levites. Second, the only person other than Moses who could actually use the Ark was the high priest Aaron (and after his death, his successors). Third, the power of the Ark could only be summoned if the high priest wore a sacred breastplate, usually referred to as the Breastplate of Judgment. It is described in detail in the book of Exodus as a square design made from twined golden linen and inlaid with twelve precious stones set in four rows:

> The first row shall be a sardius, a topaz, and a carbuncle . . . the second row shall be an emerald, a sapphire, and a diamond . . . the third row shall be a ligure, an agate, and an amethyst . . . the fourth row a beryl, and an onyx, and a jasper. (Ex 28:15–30)

Sometimes referred to as "the jewels of gold" because they were originally set in gold, these sacred gemstones were believed to have divine power, as they were fashioned by God himself at the holy Mount Sinai. The Old Testament book of Ezekiel, which refers to them as the Stones of Fire, describes them as having once belonged to Lucifer but having been taken from him by God after the fall from grace (Ez 28:13–16). They were later given to Moses because it was apparently fatal to look inside the Ark without their protection. As 1 Samuel 6:19 recounts, an entire community of inquisitive people perished for doing so:

> And he smote the men of Beth-shemesh, because they had looked into the ark of the Lord, even he smote of the people fifty thousand and threescore and ten men: and the people lamented, because the Lord had smitten many of the people with a great slaughter.

For generations the Ark was kept closed until it was finally opened in the Jerusalem Temple on King Solomon's orders, around three and a half centuries after the time of Moses. Evidently, there was nothing inside except the two stone tablets containing the Ten Commandments (1 Kgs 8:9). However, once it was opened divine forces were unleashed:

And it came to pass, when the priests were come out of the holy place, that the cloud filled the house of the Lord [the Jerusalem Temple]. So that the priests could not stand to minister because of the cloud: for the glory of the Lord had filled the house of the Lord. (1 Kgs 8:10–11)

By this time the breastplate itself seems to have perished and the stones were kept in a coffer or box, which appears to have been held by the high priest when the Ark was used. According to 1 Samuel, "the Levites took down the ark of the Lord, and the coffer that was with it, wherein the jewels of gold were" (1 Sm 6:15). The Bible does not say what happened to these sacred stones but it would appear that they remained with the Ark until its mysterious disappearance from history.

"Do you believe the Ark really did have the power the Bible says?" I asked.

"The ancient Israelites believed it could summon angels," answered Dr. Griver, without committing himself. "Unlike the Christian notion of angels as sweet little cherubs or beautiful beings with feathered wings, to the ancient Hebrews angels were often mighty, destructive instruments of God's wrath. It was an angel that killed the Egyptian firstborn when the pharaoh would not free the Israelite slaves and another that unleashed the torrents of Noah's flood. It is said that when one of God's angels was sent to destroy the corrupt cities of Sodom and Gomorrah, the devastation was so dreadful that all that remained was an immense hole in the ground and a barren country in which nothing could grow or live." Dr. Giver pointed out of the window at the Dead Sea, beside which we were now driving. "That is where Sodom and Gomorrah are said to have stood."

Burnt red mountains rose sharply from the cracked stone terraces that surrounded the green-tinged waters, and the atmosphere hung heavy with the stench of salt. It was not the familiar, healthy smell of the seaside but a pungent chemical odor, like the fumes produced by an industrial blast furnace. The aptly named Dead Sea has a salt content over seven times that of the earth's oceans—so high that marine life just cannot survive. The enormous lake, almost fifty miles long by ten miles wide, is an incredible quarter of a mile below sea level—the lowest place on land anywhere in the world. Consequently, the waters from the River Jordan that feed the Dead Sea from the north have literally nowhere to go. They simply evaporate at a rate of fifty-five inches a year in searing temperatures that hover at over a hundred degrees for months on end. The salt washed down from rocks in the north just builds up in the water, year after year, rendering not only the Dead Sea but also the surrounding land almost bereft of life. I had never been anywhere so completely barren. It was like a vast toxic ocean in some lifeless, postapocalyptic world. It was easy to see why the story of Sodom and Gomorrah should have arisen.

"You say that Lucifer had these Stones of Fire. Wasn't *he* supposed to have been an angel before he became the Devil?" I said, not sure whether Dr. Griver actually believed in angels himself. I realized that he was a devout Jew, but I did not know whether his personal faith required him to accept the existence of angels, literally.

Dr. Griver explained that Lucifer was said to have been the chief angel before he displeased God and was cast out of heaven. The story of Lucifer's fall from grace is not related in the Old Testament, but it was included in the ancient Hebrew Tanak, from which the Old Testament was compiled. For various reasons, angels among them, the Church was uneasy with some books of the Tanak. Considered mythological rather than historical, they were referred to as Apocrypha, meaning of doubtful authenticity. (Likewise, most have not been accepted by mainstream Christians, although the Roman Catholic Bible does accept as canonical seven books more than the Protestant.) The Essenes, however, relied heavily on the Apocrypha and saw themselves as the followers of Lucifer's successors in heaven.

"According to the Apocrypha, when Lucifer was cast out of heaven he was replaced by two chief angels, Michael and Gabriel, who became known as the 'kings of heaven.' They were the two cherubim represented on the Ark," said Dr. Griver. "The word *angel,* used in the Christian Bible, comes from the Greek word *angelos,* meaning a messenger—one who brings messages from God. The Hebrew word is *malakh,* meaning 'shadow side' of God. Angels do God's nasty work. However, as in the Greek word, they were also messengers and are often referred to by the Hebrew word *or,* meaning 'light.'" Dr. Griver explained that angels were called lights because it was believed that shooting stars were angels coming to earth on errands from God. "Michael and Gabriel were even represented in the sky by two permanent lights: the two tail stars of the constellation Ursa Major—the Big Dipper—the stars we now call Benetnasch and Mizar. The ancient Hebrew names for these stars were Reysh, meaning the head, as Michael was the head, or supreme of all the angels, and the other was called Kos, meaning the cup, as Gabriel was said to hold the cup of man's salvation."

Dr. Giver turned his jeep off Highway 90, which runs the length of the Dead Sea, and onto a narrow, dusty track.

"Which brings me to why I believe the Essenes were the custodians of the Ark," he said. "The Bible portrays Lucifer as the original possessor of the Stones of Fire, so, as devotees of Michael and Gabriel, Lucifer's replacement, the Essenes were alluding to possessing the stones themselves. If they had the stones, which were inseparable from the Ark, then they must also have possessed the Ark itself."

"What were these stones supposed to do?" I asked.

Dr. Griver explained that the ancient Israelites believed that at the beginning of the world, when he was still God's chief angel, Lucifer resided on Mount Sinai, from which he commanded the other angels. "The sacred stones were set into Lucifer's garments, to protect him from the might of his fellow angels," he said.

"Why were they called Stones of Fire, and why twelve?" I asked.

"The Torah—the first five books of the Old Testament—tells us they represented the twelve tribes of Israel, but why they were called Stones of Fire is something of a mystery. However, it was probably because they could control divine fire that emanated from the Ark. They were also believed to afford protection against the terrible power of the angels, which is why the high priest had them set in a breastplate." As Dr. Griver spoke I could not help envisaging the scene in *Raiders of the Lost Ark* when the Ark is opened: Beautiful angels fly out of it to transform into demonic creatures that devour the bad guys.

"So was Lucifer supposed to have possessed the Ark?" I said.

"No, that was not made until later. When the Israelites were wandering in the wilderness after the Exodus from Egypt, God led Moses to Mount Sinai where he told him to make the Ark and gave him the sacred stones to protect him from its power."

"Does the scroll you found specifically say that the Essenes had the Ark?" I asked.

Dr. Griver took his time answering. "Not in so many words."

We had arrived at the foot of the cliff, halfway up which was the cave where the scroll had been found. Leaving the jeep, I followed Dr. Griver up a narrow path, interspersed with steps cut into the rock face. I thought that I had become used to Israel's blistering temperatures, but I was wrong. The moment I left the comfort of the air-conditioned vehicle, the searing heat took my breath away. It was well over a hundred degrees.

"The Judean Wilderness is one of the hottest places on earth," said Dr. Griver, noticing my discomfort as we trudged on upward.

Finally, after about fifteen minutes, we reached the cave, which wasn't so much a cave but a deep recess in the cliff face, hollowed out by blown sand over millennia. Dr. Griver explained that before the stone steps had been carved by archaeologists the only way to reach the cave was by rappeling down from the cliff top above. He showed me the place where the jar containing the scroll had been found, at the back of the cave, buried in the dirt.

"If the Essenes had these relics, and they really worked, why didn't they use them against the Romans?" I asked.

Dr. Griver smiled. "Good question," he said. "Perhaps they'd forgotten how to use them."

"So you think the Essenes had the Ark and the Stones of Fire. What do you think happened to them?" I asked. David had told me not to expect Dr. Griver to reveal anything about his ideas concerning the whereabouts of the Ark, but I thought I'd ask anyway.

"When the Romans destroyed Qumran, they slaughtered every

person in the community," he said. "The Essenes must have been expecting it, as they hid their library of texts. If they had time enough to hide the scrolls, then they had time enough to hide other artifacts, including the Ark. Their eventual massacre must have been total, as the Dead Sea Scrolls were never recovered. The stones and the Ark of the Covenant must still be somewhere out there." Dr. Griver waved a hand in the direction of the interior of the Judean Wilderness, its barren, lifeless hills rolling away into the distant heat and haze, as far as the eye could see.

It appeared that Dr. Griver had given up hope of ever finding the Ark. He explained that his expedition, which included some of Israel's leading archaeologists, had spent two seasons searching hundreds of caves like the ones in which the scrolls were found. Not all the members of the expedition expected to find the Ark; most of them were hoping to find other scrolls. Although they searched for two long years, nothing whatsoever was found.

"If the Ark is hidden somewhere in the Judean Wilderness, as I believe it is, then I doubt its hiding place is still accessible," he said, shaking his head. "I can't imagine that there is a single cave out there that has not been searched by someone. A single fragment of an Essene manuscript would be worth a fortune. Not only archaeologists but local Arabs have spent over half a century combing the area. The problem is that many hiding places available to the Essenes two thousand years ago are now impossible to reach. The intense contrast between the heat of day and the near-freezing conditions at night causes the hills to erode away into huge mounds of rubble." He pointed down to the base of the cliff where a gigantic heap of boulders and stone shards reached halfway up the rock face. "There are millions of tons of such rubble out there in the Judean Wilderness that must be covering thousands of caves and other hiding places. In the 1980s, it took a team of British archaeologists three years to remove just one such heap. If the Ark is out there, I'm afraid it's out there to stay."

I was still was not sure whether Dr. Griver actually believed in angels or the power of the Ark, but he had certainly been a mine of information concerning ancient Jewish thinking regarding the relic.

For me, however, the most important question still remained unanswered. When had the Ark been lost to the Jews? If the Bible was right about it still being in the Jerusalem Temple during the reign of Josiah, around 622 B.C., and the first-century Jewish historian Josephus was right about it no longer being in the Temple when it was rebuilt by Herod, then there were only two obvious times it could have been lost: when the Babylonians sacked the Temple in 597 B.C., or four centuries later when the Greeks plundered it. Dr. Griver was personally convinced that the Ark had been removed from Jerusalem during the time the Greeks ransacked the Temple, but I still needed persuading. He had been vague about specific references in the Dead Sea Scrolls to the Essenes actually possessing the sacred Israelite relic. As far as I could gather, Dr. Griver was basing his theory on purely circumstantial evidence. The Essenes may have been obsessed with the Ark of the Covenant, but had they actually claimed to have had it? I decided that the best thing to do was to visit the Shrine of the Book in Jerusalem, where some of the Dead Sea Scrolls are on display, and seek a second opinion with regard to whether the Essenes really had possessed the sacred Ark.

6
The Mystery of Jeremiah

The Shrine of the Book stands close to the National Library and the Israel Museum in southwest Jerusalem. Paradoxically, although it was purpose-built to contain one of the oldest manuscript collections in the world, the Shrine's design is strangely futuristic. The main gallery is more like the inside of a flying saucer than a library—a huge round, windowless room covered by a great ringed dome and bathed in an orange luminescence that seems to radiate from the very walls. At the center of the room are the most precious of the scrolls, contained inside a circle of illuminated panels that looks like the control console of an alien vessel.

Speaking to one of the Shrine's curators, I soon discovered that Dr. Griver was pretty much alone in thinking the Essenes had possessed the Ark. Indeed, most of the staff I spoke to at the Shrine of the Book considered the scroll Dr. Griver translated to have been a religious allegory, rather than a transcript of actual events. Nonetheless, I was told that it did refer to the Ark of the Covenant and the Stones of Fire, and it did refer to the Essenes' belief that they were the spiritual successors to the archangels Michael and Gabriel. In fact, the Qumran community even referred to themselves as the Sons of Light—the reference to light being an allusion to angels. However, nowhere, I was assured, did the text make claim to the Essenes actually possessing the Ark or the Stones of Fire. Of course, Dr. Griver could still have been right: The fact that the Essenes regarded themselves as the archangels' successors might indeed have been meant to imply that they were custodians of these sacred relics. Nevertheless, there appeared to be no proof that they actually were.

Regardless of what the Essenes claimed or did not claim to have possessed, Dr. Griver's theory relied on the fact that the Ark was still in the Jerusalem Temple just before the Greek Seleucids plundered it in 167 B.C. He believed that the Essenes, as a faction of the Temple priesthood, had been given the Ark for safekeeping when it became clear that the Temple was in danger from the Seleucid king Antiochus IV. So *was* there any evidence that the Ark was still in the Jerusalem Temple in the early second century B.C.?

To answer my question, the curator led me to a PC in one of the Shrine's reading rooms, where he punched up a file listing all the historical sources concerning the Greek plundering of the Temple. As he scrolled down the list, he told me that the episode occurred at a time from which far more historical texts survive than from earlier Hebrew history. The rebellion that the incident sparked is known as the Maccabean Revolt, and it is covered in considerable detail in a number of documents and letters that were written shortly after it occurred. Collectively known as the *Pseudepigrapha,* they make repeated references to the Jerusalem Temple and its sacred vessels. However, as the curator showed me by opening the links to the various texts, not once do they refer to the Ark's presence in the Holy of Holies at the time the Temple was sacked on the orders of Antiochus IV. In fact, the most important account to survive concerning the Maccabean Revolt is found in *Jewish Antiquities*, written by the Jewish historian Josephus. Although Josephus wrote two centuries after the event, he had access to many earlier Jewish works that no longer survive. The curator opened the file containing the Josephus passage concerning Antiochus's looting of the Temple:

> So he left the temple bare, and took away the golden candlesticks, and the golden altar, and table [for unleavened bread], and the altar [for burnt offerings]; and did not abstain from even the veils, which were made of fine linen and scarlet . . . and left nothing at all remaining.

The work included, by name, the most sacred Temple treasures that were plundered, but it failed to mention the Ark. The Ark had been the Jews' most holy possession. If it *had* still been in the Temple when the Maccabean Revolt occurred, the curator explained, it is almost certain that Jewish *Pseudepigrapha* authors, and particularly the Jewish historian Josephus, would have mentioned it. In fact, he told me, he knew of no historical Jewish reference to anyone claiming to have possessed the Ark of the Covenant after the earlier Babylonian plundering of the Jerusalem Temple in 597 B.C.

It seemed that the Ark of the Covenant had to have been removed from the Temple over four centuries before Antiochus plundered it. All the available evidence pointed to its having been removed at the time of the Babylonian invasion and, for some reason, never returned. I therefore needed to consult the historical references to the Babylonian sacking of Jerusalem. Unfortunately, unlike the period of the Greek occupation of Judah, few historical sources concerning this event exist outside the Old Testament. As the curator had left me at the computer to continue my research alone, I decided to look up the relevant biblical passages. Two Old Testament passages, 2 Kings 25:13–15 and Jeremiah 52:17–19, refer to the Babylonians taking away all the sacred articles that were in the Temple. As both use almost identical words and list exactly the same items in the same order, either one account was taken from the other or the authors had both used the same earlier source. Most biblical scholars consider the Jeremiah account to have been the original, as it is attributed to a scribe called Baruch who is said to have been an eyewitness to the events. His account appears to list all the vessels that were taken:

> Also the pillars of brass that were in the house of the Lord, and the bases, and the brasen sea [a large, ornamental bowl] that was in the house of the Lord, the Chaldeans [Babylonians] brake, and carried all the brass of them to Babylon. The cauldrons also, and the shovels, and the [candle] snuffers, and the bowls, and the spoons, and all the vessels of brass wherewith they ministered, took they away. And the basins, and the firepans, and the bowls, and the cauldrons, and the candlesticks, and the spoons, and the cups; that

which was of gold in gold, and that which was of silver in silver, took the captain of the guard away.

This, and the identical list in the Kings account, seemed to be fairly comprehensive, yet it did not include the Ark. I already knew that the Ark appeared to still be in the Temple during the reign of Josiah, some twenty-five years before the Babylonian invasion, as stated in 2 Chronicles 35:1–3. If these two accounts were accurate—and there seemed no reason to doubt them, as they appear to have been written within living memory of the event—then the most logical conclusion was that the Ark had been removed from the Temple sometime between 622 and 597 B.C. But who had removed it and why?

For an answer, I turned to the very last reference to the Ark of the Covenant in the Old Testament—in the book of the prophet Jeremiah. Purporting to be the words of the prophet himself that were written down by his scribe Baruch, 3:16 reads: "The ark of the covenant of the Lord: neither shall it come to mind: neither shall they remember it: neither shall they visit it."

Many biblical scholars infer from this verse that the prophet is warning the Jewish people that the Ark will be taken from them if they do not change their ways. Personally, I could not help wondering if the verse implied that the Ark had already been taken away. Jeremiah was the most prominent Jewish religious figure of the era, so if anyone had the authority to removed the Ark from the Temple, it was he. I clearly needed to find out more about Jeremiah.

According to the Old Testament, Jeremiah was the leading Jewish prophet at the time of the Babylonian invasion. He had begun his ministry thirty years earlier, during the reign of Josiah, when he seems to have been responsible for a number of significant religious reforms. From then until the time of the conquest, he was the most important religious figure in Judah. During this time, Judah had been enjoying a period of fortune and prosperity, the likes of which it had not known for generations. However, foreseeing danger ahead, Jeremiah continually warned the Jews to prepare themselves to face the Babylonians, whose empire to the north was expanding year by year. Few people, however, heeded his advice.

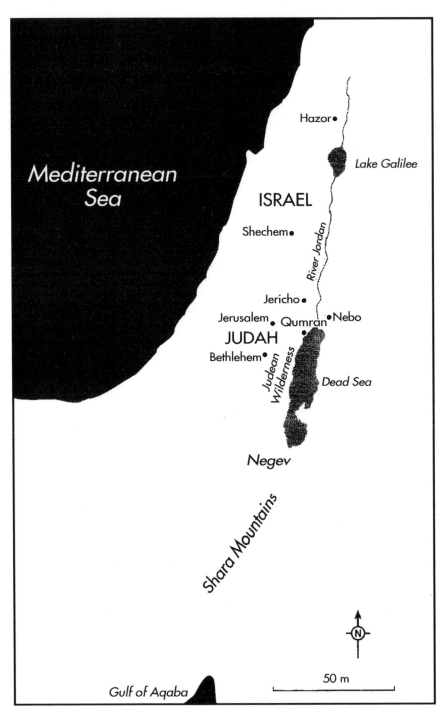

Ancient Israel and Judah

In 605 B.C., Jeremiah's predictions began to come true when the Babylonians invaded northern Judah. The Judean king Jehoiakim was forced to swear his allegiance to Babylon, but, in return, Jerusalem and southern Judah were left under his control. For the next eight years, life in Jerusalem continued as normal and the Temple remained safe. However, in 597 B.C. a revolt took place in the Babylonian army and, against Jeremiah's advice, Jehoiakim seized the opportunity to try to force the invaders out of northern Judah. The brief campaign was catastrophic for Jehoiakim, and when the Judean army was defeated, the Babylonian king Nebuchadnezzar captured Jerusalem and sacked the Temple. It therefore seemed that Jeremiah was not only in the position to have hidden the Ark, but his repeated warnings regarding the Babylonian peril show that he had the foresight to have done so.

Searching through the Shrine's comprehensive database, it was not long before I found that there was an early apocryphal text that actually did allege that Jeremiah had hidden some of the Temple treasures shortly before the Babylonians arrived. This was a rare first-century Greek manuscript known as *The Paralipomena of Jeremiah*—"The 'Remaining Words' of Jeremiah." Attributed to an anonymous Greek convert to Judaism, it claimed to be a copy of an earlier Hebrew text written by Baruch, who is described in this text as a servitor at the Jerusalem Temple who acted as Jeremiah's personal scribe. According to the manuscript, once it became apparent that Babylon would invade Jerusalem, God spoke to Jeremiah and told him to hide certain holy items from the Temple:

> And Jeremiah said, Behold, Lord, now we know that you are delivering the city into the hands of its enemies, and they will take the people away to Babylon. What do you want me to do with the holy vessels of the temple service? And the Lord said to him, Take them and consign them to the earth, saying: Hear, Earth, the voice of your creator who formed you in the abundance of waters, who sealed you with seven seals for seven epochs, after this you will receive your ornaments. Guard the vessels of the temple service until the gathering of the beloved.

Regardless of whether this text really was written by the scribe Baruch, it proved the existence of an early Jewish tradition that Jeremiah saved at least some of the Temple treasures from the Babylonians. While *The Paralipomena* does not specifically mention the Ark or any other Temple vessel by name, it makes historical sense that the Ark would be among them. Surely, suspecting that the Babylonians were going to invade, Jeremiah would not have stood idly by and let the most sacred Jewish relics be left in the Temple to be looted. Moreover, the mention in the passage of "holy vessels," rather than "vessel," made me think again about the two Old Testament accounts concerning the Babylonian plundering of the Temple. The list there is comprehensive and detailed, but it fails to reference the Ark as well as other important items that the Bible says had previously been in the Temple: the golden incense altar and the sacred tabernacle (the tent that served as a portable temple while the Israelites had wandered in the wilderness). It also failed to name the menorah, although this may have been included in the Old Testament list as one of the "candlesticks." It seemed to me most unlikely that the Old Testament authors would have failed to mention the incense altar and the tabernacle had they been in the Temple to be pillaged with the other vessels. It appeared that someone—presumably Jeremiah—had made sure that, along with the Ark, they had already been removed to a safer place.

However, if Jeremiah had hidden these Temple treasures, why were they not retrieved when the Persians overthrew the Babylonians and the Temple was rebuilt some seventy years later? The Old Testament assures us that all the sacred vessels that the Babylonians had taken were returned by the Persians and were again housed in the Jerusalem Temple (Ez 1:7–11). Why, then, not the Ark and the other missing items?

When I further examined the biblical accounts of Jeremiah's life, an answer suggested itself. Many Jews died during the Babylonian capture of Jerusalem, and thousands of others were enslaved and carted off to exile in Babylon. Jeremiah, however, not only survived, he avoided imprisonment and slavery. Although he was initially arrested, he was freed because he cooperated with the enemy by urging his people to avoid bloodshed and lay down their arms. He remained in Judah for some years before moving to Egypt, where he lived until his death around 562 B.C. A possible reason any Temple vessels he might have hidden were not recovered may have been that he died before the Babylonians left. Perhaps, by the time the Temple was rebuilt, no one survived who knew where they were. Obviously, Jeremiah would have needed help moving heavy artifacts like the Ark, but his helpers could well have died during the Babylonian invasion, or in slavery thereafter, without ever revealing the secret location.

Unfortunately, *The Paralipomena* provided no clue to the whereabouts of Jeremiah's hiding place for the Temple vessels. However, as I continued to search the database, I noticed a tantalizing reference to an early Jewish tradition that Jeremiah had hidden them in a secret cave. I had just begun to hunt this down when one of the Shrine's attendants told me that they were closing for the day. I only had time to note the source of the reference on a piece of paper.

As I left the Shrine of the Book, I glanced at the scrap of paper in my hand. The tradition that Jeremiah had hidden the vessels in a secret cave apparently came from an early version of the Bible, compiled by the fourth-century bishop Saint Jerome. Evidently, an early copy of Jerome's Bible still survived in the church where the saint had lived—the Church of the Nativity in the town of Bethlehem. I decided that I would take the bus there the following morning.

I had been to Bethlehem a couple of years previously, but everything had changed. Some seven miles south of Jerusalem, it is a small Arab town that now lies in the semiautonomous Palestinian region of what is still officially Israel. It had had a fairly relaxed atmosphere during my first visit, but that was before the present troubles. I would probably have been better off walking to Bethlehem like the pilgrims traditionally do, as a massive traffic jam had formed on the Hebron Road. Israeli soldiers were searching all vehicles at a checkpoint on the outskirts of Jerusalem, and it took almost three hours to reach my destination. When the bus eventually did make it into Bethlehem, all passengers and luggage were again searched, this time by Arab officials.

According to the Bible, Bethlehem was the birthplace of Jesus, and the Church of the Nativity is said to mark the place where he was born. It is situated in Manger Square, at the heart of the town, and the last time I had been here it was bustling with tourists who filed enthusiastically in and out of cafes and souvenir shops. Many of the 20,000 Arab inhabitants—half of whom are Christian and half of whom are Moslem—make their money from the tourist trade, in particular the manufacture and sale of images of the holy family. It had been a lucrative business, but I doubted it still was. Instead of the throngs of sightseers and parties of pilgrims being shown around by nuns from the town's Sisters of Saint Joseph's Convent and by monks from the nearby Franciscan monastery, Manger Square was ringed by armed Palestinian police. There were no more than a couple of dozen Westerners anywhere in sight.

Dominating the east end of the square is the Church of the Nativity, which stands over the site of Christ's birth. It actually looks more like a fortress than a church, as the present structure, built by the Roman emperor Justinian in the sixth century, was fortified by Crusaders in medieval times. Justinian was not responsible for the original church; that responsibility belonged to the first Christian Roman emperor, Constantine the Great, who built it over a cave in the late 320s. Evidently, Constantine's mother, Helena, had confidently informed him the cave was the site of the Nativity. She had been told of it by a local hermit.

Bowing my way through the single low entrance into the church, I found that there was more activity inside. The routine was continuing much as it had done for centuries. All around me, the church attendants were busy lighting incense and candles and seeing to flowers: the Greek Orthodox priests in their black robes, the Armenian priests in their cream and purple robes, and the Catholic Franciscan monks with their hooded brown habits. All three denominations tend the church, but incredibly, no one is actually in overall charge. Finding a Franciscan monk who spoke English, I learned that Jerome's Bible was on display in a glass case in the Nativity Grotto. Situated underground, beneath the high altar, this is where Jesus is said to have been born.

Last time I was here I had to queue for about an hour to see the grotto. This time I was able to walk straight in and descend the flight of narrow stone steps that lead down into the supposed site of Christ's birth. The grotto itself is a dimly lit cavern, reeking with the incense smoke that belches from overhanging burners. The Bible tells us that Jesus was born in a stable, yet the grotto looks nothing like the familiar hut from a children's Nativity play. Whether Jesus actually was born here has been the subject of much debate. Nevertheless, the guidebooks assure visitors that there is plenty of evidence that the cave *was* used as a stable at the time Jesus is said to have been born. The precise spot where the birth is believed to have occurred is marked with a silver star on the floor, bearing the Latin inscription that translates as "Here Jesus Christ was born of the Virgin Mary." However, what interested me was the glass case set against the wall to one side of the star. Inside was the copy of Jerome's Bible, opened, so I discovered, to the page from Saint Luke's gospel that tells of Christ's birth. An inscribed plaque below, written in a number of different languages, informed visitors that the book dates from around A.D. 400 and is one of the oldest Bibles in the world.

Obviously, I would not be allowed to take it out of its case. Even if I could, I would have had to understand fourth-century ecclesiastical Latin to read it. Luckily, one of the attendants informed me that there was a modern English copy of Jerome's Bible in the church library. However, I would have to wait until the only librarian came back from his lunch. About three quarters of an hour later he appeared, but he was an Orthodox priest who evidently spoke only Greek. Finally, I managed to find someone to interpret for me and was able to tell him what I wanted. As it turned it, he was happy to let me browse through the book at my leisure, but my task seemed impossible; the work was over a thousand pages long, and I had no idea where to begin looking for a reference to Jeremiah hiding the Temple treasures in a cave. Eventually, I was helped by the Franciscan monk whom I spoke to when I first entered the church, and it did not take him long to work out where I might find what I was looking for.

The monk told me that Jerome's Bible contains a number of books in its Old Testament that are not included in modern Protestant Bibles like the King James version. These were some of the so-called Apocrypha, the texts of the Jewish Tanak that the Protestant Church had eventually decided to exclude. One of these was known as the second book of Maccabees, and it was here that there was indeed a passage concerning Jeremiah hiding some of the sacred Temple vessels. To my astonishment, these items were actually said to have included the Ark.

2 Maccabees 2:4–8 relates how, before the fall of Jerusalem to the Babylonians, Jeremiah left the city with the three Temple relics that were absent from the current Old Testament list: the tabernacle, the high altar, and the Ark of the Covenant. Apparently, God told Jeremiah what to do: "The prophet [Jeremiah], being warned by God, commanded that the tabernacle and the ark should accompany him." What was even more exciting was that the passage actually explains what Jeremiah did with them:

> He came forth to the mountain where Moses went up and saw the inheritance of God. And when Jeremiah came thither he found a hollow cave and he carried in thither the tabernacle and the ark and the altar of incense, and so stopped the door.

Here, it seems, the Ark remained:

> Then some of them that followed him, came up to mark the place; but they could not find it. And when Jeremiah perceived it, he blamed them saying: the place shall be unknown, till God gather together the congregation of the people and receive them to mercy.

Evidently, Jeremiah decided that the Ark should remain hidden in this mountain cave and made sure that no one else should know its precise location. Apparently, he believed that it was God's will that the Hebrew people should no longer possess these holy relics, as they had transgressed.

This was a thrilling discovery: I had found an ancient text that not only confirmed my suspicions that Jeremiah had hidden the Ark, it actually revealed *where* he had hidden it. Nevertheless, I had to curb my excitement until I could discover just how old and how authentic the 2 Maccabees account really was.

Back in Jerusalem, at the National Library, I learned that the text purportedly found its final form during the second century B.C. However, sections of it were certainly in existence, at least in oral form, in the early first century because it was quoted from by Philo of Alexandria, a Jewish Greek philosopher and historian who died in A.D. 40. No original Hebrew version of the text survives, but based on various references in the text, it is believed to be a composite work compiled from earlier documents dating from around 130 B.C. It is not, it seems, a contemporary account, so just how reliable it is seemed open to question. Nevertheless, as far as I could discover, it is the oldest known reference to the Ark of the Covenant outside what is now the Old Testament. In fact, it is the *only* ancient reference in existence to specifically refer to the hiding place of the Ark.

As I sat in the National Library, looking around me at the students and scholars meticulously studying books and diligently peering into computer screens, I realized that many Ark hunters before me must have been inspired by the book of Maccabees. I can't have been the only one to find it. It actually revealed where the Ark was hidden—in a cave on "the mountain where Moses went up and saw the inheritance of God." In the Old Testament, Moses leads the Israelites out of Egyptian captivity, and after forty years in the wilderness, they enter what the Bible calls the Promised Land of Canaan. Moses never sets foot in Canaan himself, but just before he dies, he climbs a mountain where he has a vision of the Promised Land and reveals the last of God's commandments to the Israelites. The Promised Land of Canaan, it seems, is what is implied by the words "inheritance of God" in the book of Maccabees account. Nearly every guidebook to the Holy Land confidently informs the reader that Moses's vision of the Promised Land occurred on Mount Nebo, modern Jebel en Neba, ten miles east of the northern end of the Dead Sea—a site that is now in the kingdom of Jordan. Indeed, as I suspected, many researchers had visited this site in the hope of finding the Ark.

There had, I soon discovered, been a number of expeditions to

Jebel en Neba in search of the Ark, the first in modern times being by the American evangelist and explorer Antonia Frederick Futterer in the 1920s. In 1981, one expedition to the area actually claimed to have found the Ark. It was led by another American, Tom Crotser from Winfield, Kansas. Apparently, close to a Franciscan monastery that stands on the summit of the mountain, Crotser and his companions discovered a cave that they believed was the cave described in the Maccabees account. They professed to have found a golden box inside that they believed was the lost Ark. For reasons best known to themselves, the team left it where it was and refused to reveal its location. Needless to say, Crotser's claim was greeted with skepticism by archaeologists. Photographs of the supposed find were shown to the eminent archaeologist Siegfried Horn, who was not impressed. Apparently, Crotser's color slides were not only unclear, but only two showed anything at all. One of these was fuzzy but did show what appeared to be a chamber with a yellow box in the center. The other slide was clearer and gave a good front view of the box. According to Horn, the workmanship of the box was so uniform that it could only have been done by machine. Furthermore, a nail sticking out of the top of the box had, in his opinion, a modern-looking head. He concluded that it appeared to be an artifact of modern fabrication.

After reading of Crotser's purported discovery, I was as skeptical as Professor Horn. In fact, when I consulted the biblical references to the mountain where Moses is said to have apparently seen "the inheritance of God," I began to wonder whether the book of Maccabees account referred to Mount Nebo at all.

There are three Old Testament accounts of Moses's vision of the Promised Land, found separately in the books of Leviticus, Numbers, and Deuteronomy, and they each provide different locations for the event: on Mounts Nebo, Abarim, and Sinai. Deuteronomy 32:49 actually gives two locations, naming both Mount Abarim and Mount Nebo in God's command to Moses: "Get thee up unto this mountain Abarim, unto mount Nebo, which is in the land of Moab, that is over against Jericho." The author seems to have considered the two mountains to be the same, whereas, in fact, Mount Nebo is modern Jebel en Neba, ten miles east of the northern end of the Dead Sea, while Mount Abarim is modern Jebel el Hamra, some twenty-one miles farther south. The author not only wrongly assumed that Abarim and Nebo were the same mountain, he also appeared to believe that the site in question was near Jericho, which is actually miles from either location. Mount Nebo is nineteen miles from Jericho, and Mount Abarim is over thirty miles away. It seems that the author was totally unfamiliar with the area. Whoever he was, he must have been writing years after the event and in a different country.

Although the Numbers account of the same event is less confusing, naming only Mount Abarim, when the author summarizes the episode in the final verse of this book, he reveals that he is equally unfamiliar with the topography of the area:

> These are the commandments and the judgments, which the Lord commanded by the hand of Moses unto the children of Israel in the plains of Moab by Jordan near Jericho. (Nm 36:13)

In this verse, the author mistakenly places Jericho in the land of Moab. Moab was a foreign kingdom to the east of the River Jordan, while Jericho is fifteen miles to the west of the river—well inside ancient Canaan.

The same account is found in the book of Leviticus, which also summarizes the event in its last verse. Here it takes place on Mount Sinai: "These are the commandments, which the Lord commanded Moses for the children of Israel on Mount Sinai" (Lv 27:34).

I was pretty much persuaded that the Ark of the Covenant had been removed from the Jerusalem Temple just before the Babylonian invasion in 597 B.C., and that Jeremiah was the most likely person to have been responsible. Whoever removed it, it was never retrieved, and so it was presumably hidden somewhere. As the only ancient text to name a hiding place, the book of Maccabees account was all I had to go on. Whether it was reliable was open to debate. Nevertheless, it seemed well worth following up. The problem was that I had three possible locations to investigate. I had to decide which of these seemed the most likely to have been the site of

Moses's vision of the Promised Land. As both the Deuteronomy and Numbers accounts contained geographical mistakes that did not appear in the book of Leviticus, the Leviticus account of the event occurring on Mount Sinai seemed the best bet. The more I thought about it, the more likely it seemed that Mount Sinai was the place where the Ark would have been hidden: It was, after all, where its story began. Moreover, the Ark was the Hebrews' most sacred possession, which from the time of King Solomon had to be kept on only the most sanctified ground. God himself was believed to have instructed the Temple to be built especially to house it. Before that time, the most sacred Hebrew site was Mount Sinai. With the Temple threatened, Mount Sinai would be the next logical choice for the Ark's resting place. I was sure that others must have reached the same conclusion. Even if they had, however, I now understood why the Ark had never been found: The true location of Mount Sinai has itself been long forgotten.

7
Mountain of God

Before I spent time trying to identify Mount Sinai, I needed to determine whether the book of Maccabees account of the hiding of the Ark was historically plausible. It said that Jeremiah had hidden the Ark at the mountain where Moses had experienced his vision of the Promised Land, and the Leviticus account identified the site as Mount Sinai. As I had already decided, Jeremiah was by far the most likely person to have been responsible for the Ark's removal from the Jerusalem Temple, so there was nothing improbable about that aspect of the Maccabees account. But what about Mount Sinai as a location for its secret hiding place?

The more I continued my research, the more Mount Sinai did in fact seem the most logical place for Jeremiah, or any other Jew of the time, to have brought the Ark. According to the Bible, Mount Sinai was the ancient Israelites' most sacred site before the Jerusalem Temple was built. It was here that God first spoke to Moses from the burning bush; it was here that Moses led the Israelites after their flight from Egypt; and it was here that God gave the Israelites their religious laws, made the Ten Commandments, and ordered the making of the Ark. All this may have been reason enough for Jeremiah to have considered it a fitting hiding place for the Ark. However, the Jerusalem Temple and the sacred mountain had something in common that appeared to make Mount Sinai the *only* place the Ark could have been taken. Both sites—and only these sites—were thought to have been inhabited by God.

In the Old Testament, Mount Sinai is often referred to as the Mountain of God because God was, quite literally, thought to have resided here. Repeatedly, the mountain is described as God's "holy habitation" (e.g., in Exodus 15:13 and Deuteronomy 26:15) while other references specifically state that God lived on the sacred mountain. For example, Exodus 24:16 relates that "the Lord abode upon mount Sinai." The first-century Jewish historian Josephus confirms that this was no metaphor and that the ancient Israelites really did believe that God resided on the mountain. Concerning the place where Moses encountered the burning bush, he wrote: "Now this is the highest of all the mountains thereabouts, and the best for pasturage, the herbage being there good; and it had not been before fed upon, because of the opinion men had that God dwelt there." (*Antiquities* 1981)

However, after it was built, the Israelites considered that the Jerusalem Temple was God's new "holy habitation." In the second book of Chronicles, Solomon explains why he has built the Temple: "I have built a house of habitation for thee [God], and a place for thy dwelling for ever" (2 Chr 6:1). According to 2 Chronicles then, the Jerusalem Temple was to be forevermore the one and only house of God. Unlike later Christian or Jewish notions of all churches or synagogues being the house of the Lord, to the ancient Israelites there was only one such place. There were other temples and shrines where God could be worshiped, but there could be only one "house of God." Right up until the time of the Babylonian invasion, the Temple continued to be referred to as the House of God. In the reign of the Judean king Ahaz, in the eighth century B.C.: "And Ahaz gathered together the vessels of the house of God" (2 Chr 28:24). In the reign of Hezekiah, in the seventh century B.C.: "And in every work that he began in the service of the house of God" (2 Chr 31:21). And at the time the Babylonians sacked the Temple, in the sixth century B.C.: "And they burnt the house of God" (2 Chr 36:19).

With the Temple under threat, Mount Sinai would have been the most appropriate place for Jeremiah to have brought the Ark: It was the only other "holy habitation" of God. However, as I continued to examine the Old Testament texts, I began to realize that there was a compelling and far more specific reason for Jeremiah to have taken the Ark to Mount Sinai. It was not so much the Ark itself that had to be removed from the Temple, but the presence of God that it was constructed to contain.

According to the book of Exodus, God physically appeared to the Israelites for the first time on Mount Sinai:

> And the Lord said unto Moses, Lo, I come unto thee in a thick cloud, that the people may hear when I speak with thee . . . And be ready against the third day: for the third day the Lord will come down in the sight of all the people upon mount Sinai. (Ex 19:9–11)

It is not clear in exactly what form God appeared, but he somehow manifested inside a dense cloud of smoke:

> And mount Sinai was altogether in a smoke, because the Lord descended upon it in fire: and the smoke thereof ascended as the smoke of a furnace, and the whole mount quaked greatly . . . And the Lord came down upon mount Sinai, on the top of the mount. (Ex 19:18–20)

Each time God appeared on Mount Sinai, the cloud materialized and the presence of God that manifested within it is described as the "glory of the Lord"—apparently a kind of divine fire:

> And the glory of the Lord abode upon mount Sinai, and the cloud covered it six days: and the seventh day he called unto Moses out of the midst of the cloud. And the sight of the glory of the Lord was like devouring fire on the top of the mount in the eyes of the children of Israel. (Ex 24:16–17)

Before the Israelites left Mount Sinai to continue their journey through the wilderness, God ordered them to make the Ark. As strange as it may seem to modern theological thought, the Ark was actually made to contain God himself. In the Exodus account God told Moses what to do:

> And let them make me a sanctuary; that I may dwell among them. According to all that I shew thee, after the pattern of the tabernacle,

and the pattern of all the instruments thereof, even so shall ye make it. And they shall make an ark of shittim wood: two cubits and a half shall be the length thereof, and a cubit and a half the breadth thereof, and a cubit and a half the height thereof. (Ex 25:8–10)

The most essential part appears to be the mysterious mercy seat, upon which God would be able to manifest:

And thou shalt make a mercy seat of pure gold . . . And thou shalt put the mercy seat above upon the ark . . . And there I will meet with thee, and I will commune with thee from above the mercy seat. (Ex 25:17–22)

The presence of God was now within the Ark, for when the Israelites left Mount Sinai, the miraculous cloud of smoke hung over it:

And they departed from the mount of the Lord three days' journey: and the ark of the covenant of the Lord went before them in the three days' journey, to search out a resting place for them. And the cloud of the Lord was upon them by day, when they went out of the camp. (Nm 10:33–34)

Each time the Israelites made camp, the Ark was placed in the tabernacle or "tent of the congregation" behind a special veil or curtain.

And the Lord spake unto Moses, saying, On the first day of the first month shalt thou set up the tabernacle of the tent of the congregation. And thou shalt put therein the ark of the testimony, and cover the ark with the veil. (Ex 40:1–3)

It seems that this veil divided the sacred place of the Ark from the rest of tabernacle:

And thou shalt hang up the veil under the taches [clasps], that thou mayest bring in thither within the veil the ark of the testimony: and the veil shall divide unto you between the holy place and the most holy. (Ex 26:33)

On Mount Sinai, when God had communed with Moses, he appeared on the summit of the mountain. Now, however, he appeared where the Ark was, from behind the veil in the tabernacle. His presence, however, could be fatal to anyone who came too near, as Moses's brother Aaron was warned:

> And the Lord said unto Moses, Speak unto Aaron thy brother, that he come not at all times into the holy place within the veil before the mercy seat, which is upon the ark; that he die not: for I will appear in the cloud upon the mercy seat. (Lv 16:2)

Just as at Mount Sinai, the presence of God upon the Ark was called the glory of the Lord—already described as devouring fire: "Then a cloud covered the tent of the congregation, and the glory of the Lord filled the tabernacle" (Ex 40:34).

Biblical passages such as these clearly show that the presence of God, which was previously believed to have dwelled exclusively on Mount Sinai, was now thought to reside with the Ark. Like the Egyptian bark that carried the statue of the god Amun when it left the Temple of Karnak, the Ark of the Covenant seems to have been considered a means of carrying God—or something through which God could manifest—from his holy habitation on Mount Sinai.

When Mount Zion was later consecrated as a new holy mountain and the Jerusalem Temple was eventually built as the "house of God," it seems that the presence of God left the Ark to inhabit the Temple's inner sanctum. The first book of Kings describes how the Ark was carried inside the Temple once it was finished: "And the priests brought in the ark of the covenant of the Lord unto his place, into the oracle of the house, to the most holy place" (1 Kgs 8:6). At this point, the Ark was opened for the first time in years:

> There was nothing in the ark save the two tables [tablets] of stone, which Moses put there at Horeb, when the Lord made a covenant with the children of Israel, when they came out of the land of Egypt. (1 Kgs 8:9)

Yet as soon as the Ark was opened, something miraculous occurred:

> And it came to pass, when the priests were come out of the holy place, that the cloud filled the house of the Lord, so that the priests

could not stand to minister because of the cloud: for the glory of
the Lord had filled the house of the Lord. (1 Kgs 8:10–11)

King Solomon then explained what has occurred: "The Lord said
that he would dwell in thick darkness. I have surely built thee a
house to dwell in, a settled place for thee to abide in for ever" (1 Kgs
8:12–13). Solomon is quite clearly interpreting the cloud and "glory
of the Lord" filling the building as God's presence leaving the Ark
to dwell permanently in the Temple.

From my perspective, it did not matter whether these miraculous
episodes historically occurred or not. The important point was that
the Jews at the time of the Babylonian invasion believed they had.
Their holy scriptures asserted that the presence of God had been carried from Mount Sinai and had ultimately been brought to the
Jerusalem Temple in the Ark of the Covenant. Jeremiah knew that
the Babylonians would invade Jerusalem and would probably
destroy the Temple as an act of reprisal. If the Jerusalem Temple was
no longer a safe place for the presence of God to inhabit, then surely
it would have to be returned to the place from where it originally
came: Mount Sinai. The only way to transport this divine presence
was in the Ark of the Covenant. In short, it seemed that the Ark had
to be returned to Mount Sinai and nowhere else.

I was satisfied that Mount Sinai was the most likely place for
Jeremiah to have hidden the Ark. The big question then was, Where
exactly was Mount Sinai? Strangely, considering the religious signif-
icance of the Mountain of God, the Bible is far from clear regarding
its actual location. All we are told in the Exodus account is that it is
somewhere in the Sinai Wilderness:

In the third month, when the children of Israel were gone forth out
of the land of Egypt, the same day came they into the wilderness
of Sinai. For they were departed from Rephidim, and were come
to the desert of Sinai, and had pitched in the wilderness; and there
Israel camped before the mount. (Ex 19:1–2)

Unfortunately, the inclusion of the name Rephidim, where the
Israelites had just been, is of no help. This is not a place-name; it

simply means "place of rest." It was where the Israelites camped for a while to recuperate and allow their animals to graze. All we learn from this passage is that the Mountain of God is somewhere in the Sinai Wilderness. From the known locations referred to in the Old Testament, we can gather that the area known as the Sinai Wilderness covered a large territory, including the modern-day Sinai Peninsula in eastern Egypt, parts of southern Israel and Jordan, and even a part of Saudi Arabia. It was not a desert, like the Sahara, with great stretches of sand, but a stony, dusty, rough country with sparse vegetation, interspersed with the occasional oasis of fertile ground. It measures some 250 miles from north to south and 220 miles from east to west. This is around 55,000 square miles. There were many mountains in this considerable expanse, and the Mountain of God could have been any of them. Indeed, by the Christian era its true location seems to have been completely forgotten.

In the fourth century A.D., the first Christian Roman emperor, Constantine the Great, believed he had discovered where Mount Sinai was. He confidently proclaimed that it was a particular mountain at the southern end of the Sinai Peninsula in Egypt. By all accounts, he learned of the location from a vision or dream experienced by his mother, Helena (the same Helena who affected the construction of the original Church of the Nativity). Constantine renamed the site Mount Sinai, and soon after, the monastery of Saint Catherine's was founded there and quickly became a major center of pilgrimage. Even today, the monastery is still occupied by monks who claim it to be the oldest continuously inhabited building in the world. What the mountain had previously been called is now unknown. Most Western maps still refer to it as Mount Sinai, while Arab maps call it Jebel Musa—the "Mountain of Moses." However, despite the fact that the site still attracts thousands of tourists every year, modern scholars have failed to discover any biblical or historical evidence to support Constantine's or his mother's belief.

Skeptical of Jebel Musa, a number of modern archaeologists have proposed other locations for Mount Sinai. One of the more recent theories has come from respected Italian paleoethnologist Emmanuel Anati, who proposed Mount Karkom, near El Kuntilla in

Israel, about twenty-five miles north of Elat. Anati based his conclusion on his discovery at the foot of the mountain of the remains of circular dwellings and an altar surrounded by twelve standing stones. According to Exodus 24:4, Moses erected an altar and twelve pillars below the Mountain of God to represent each of the twelve Hebrew tribes. Despite the initial excitement, however, a recent excavation has dated the remains to around 2000 B.C., five centuries before even the earliest dating of the Exodus.

Another recent theory identified the Mountain of God as Jebel al-Lawz in Saudi Arabia. In 1986 two American explorers, Ron Wyatt and David Fasold, traveled to the mountain, hoping to find the Egyptian jewelry the Bible says the Israelites had with them during the Exodus. However, they were almost immediately arrested for illegal excavation, threatened with imprisonment by the Saudi authorities, and deported. Their identification of Jebel al-Lawz with the Mountain of God was based on their hypothesis that it is located in what was once the land of Midian. According to Exodus, this is where Moses fled after his exile from Egypt. As Jebel al-Lawz is the highest mountain in this region, it seemed logical to Wyatt and Fasold that this would be the place where God would have communed with Moses.

More recently, another pair of American explorers decided to follow in Wyatt and Fasold's footsteps. Wall Street millionaire Larry Williams and ex–police officer Bob Cornuke illegally crossed into Saudi territory to search the mountain for evidence that it really was Mount Sinai. Breaking into the now fenced-off area, Williams and Cornuke searched for correspondences with the biblical record. Near the foot of the mountain, they spotted a stack of boulders bearing rock drawings of bulls. This, Williams and Cornuke decided, might be the altar where the Israelites were said to have worshiped the golden calf. Higher up the slope, Williams and Cornuke found a large stone structure, next to which were the remnants of what appeared to be twelve stone towers, each about eighteen feet in diameter. They identified the stone structure as the altar constructed by Moses and the towers as the twelve pillars he erected nearby.

Unlike their predecessors, Williams and Cornuke managed to evade the Saudi authorities, but their findings failed to convince their critics, and various archaeologists questioned their theory. Biblical scholar Allen Kerkeslager, for instance, pointed out that the stack of stones that Williams and Cornuke identified with the golden calf altar—because of the bull pictographs—was actually a common construction in the area, intended in ancient times to communicate messages concerning hunting and other pastoral activities. What the explorers identified as stone towers, Kerkeslager suggested, were burial mounds common throughout northwest Arabia.

Fierce academic debate still surrounds many proposed sites for Mount Sinai, and its true location remains one of the Bible's most contested mysteries. However, when I examined the various Old Testament references to the Mountain of God more carefully, I realized that they did provide some important clues that seemed to have been completely overlooked.

The Mountain of God is referred to by two different names in the Old Testament: Mount Sinai and Mount Horeb, or simply Horeb. The Bible leaves no doubt that these were both the same mountain. The holy laws that God is said to have revealed to the Israelites at the Mountain of God are referred to in the Bible as "the Covenant," and repeatedly when the book of Deuteronomy talks of the Covenant it refers to Horeb. For example: "God made a covenant with us in Horeb" (Dt 5:2). Indeed, 1 Kings 19:8 says quite specifically that Horeb is the Mountain of God. Concerning the prophet Elijah, this verse tells us: "And he arose, and did eat and drink, and went in the strength of that meat forty days and forty nights unto Horeb the mount of God."

Why the mountain has two different names is something of a mystery, but it may have been because, like God himself, the mountain was considered too sacred to call by name. As the term suggests, Mount Sinai merely refers to a mountain in the Sinai Wilderness, while in Hebrew the word *horeb* simply means something like "mountain in the desert." (Biblical linguists have suggested that it is a combination of two Hebrew words: *hor,* meaning "mount," and *choreb,* meaning a dry or desert place.) Deuteronomy only once refers to the holy mountain as Mount Sinai; on other occasions it is referred to only as "the mount" or "mount of God." In other words, neither of these names identifies a specific site; the Mountain of God could be any mountain in the Sinai Wilderness. What I needed to discover was its real name, which meant ascertaining more precisely where it was thought to have been. Were there any clues in the Bible? As it turned out, there were in fact two incidents that were said to have occurred on the Mountain of God that pointed to a specific area of the Sinai Wilderness—not Midian, in the south of the wilderness, as Wyatt and Fasold proposed, but Edom in the north.

The first indicator I discovered was in the book of Exodus, in the passage that concerned Moses and the burning bush. According to Exodus 2:15–21, after he was forced into exile from Egypt, Moses settled in the land of Midian, where he married the daughter of a local priest called Jethro. Some years later, Moses was tending his father-in-law's flock when he was confronted by a bush that burned without being consumed. It was from within this miraculous fire that Moses first heard the voice of God. According to Exodus 3:1, this event took place at Horeb, the Mountain of God:

> Now Moses kept the flock of Jethro his father-in-law, the priest of Midian: and he led the flock to the backside of the desert, and came to the mountain of God, even to Horeb.

Midian was the ancient name for the area to the immediate east of the Gulf of Aqaba, in what is now the extreme northwest of Saudi Arabia. Just like today's Bedouin, the peoples of Midian were nomadic shepherds. Entire family groups would lead their flocks of sheep and goats hundreds of miles in the course of a year around the Sinai Wilderness to the north of Midian, continually moving on to fresh grazing land. This, it seems, is what Moses was doing when he encountered the burning bush. If the desert referred to in the above verse was the Sinai Wilderness, then the words "backside of the desert"—where the Mountain of God was from the Midian perspective—must have been to the extreme north of the region. This would be somewhere in what is now the Negev Desert, in southern Jordan—a land that in biblical times was called Edom.

The second clue to the location of the Mountain of God I found later in the Exodus account. After Moses went back to Egypt and led the Israelites to freedom, he returned with them to Horeb to again commune with God on the sacred mountain. By the time they arrived, the Israelites had run out of water and were dying of thirst. Moses, however, saved them with a miracle:

> And the Lord said unto Moses, Go on before the people, and take with thee of the elders of Israel; and thy rod, wherewith thou smotest the river, take in thine hand, and go. Behold, I will stand before thee there upon the rock in Horeb; and thou shalt smite the rock, and there shall come water out of it, that the people may drink. (Ex 17:5–6)

Although this particular passage provides no clue about where Horeb actually is, the same incident is mentioned in the book of Numbers:

> And Moses took the rod from before the Lord, as he commanded him . . . And Moses lifted up his hand, and with his rod he smote the rock twice: and the water came out abundantly, and the congregation drank. (Nm 20:9–11)

This passage does not say that the incident occurred at the Mountain of God—which is why it seems to have been overlooked—but it is clearly the same event. However, a few verses later we *are* told where it occurred. Once the Israelites have refreshed themselves, Moses sends a messenger to ask the local king for permission to pass through his land:

> And Moses sent messengers from Kadesh unto the king of Edom, Thus saith thy brother Israel . . . Let us pass, I pray thee, through thy country. (Nm 20:14–17)

The Exodus passage says that the miraculous water from the rock episode took place at Horeb, the Mountain of God, while the Numbers passage tells us that this same event took place at Kadesh. In Hebrew the word *kadesh* means "holiness," or in this context "a holy place." It seems then that this is not the name of the place but rather a description. The English translation should have been "Moses sent messengers from the holy place unto the king of Edom." It would appear then that this verse simply referred to Horeb, the Mountain of God. Although the precise location of Kadesh is a mystery, it must have been somewhere on the border of the land of Edom, as Moses seeks permission from the king of Edom to proceed further. It is quite clear, therefore, if the current Old Testament is right, that the Mountain of God is in or near the land of Edom—a land in what is now southern Jordan.

As I pored over ancient maps in the National Library, I scanned the area for clues to the mountain that Old Testament authors might have called Mount Sinai or Mount Horeb—and to which Jeremiah would have taken the Ark. A mountain range in southwest Jordan runs right through what was once the land of Edom—the Shara Range. Could one of its mountains have been referred to by the Old Testament authors as Mount Sinai or Horeb?

Edom was a small kingdom in the northwest of the Sinai Wilderness. Archaeology has shown that it was inhabited by a Semite people known as the Edomites from around 1700 B.C. until the area was occupied by the Nabateans from Arabia in the fourth century B.C. From the various finds, it has been determined that the Edomites had migrated south from Canaan at around the same time that other Semites (including, it seems, the Israelites) settled in Egypt. The Edomites were therefore closely related to the original Israelites, and this, plus their migration into the Sinai Wilderness, seems to be reflected in the Old Testament story of Jacob and Esau.

According to the book of Genesis, Jacob and Esau were brothers who lived in Canaan, but separated because Jacob tricked Esau out of his inheritance. Jacob and his family moved east to Egypt, where his descendants became the Israelites, while Esau moved south into Edom, where his descendants became the Edomites. Although this was no doubt a simplification, or allegory, of events, DNA tests on the skeletal remains of both the Israelites and Edomites have shown that they did have a common ancestry. On reading the Genesis account of Esau settling in the land of Edom, I was immediately struck by something interesting—the passage made reference to a specific mountain around which the Edomites lived: "Thus dwelt Esau in mount Seir . . . And these are the generations of Esau the father of the Edomites in mount Seir" (Gn 36:8–9).

Mount Seir is mentioned a number of times in the Old Testament, and when I read the various references I realized that I was on to something. It seemed that, like Mount Sinai, Mount Seir was considered a holy mountain associated with God. In the book of Isaiah, the prophet Isaiah (circa 700 B.C.) says that when God speaks to him, "He calleth to me out of Seir" (Is 21:11). God, it seems, called to the prophet from where he was residing, at Mount Seir. Another Old Testament passage further suggests that God was thought to have resided on Mount Seir, as when God was called by the Israelites he again responded by coming from that mountain. However, this passage actually seems to link Mount Seir with Mount Sinai. Judges 5:4–5 includes the prayer:

> Lord, when thou wentest out of Seir, when thou marchedst out of the field of Edom, the earth trembled, and the heavens dropped, the clouds also dropped water. The mountains melted from before the Lord, even that Sinai from before the Lord God of Israel.

What the link between the two mountains may have been is difficult to tell from this passage alone. However, Deuteronomy includes a verse that appears to imply that the two mountains are actually one and the same. When Moses was dying, he asked God to come and bless the Israelites, and "the Lord came from [Mount] Sinai and rose up from [Mount] Seir unto them" (Dt 33:2). As mentioned, the Old Testament frequently gives two names when it mentions Mount Sinai. When Moses first visited Mount Sinai in the burning bush episode, for example, he is described in the widely used King James Bible as having gone to "the mountain of God, even to Horeb" (Ex 3:1). As "even" means "that is" or "in other words" in this context, the author is using both the terms "Mountain of God" and "Horeb" for the site. In the same way, the author of the Deuteronomy passage appears to be using both the names Sinai and Seir for the sacred mountain.

The Mountain of God certainly appeared to have been in the

land of Edom, somewhere in the Shara Range. At least, that is what the Old Testament scribes who compiled the relevant accounts around 650 to 500 B.C. seem to have believed. It also seemed that at least some of these scribes believed that Mount Seir and Mount Sinai were one and the same. I may well have narrowed down the area of the Sinai Wilderness in which the holy mountain was. However, I still had a problem. The precise location of Mount Seir was as much a mystery to biblical scholars as Mount Sinai. Which of the Shara Mountains was Mount Seir?

The Valley of Edom

8

What exactly was known about the ancient land of Edom? Not only the Bible but also texts from Middle Eastern countries other than Judah refer to it. Going by these various accounts, the area described as Edom was roughly the southern half of the Negev Desert, which in biblical times formed the northern and least hospitable part of the Sinai Wilderness. It remains unchanged today. As far as the eye can see, the sun beats mercilessly down upon dusty white rocks and searing, lifeless sand. Day after day, year after year, the ground bakes in the shimmering heat. In this dry, stony desert, 125 miles long and 125 miles wide, temperatures can rise to well over a hundred degrees in the shade. At night, however, the temperature plummets close to freezing, and a bitter chill descends over this barren country.

The Shara Mountains run right through this arid wasteland, and nestling within them is a valley once called the Valley of Edom. Nourished by cool mountain streams and shaded by towering cliffs, it was a haven for life in otherwise hostile terrain. Today, although the valley is far more life-bearing than the surrounding desert, it is nowhere near as fertile as it was three thousand years ago when rainfall was higher and numerous streams fed the valley floor. Located some twelve miles inside what is now the kingdom of Jordan, the Edom Valley is around half a mile wide and three miles long. Although the entire southern Negev was known as the land of Edom, at the time of the ancient Israelites the kingdom of the Edom was a tiny realm, centered on this fertile vale. It seems, then, that

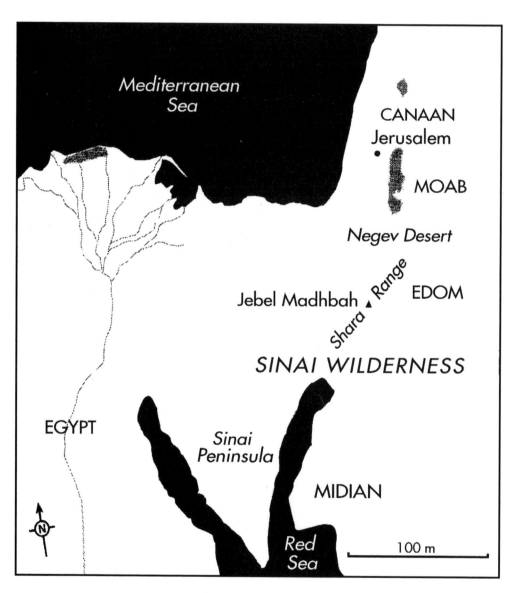

The Sinai Wilderness

this isolated valley was the land that Moses asked the king of Edom for permission to pass through after he had created the miraculous spring. As the incident had taken place at Horeb, and Horeb was another name for Mount Sinai, it seems that one of the mountains that encircled the Valley of Edom was the mysterious Mountain of God.

In ancient times an important trading route ran right through the Valley of Edom from east to west. It connected Egypt and Africa with the Arab world and the East, and the Edomites who controlled it for more than a thousand years until the fourth century B.C. prospered from the tariffs they charged. The valley was a natural fortress with easily guarded passes, and the entrances to the trade route were gorges so narrow in places that pack animals could only be led through in single file. According to the Exodus account, the miraculous spring incident took place at "the rock in Horeb" (Ex 17:5–6), and from the Numbers account we can gather that the same incident took place at a location called Kadesh—the holy place—on the border of the Edomite kingdom (Nm 20:9–17). If the Israelites had come from the southern Sinai Wilderness, then they would have arrived at the border of the Edomite kingdom at a gorge that is today known as Siq al Barid, Arabic for "cold canyon" and called the Siq for short. If my theory was correct, then it was here that Mount Sinai was to be found.

Traveling south from Jerusalem by bus, I crossed the border from Israel into Jordan to arrive soon after at the town of Elji that lies at the outer end of the Siq gorge. Elji was hardly what I had been expecting. I had envisaged a quiet little village, inhabited by just a few local farming families, whereas it turned out to be a popular tourist site with modern hotels and gift shops. Having checked into one of the hotels, I looked out my window at the mountains that rose to either side of the entrance to the gorge. In stark contrast to the desert, their rocks were a vista of color: golden brown, yellow, orange, and red. If I was right, then one of these two mountains had to have been Horeb, where Moses had created the miraculous spring. Which one, I wondered, had been the real Mount Sinai, the Mountain of God?

Next day, I hired a local guide named Abdul who almost immediately told me something that left me stunned. The Valley of Edom is now called Wadi Musa, which in Arabic means "the valley of Moses." It was so named, Abdul told me, because there was a local Bedouin tradition that it was here that Moses had created the miraculous spring in the Old Testament story. I thought that I had been really clever in working out that this was where the incident occurred—only to find out that the local people had believed it for years. In fact, they had built a shrine on the exact site where they thought the incident occurred, near the entrance to the Siq. Called Ain Musa—the Spring of Moses—it was a small domed mosque erected over a rectangular pool, still supplied by a freshwater spring.

The Ain Musa tradition was indeed ancient, as I later discovered. It is attested to by the medieval Arab chronicler Numairi. Numairi was an Egyptian and his chronicle, dating from the thirteenth century, still survives at the National Library of Egypt in Cairo. Referring to the approach to Petra, Numairi wrote:

> At the foot of a mountain there is a spring, which is said never to run dry. The people thereabouts say that Moses, Prophet of God, peace upon him, did bring it forth with his staff.

If this spring had really been the one in the Exodus account—a spring that came from a rock "in Horeb"—then presumably the mountain rising above it was none other than Mount Horeb itself. Standing outside the shrine, I looked up at the sandstone cliffs that towered above me. Was this really the Mountain of God?

I asked Abdul if there were any traditions associating the mountain with Mount Sinai. Unfortunately, he knew of none. However, he told me that it had long been considered a sacred place by the Bedouin of the area. It was called Jebel Madhbah—Mountain of the Altar—as there was an ancient shrine on its summit that dated back over three thousand years. What struck me as strange was that, as far as I could tell, no biblical scholar, archaeologist, or historian who had attempted to search for the Mountain of God appeared to have appreciated the relevance of the Ain Musa shrine. All I could assume was that they had not coupled the book of Numbers account of Moses creating the miraculous spring with the same account in the book of Exodus.

Abdul offered to take me up Jebel Madhbah and show me the shrine at the summit. The only way up the mountain was from within the Wadi Musa, and the quickest way to get there was on horseback or by camel. Abdul had a number of horses at his disposal, but I had only ridden once in my life and doubted I would be able to stay on a horse, let alone control it. However, it was not as bad as I expected; the animal seemed to know what to do and simply followed Abdul's horse and stopped when it did.

Just as it would have been for the ancient Israelites, the only way to enter the Valley of Edom from the southern side, avoiding the grueling haul over the mountains, was through the Siq that wound its way eastward through a mile of solid rock. This deep, narrow cleft was created millions of years ago when some gigantic geological upheaval literally tore a mountain in two. At the start, this long, winding gorge was around fifteen feet wide, but the further we progressed, the narrower it became until sunlight no longer shone down between the sheer walls to either side. Apparently, this is why it was called the "cold canyon." Finally, after riding for what seemed forever and just when the deep, dark corridor seemed about to close completely in on us, it turned abruptly and opened out onto one of the most spectacular sights I had ever seen. Rising high above us in the opposite cliff was the 130-foot edifice of a gigantic monument: two tiers of towering columns, colossal pediments, statue niches, and carved urns, all cut into the sheer rock face. It was, I was told, the entrance to a number of vast chambers cut deep inside the mountain. Immediately, I realized that I had seen this monument before. It had been used by Steven Spielberg as the lost repository for the Holy Grail in his movie *Indiana Jones and the Last Crusade*. Now called Al Khazneh—the Treasury—its original function is something of a mystery, but it is thought to be the remains of a two-thousand-year old tomb.

As old as it may be, the Treasury would not have been here when the Edomites occupied the valley in Old Testament times. Abdul explained that it was one of the many monuments built by the Nabateans who moved into the Valley of Edom in the fourth century B.C. Forced westward by the expanding Babylonian empire, the Nabateans had originated around the Arabian Gulf and were first compelled to a nomadic existence in the Arabian Desert. Something, perhaps incursions by the Babylonians, weakened the Edomites between the sixth and fourth centuries B.C. enough for the Nabateans to move into the Valley of Edom and make it their own. By the end of the fourth century B.C., Alexander the Great had established Greek influence throughout the eastern Mediterranean, and the Nabateans quickly took control of new trade routes that came into existence through the Shara Mountains. Standing on a crossroads between the lands of the Mediterranean and the lands of the Near East and Asia, the Nabatean kingdom became rich and powerful, and a great city, the city of Petra, grew up at the heart of the valley. One of the most important cities of the Middle East, Petra remained independent until it was annexed by the Romans in A.D. 106.

Abdul wanted to show me around the Treasury, so we dismounted and went inside. Passing into the dark interior, through a huge entrance some twenty feet high, I found myself inside a vast hall, leading off into cold, empty chambers, deep inside the mountain. As I followed my guide from chamber to chamber, he told how archaeologists believed that it had been the tomb of an important Nabatean king who had lived in Petra in Roman times. When I asked why it was called the Treasury, Abdul told me a fascinating story about hidden treasure. Apparently, in the twelfth century, European Crusaders had found jewels and artifacts of pure gold hidden in a nearby cave. Since that time, countless numbers of treasure hunters had excavated all around the monument in the hope of finding more.

By the time we left the Treasury, two parties of Western tourists had arrived. Hearing English voices, I was about to go over and chat with some of them when the most peculiar thing happened. A sudden and fierce wind whipped up the dust of the valley floor, making the horses whinny, forcing the tourists to cover their faces, and blowing hot, dry sand right into my eyes. It was then that there came the most eerie sound I had ever heard. It was a deafening noise, like a bizarre cacophony of Buddhist prayer horns being blown in unison. Unable to see, I wondered what the hell was going on. A few seconds later the wind subsided and the noise ceased. When I was finally able to open my eyes, I could see that the tourists were as mystified as I. They were looking about them in stunned silence, while two Arab guides were laughing their heads off. Behind me, Abdul joined in.

"That always frightens the sightseers," he laughed. He explained that the strange sound was an unusual but natural phenomenon created by a strong wind that sometimes howls through the Siq. The local Bedouin, he told me, refer to it as "the trumpet of God."

At first, I joined in the laughter. The guides had obviously not yet told the tourists the cause of the noise, and they were still visibly shaken by the unearthly sound. All of a sudden, however, the scene reminded of something that I had only that morning read in the Bible. I had been rereading the relevant verses of the Old Testament concerning the Israelites' first visit to the Mountain of God. According to Exodus 9:11–27, while Moses prepared the Israelites to witness the manifestation of God, they camped at the foot of the mountain. On the third day, God finally descended upon Mount Sinai:

> There were thunders and lightnings, and a thick cloud upon the mount, and the voice of the trumpet exceeding loud; so that all the people that was in the camp trembled. (Ex 19:16)

A trumpet exceedingly loud! Could this have been an ancient description of the very same sound I had just heard? If the Israelites made camp at the foot of Jebel Madhbah, then they could well have camped where I was now standing. The Exodus passage suggested that a violent storm was raging—and with storms come winds. (Today, such storms are a rarity in the area, although when it does rain it can be torrential.) If the wind had howled down the gorge as it had just done, then the ancient Israelites might well have been as frightened as the bewildered tourists. The Israelites had considered the sound they heard to be a sign from God. The local Bedouin even called the phenomenon the trumpet of God. A coincidence, perhaps, but a fascinating one nevertheless!

As we continued our trek into the valley, I stared up at Jebel Madhbah, rising high above the Treasury. Had the ancient Israelites really seen something spectacular up there among the primeval, weathered rocks—a manifestation so awesome that, for them, it could have been nothing other than God himself?

Beyond the Treasury, there was another gorge, known as the Outer Siq, flanked on each side by a sheer cliff face. However, it was nowhere near as narrow as the Siq itself, averaging some two hundred feet wide. It led downward into the Wadi Musa, about three-quarters of a mile to the north, where a broad, flat plain, set between craggy mountains, stretched out before us. At the time of Moses, this had been the home of the Edomites, but the ruins that now dominate the valley are the remains of the Nabatean city of Petra. They are in fact classical ruins, the buildings having been influenced by Greek and Roman design—an amphitheater, the walls of homes, administrative buildings, and temples, all set around a series of paved roads. To either side of these straight avenues, stone pillars, colonnades, and broken statues line the ways that would long ago have been the thoroughfares of the ancient city. Cut into the cliffs surrounding Petra are hundreds of ornate and lavish tombs, many of them similar to the Treasury, although not so large.

Before the Nabateans moved into the valley, the Edomite capital had stood on this site. It may have been less elaborate, but it was a sophisticated city for its time. Excavations of Edomite settlements have unearthed decorative pottery, inscribed clay tablets, and many other highly crafted artifacts, revealing a prosperous and well-defended population. Although this had been a settlement of simple mud-brick houses, there was a central palace complex from which the Edomite leaders controlled their valley kingdom. The earliest level of occupation was found to have dated from around 1500 B.C., which showed that there had been an Edomite presence in the valley when the Israelites may have arrived here around 1360 B.C.

"The ancient Edomites were an advanced culture," Abdul told me as we left our horses with one of the attendants at the Roman-style amphitheater at the end of the Outer Siq. "The shrine on top of Jebel Madhbah was built by them, and to get to it they made these." He pointed to a flight of steps cut into the cliff face that zigzagged up the side of the mountain. Abdul was a lot fitter than I was, and by the time we had climbed to well over a thousand feet above the valley floor, I was exhausted. Finally we reached a plateau of flat rock, about two hundred feet long by a hundred feet wide. It was known as the Obelisk Terrace, Abdul explained, because of two huge monuments that stood there. Rising from the terrace, about a hundred feet apart, were two towering obelisks: huge pillars of solid rock, each over twenty feet high.

After I had caught my breath and examined the monuments, I quickly realized that the work necessary to create these giant structures was even more impressive than I had first thought. They had been sculpted from the mountain bedrock. To create these obelisks, the makers had hacked away solid rock from all around them, Abdul explained. The entire terrace, 20,000 square feet of it, was an artificial construction—an astonishing achievement for a people without modern technology. Incredibly, it was not the Nabatean civilization who had created it, but the much earlier Edomites. Excavations of the quarried stone found around the plateau had uncovered organic remains—such as animal bones—that had been radiocarbon dated to around 1500 B.C. Remarkably, therefore, these monuments would have been here at the time the Israelites appear to have left Egypt to wander in the Sinai Wilderness around 1360 B.C.

The site must have been even more impressive when it was first made. Archaeologists had found large, broken slabs of worked slate in the scree around the plateau and had concluded that the slate, which was not indigenous to the area, had been used to form a paved area around the obelisks. After examining the slate fragments in detail, the archaeologists reckoned that they had been polished to create a shiny blue surface for the concourse where, it would seem, religious ceremonies took place.

"These obelisks seem to have been the processional entrance to the shrine that is up there on the summit," said Abdul, indicating the mountaintop, which was joined to the terrace by a narrow ridge about six hundred feet long. "The Bedouin still consider this plateau to be sacred ground; they even call these monuments Al-Serif, meaning 'the feet,' as they have a tradition that God once stood astride it."

I had been hoping to find local legends that linked Jebel Madhbah with the biblical appearance of God, and here I had one. Moreover, the topography of the mountain even matched the descriptions of the Mountain of God in the Old Testament. The split level of the Jebel Madhbah site—the obelisk terrace below the shrine at the summit—certainly fitted with what we are told of the Israelites' first encounter with God on Mount Sinai. After he had produced the miraculous spring, and the Israelites made camp at the foot of the mountain, Moses prepared his people to meet with God himself:

> The Lord will come down in the sight of all the people upon mount Sinai . . . And Moses brought forth the people out of the camp to meet with God; and they stood at the nether part of the mount. (Ex 19:11, 17)

The implication here is that there were two levels to the sacred site where God was to be encountered. As "nether" means "lower," the people stood on some lower precinct to the sacred mountaintop where Moses later received the Ten Commandments—precisely as the case would have been if the Israelites had ascended Jebel Madhbah, arrived at the Obelisk Terrace, and looked up to the summit, six hundred feet to the north.

On another occasion the Israelite elders were again invited up into the nether part of the mountain:

> And he [God] said unto Moses, Come up unto the Lord, thou and Aaron, Nadab, and Abihu, and seventy of the elders of Israel; and worship ye afar off. And Moses alone shall come near the Lord: but they shall not come nigh; neither shall the people go up with him . . . And went up Moses, and Aaron, Nadab, and Abihu, and seventy of the elder of Israel: And they saw the God of Israel: and there was under his feet as it were a paved work of a sapphire stone. (Ex 24:1–10)

Amazingly, this passage could be a precise description of the Obelisk Terrace. The polished blue slate that archaeologists had found may well have caused the terrace to shine in the sunlight "as it were a paved work of a sapphire stone." God's feet are even mentioned, further linking the scripture to the old Bedouin tradition. The legend could well have arisen from an early association between the biblical account and the Obelisk Terrace. Often in the Old Testament sacred landmarks are named as appendages of God. For example, the hill on which the city of Samaria stood was called the "fist of God," and there is *Penuel*, the "face of God"—a cliff in the valley of Jordan (Jgs 8:8).

When Abdul finally led me up the ridge to the shrine on the summit, I was confronted with yet another remarkable piece of ancient engineering. Known as the High Place, it was an ancient open-air temple, over three thousand feet above sea level. Like the obelisks, it was cut from the solid bedrock and was thought to date from the same period. A large rectangular depression, measuring approximately forty-five by twenty feet, had been neatly cut from the sandstone to a depth of some fifteen inches, and all around it were the remains of rock-cut benches where worshipers would once have sat. Near the center of this courtyard, as archaeologists refer to it, there was a raised stone platform, six feet by three, which was probably used for offerings, and at the west end there was a solid stone altar, three and a half feet high and six feet wide, standing next to a huge stone basin about the same size. The main altar had steps carved up to it and was probably where the Edomite priesthood presided over rites, while the basin is thought to have been used to contain the blood of sacrificial animals.

If Jebel Madhbah was Mount Sinai, then this open-air temple is where Moses would have come alone to receive the Ten Commandments:

And the Lord said unto Moses, Come up to me into the mount, and be there: and I will give thee tables [tablets] of stone, and a law, and commandments which I have written; that thou mayest teach them. (Ex 24:12)

If this shrine did date from the same period as the Obelisk Terrace, as archaeologists believed, then it would have been here at the time the Moses story appears to be set. And if the Jewish historian Josephus was right, then the people of the area around Mount Sinai already considered it a sacred mountain before Moses or the Israelites ever arrived. Josephus tells us that, at the time Moses first set foot on the mountain, the local people did not allow grazing on its slopes because "of the opinion men had that God dwelt there." If the mountain was already considered sacred, then there would presumably have been some kind of temple there, and the High Place on the summit of Jebel Madhbah may well have been it. The Edomites were closely related to the Israelites, so their religion may even have been similar. Regardless of whatever deity the Edomites may have worshiped on Jebel Madhbah, however, if this was Mount Sinai, then the shrine may have been where God was believed to have appeared to Moses:

> And Moses went up into the mount, and a cloud covered the mount. And the glory of the Lord abode upon mount Sinai, and the cloud covered it six days: and the seventh day he called unto Moses out of the midst of the cloud. And the sight of the glory of the Lord was like devouring fire on the top of the mount in the eyes of the children of Israel. (Ex 24:15–17)

When I asked Abdul if he knew of any legends concerning the shrine, he told me something that could well explain what the Israelites had actually seen. Abdul knew of no specific legends, but he did know of a peculiar phenomenon—a strange light that had been reported on the summit of Jebel Madhbah. The last time it had been reported was in 1993. A team of British archaeologists were working around the shrine when they were caught in a rare thunderstorm. According to more than a dozen witnesses, the archaeologists were hurrying to get off the mountain to avoid being struck by lightning when they saw a ball of fiery red light, estimated to be around six feet in diameter, hovering a few feet in the air above the temple ruins. It was visible for about five minutes, moving slowly back and forth before disappearing. Abdul assured me that he knew of many people who had witnessed the spectacle, and I later spoke to over half a dozen older residents of Elji who swore to have seen it themselves.

This strange phenomenon could well have been described as being "like devouring fire"—the glory of the Lord that the Israelites are said to have seen—but what on earth was it? The first possibility was that it was what is known as ball lightning, spheres of highly charged particles created by the electrified atmosphere of a thunderstorm. Ball lightning does occur more frequently in high places, such as mountain peaks, tops of skyscrapers, and around radio masts. However, the color, size, and longevity of the spectacle did not appear to fit with ball lightning. Ball lightning is bluish in color, no larger than a football, and only remains visible for a few seconds. The witnesses to the Jebel Madhbah phenomenon described it as red or yellow, much bigger, and visible for up to five minutes. There is, however, another natural phenomenon that seemed to fit more with what was being reported—a rare electromagnetic anomaly known as geoplasma.

Plasma is an electrically charged gas that has peculiar properties. In an ordinary gas, each atom contains an equal number of positive and negative charges, and the positive charges in the nucleus are surrounded by an equal number of negatively charged electrons. If an external energy source causes the atoms of a gas to release electrons, the atoms are left with a positive charge and the gas is said to be ionized. When enough atoms are ionized, the gas ignites with a "cold flame" that carries a strong static charge. This is known as plasma. Because it is as light as the air around it, plasma can hover or hang in the air as a sphere or column of luminous gas that can move or remain stationary, depending on conditions, and can continue in this state for many minutes. Geoplasma is believed to be such a phenomenon caused by geodynamics—in plain English, certain types of rocks being rubbed together by seismic activity to ionize the air above them.

Because of the rarity and unpredictability of geoplasma, scientific research into it has only been properly conducted in the last couple of decades. In 1981 Brian Brady, then of the US Bureau of

Mines, was the first to produce what appeared to be miniature geo-plasma in the laboratory. When a carnelian granite core was crushed in darkened conditions, tiny sparklike red and yellow lights were observed flitting around the chamber of the rock crusher.

Strange lights, such as those described at Jebel Madhbah, have been reported at various locations throughout the world, usually in regions prone to earthquakes and tremors and in areas of particular sorts of rocks that contain large amounts of iron oxide and quartz, such as arenite sandstone and carnelian granite. Although earth-quakes are rare around Jebel Madhbah, the mountain is prone to mild tremors, and the summit is composed of arenite sandstone. When I later read up on the reports of such anomalies and the research into geoplasma, I could not help wondering if it was because of such phenomena that Jebel Madhbah had been consid-ered sacred. If the ancient Edomites had witnessed such phenomena, they would undoubtedly have considered them supernatural in ori-gin. This may have been why, if Josephus was referring to this mountain, men thought that God dwelled here. It could certainly account for why the shrine and Obelisk Terrace were built.

In the 1990s some geologists proposed that factors beyond rock type and seismic activity were necessary to produce geoplasma in the natural environment. Norwegian geologist Erling Strang considered that local variations in the earth's magnetic field were a contributing factor, and John Derr, of the US Geological Survey, suggested that water was an essential element in the production of geoplasma in the landscape. Heat produced by tectonic movement, he argued, creates a sheath of steam that coats the edges of a geological fault and serves to insulate the buildup of an electromagnetic charge.

Most geoplasmic phenomena are indeed reported during or after heavy rainfall. The event witnessed by the archaeologists on Jebel Madhbah in 1993 is a case in point. Heavy rainfall also accompa-nied the appearance of "the glory of the Lord" as witnessed by the ancient Israelites. Exodus 19:16 tells us that there were "thunders and lightnings, and a thick cloud upon the mount." In fact, the Exodus comparison of "the glory of the Lord" to "devouring fire" is an excellent description of a geoplasmic phenomenon.

I was now convinced that Jebel Madhbah was the biblical Mountain of God. The Old Testament passages suggested that the mountain was in the land of Edom, specifically on the border of the kingdom of Edom where Moses created the miraculous spring. The local Bedouin had long believed that the shrine near the entrance to the Siq, at the foot of Jebel Madhbah, was the site of the miraculous spring. The two levels of the mountain fitted the physical descriptions of Mount Sinai, and it had been considered a sacred place when the Israelites arrived. There were even two strange natural phenomena that could account for the descriptions in the Old Testament account of God's appearance on the holy mountain— namely, the bizarre trumpeting sound in the Siq and the peculiar lights reported on the summit. If this was the real Mountain of God, then this was where the prophet Jeremiah was said to have hidden the Ark. But Jebel Madhbah was a huge mountain. Could I find the cave in which the book of Maccabees said Jeremiah hid the Ark? I would need to resolve a crucial dilemma first. Why would the ancient Israelites have considered an Edomite mountain to be the dwelling place of their own God?

9

The Forgotten Cave

The location and topography of Jebel Madhbah certainly seemed to fit with the biblical Mountain of God. Furthermore, there were rare natural phenomena at the site that could account for the miraculous events said to have surrounded God's appearance on the sacred mountain. However, if Jebel Madhbah really was Mount Sinai, then the holy places Moses associated with God were already being used by the Edomites. This left me with two important questions. The Bible appeared to portray the Edomites as a hostile people who practiced pagan idolatry. How had the Israelites managed to gain access to Jebel Madhbah and, more significant, why would they want to? Why would they have thought that an Edomite religious site was a place where their own God resided? To resolve this dilemma, I first needed to examine the Old Testament's portrayal of events that led to the Israelites getting to the Mountain of God in the first place.

According to the book of Numbers, when the Israelites arrived in Kadesh, at what appears to have been the entrance to the Siq at the southeastern end of the Valley of Edom, Moses created the miraculous spring at Horeb, the Mountain of God. He then sent a message to the Edomite king asking for permission to enter his lands. However, the king refused: "Thus [the king of] Edom refused to give Israel [the Israelites] passage through his border: wherefore Israel turned away from him" (Nm 20:21).

From this verse, it seems that the two peoples failed to get on

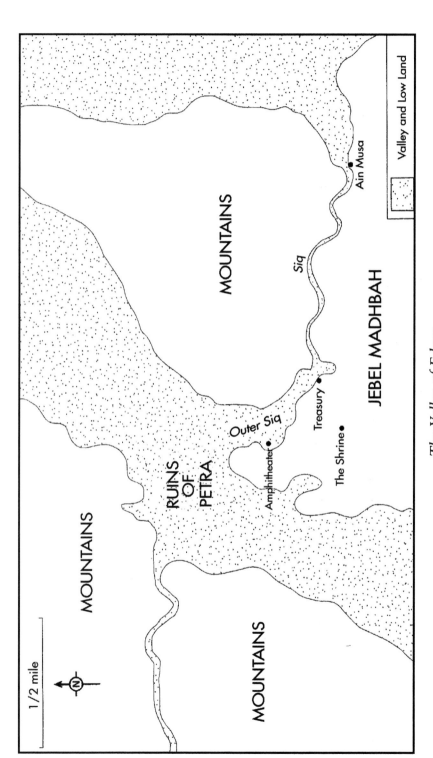

The Valley of Edom

and the Israelites had to turn back. From my own excursion up Jebel Madhbah, I knew that the only way to climb the mountain was from within the Wadi Musa. The Israelites would have needed to find an alternate way into the valley—which is precisely what they seem to have done. In the next verse the Israelites move on to a different location: "And the children of Israel, even the whole congregation, journeyed from Kadesh, and came unto mount Hor" (Nm 20:21). Later in Numbers, in a summary of the same event, we are told that Mount Hor was situated on another part of Edom's borders: "And they removed from Kadesh, and pitched in mount Hor, in the edge of the land of Edom" (Nm 33:37).

Although the Old Testament does not specifically say where Mount Hor is, it appears to be at the other end of the Valley of Edom. Also according to Numbers, soon after the Israelites arrived at Mount Hor, Moses's brother Aaron died on the mountain and was apparently buried there (Nm 20:25–29). The Jewish historian Josephus was in no doubt that the mountain on which the prophet Aaron died was a mountain that overlooked what was by his time the city of Petra:

> And when he came to a place which the Arabians esteem their metropolis, which was formerly called Acre, but has now the name Petra, at this place, which was encompassed by high mountains, Aaron went up one of them in the sight of the whole army, Moses having before told him that he was to die . . . and died while the multitude looked upon him. (*Antiquities* 1981)

The Bedouin of southern Jordan have long considered this mountain to have been Jebel Haroun—Aaron's Mountain—which stands at the northwestern end of the Wadi Musa. As with Ain Musa, the Spring of Moses at the foot of Jebel Madhbah, the local Arabs have marked the purported site of Aaron's tomb with a shrine. Just below the summit, overlooking a sheer cliff, the small whitewashed mosque stands over a cave where Aaron is said to have been laid to rest. It is a simple domed building with an Arabic inscription above the door saying that it was erected by the Sultan of Egypt almost eight hundred years ago.

If Jebel Haroun was Mount Hor, then it seems that the Israelites, having failed to gain entrance to the Valley of Edom from the southeast, journeyed around to the other end of the valley and crossed over the mountains in the northwest. Although the Old Testament provides no details of events, it seems that the Israelites somehow managed to defeat the Edomites—perhaps by a sneak attack—and occupied the Valley of Edom. In Numbers, God promises that the Israelites will overcome the Edomites: "And Edom shall be a possession, Seir also shall be a possession for his enemies; and Israel shall do valiantly" (Nm 24:18).

If Mount Seir was the Edomite name for Mount Sinai, as it seems to have been, then it appears that the Israelites had no trouble seizing the sacred mountain along with the rest of the kingdom. Exodus also recounts the Israelites overcoming the Edomites and occupying their land:

> Then the dukes of Edom shall be amazed . . . Fear and dread shall fall upon them . . . till thy people [the Israelites] pass over [into Edom] . . . Thou shalt bring them in, and plant them in the mountain of thine inheritance, in the place, O Lord, which thou hast made for thee to dwell in, in the Sanctuary, O Lord, which thy hands have established. (Ex 15:15–17)

In fact, this passage not only confirms that the Israelites were believed to have conquered the Valley of Edom; it also gives the reason for the invasion—so that they could occupy a mountain that is quite clearly the Mountain of God. A mountain that God made for himself to dwell in! What else could it be but Mount Sinai? Interestingly, the passage even mentions "the sanctuary" on the mountain. *Sanctuary* is the word used specifically in the Old Testament for two other places: the inner sanctum of the tabernacle and the Holy of Holies in the Jerusalem Temple—both shrines in which God was thought to dwell. If Jebel Madhbah was Mount Sinai, then this Sanctuary must surely have been the Edomite shrine on its summit.

It seemed, then, that the Israelites had to conquer Edom in order to secure the Mountain of God. They were obviously not in a strong enough position to remain in control of the area for long, as they soon left the valley and continued their trek through the Sinai Wilderness. However, a mystery still remained. Why would Moses or the ancient Israelites have considered an Edomite religious site to be the home of their own God? The answer would appear to be that both religions shared a common origin. Indeed, they may even have worshiped the same God.

As noted, modern DNA tests on ancient skeletal remains have shown that the Edomites and Israelites were closely related. Even the Old Testament admits that the two peoples were descended from common ancestry. Although the Bible depicts the Edomites as heathen idol worshipers, historical evidence seriously challenges these allegations. Little is known about the specifics of Edomite religion, as no Edomite records exist, but early Greek accounts do survive concerning the Edomites at the time their valley was being annexed by the Nabateans in the fourth century B.C. From these documents we learn that that the Edomites had only one god, which they called Dhu-esh-Shera—meaning "Lord of [Mount] Seir." This title shows that, like the Israelites, the Edomites were monotheistic and that they were still worshiping the same god as they had been centuries earlier. Furthermore, their use of a title for their deity, rather than a name, links them even more closely to the Israelites. In fact, many of the Edomites' customs were uniquely shared with the contemporary Jews. They were forbidden to consume blood (meaning that animal carcasses had to be prepared by ritual draining); they were not allowed to keep slaves; and they were not permitted to do any work for one day each week. Of all the other cultures of the Middle East at the time, only the Jews prepared kosher foods, abhorred slavery, and observed the Sabbath.

From a historical perspective, the Edomite religion was far closer to the Israelite religion than the Old Testament authors cared to admit. Neither is there any archaeological evidence for the Edomites being idolaters as the Bible claims. Many Edomite sites have been excavated over the years, but not a single statue or effigy of a god has ever been unearthed. The Old Testament's depiction of the Edomites as a godless people was clearly wrong and probably stemmed from animosity between the Edomites and the Jews at the time the Old Testament was committed to writing, particularly because the Edomites had refused to come to the aid of the Jews when the Babylonians invaded in the sixth century. The resultant enmity can clearly be seen in the many tirades against the Edomites in Old Testament books about the Babylonian period and may have affected the portrayal of the Edomites in yet earlier times. It seemed, therefore, that there was actually no reason the ancient Israelites would not have considered an Edomite holy site to be sacred to their own God. For all intents and purposes, the Edomite and Israelite religions were the same.

I was now more convinced than ever that Jebel Madhbah was the Mountain of God. If I was right, then the Ark of the Covenant may once have been hidden here, somewhere in a secret cave. The only problem was, Where? The mountain measured over a million square feet at its base and was over three thousand feet high. To travel completely around its base alone would be a journey of almost fifteen miles. It would have taken a massive team of archaeologists, geologists, and experienced mountaineers months to search the entire mountain. Even if I had the resources to organize such an expedition, the chances of finding anything seemed remote, to say the least, because the Maccabees account had said that Jeremiah sealed the cave entrance. If the cave had managed to remain undisturbed, presumably a boulder or rubble blocked its entrance. On my trek through the Siq and Outer Siq, only a couple of miles around the bottom of the mountain, I had seen dozens of rock piles stacked against the cliff faces, each of which could have been concealing caves. To remove the debris from just one of these piles would have taken hours, even with heavy lifting gear, and most of the mountain would have been completely inaccessible to such equipment. In fact, the more I thought about it, the closer the chances of finding any trace of the Ark dwindled to zero. The Nabateans had spent centuries carving and crafting the cliffs of Jebel Madhbah, cutting deep into the rocks to build their tombs. If the Ark of the Covenant was hidden in a cave on Jebel Madhbah, these ancient tomb builders may well have found it long ago.

It was, however, when I was contemplating the likelihood of the Temple treasures having already been found that I suddenly remembered what Abdul had told me about the Treasury. I hadn't thought much about it at the time, but Abdul had said that the Crusaders had found a treasure trove of some kind in a cave in the vicinity of the monument. Evidently, among the treasure there were golden artifacts. I did not think for one moment that these would have included the Ark but, with nothing else to go on, I decided to question him further about it.

Unfortunately, Abdul knew little more than he had already told me, but he introduced me to an Australian historian who was staying in one of the local hotels. Jonathan Warren—Jack for short— was working on a Ph.D. thesis on the history of Petra and knew all about the purported discovery by the Crusaders. When I met up with him at his hotel he was extremely helpful. He told me that there was no contemporary record of the Crusaders' purported find, but the oldest historical reference to it did date back to the early 1800s. Apparently, the story had been told to the Swiss explorer Johannes Burckhardt, who was the first Westerner to visit the ruined city of Petra since the Crusaders abandoned their forts on the site in 1189. The city of Petra had declined with the Roman Empire, and by the time of the conversion of the Arabs of the area to Islam in the seventh century, it was abandoned altogether. The Crusaders (Christian soldiers from Europe) occupied the valley briefly and built a series of forts, but thereafter the ancient city was forgotten by Europeans until it was rediscovered by Burckhardt, completely by accident, in 1812.

Burckhardt's original design was to discover the source of the River Nile, something that no Westerner had yet done. In fact, no European had even attempted such an expedition, as there had been great animosity between the Moslems and Christians since the time of the Crusades, those medieval wars fought between the Christian Europeans and the Moslem Arabs for control of the Middle East. For a European to travel through northern Africa at the beginning of the nineteenth century was conduct approaching suicidal. To prepare for his solo expedition, therefore, Burckhardt spent three years learning Arabic and studying Islam in order to pass himself off as a Moslem trader. His studies completed, and assuming an Arab name, he took a boat to Turkey, where he began his arduous journey south along the eastern Mediterranean coast, keeping a secret diary as he went. In 1812 Burckhardt was traveling through the Negev Desert with a caravan bound for Cairo when he began to hear tales of the ruins of a magnificent city hidden away in the Shara Mountains. His curiosity aroused, he found an excuse to make a detour, and in August of that year, he became the first Westerner for over half a millennium to enter the Valley of Edom and see the ruins of Petra.

Accompanied by a Bedouin guide, Burckhardt rode through the Siq and into the Wadi Musa, where he was confronted by the extraordinary Treasury monument. In his diary he noted that his guide told him about the legend of the treasure supposedly found by European Crusaders just before they were forced out of the area by the Arabs. He did not specifically state where it was discovered, but he did say what had supposedly been found.

"If I remember rightly, the treasures included jewels and a gold chest," Jack told me after he had finished his account of Burckhardt's journey. My ears could not help but prick up at the mention of a gold chest. The Ark of the Covenant could be described as a gold chest. Jack could tell that I was showing more than a casual interest.

"I wouldn't take the story too seriously," he said. "It was probably concocted by the Crusaders. The monument's full Arabic name is Khaznat al-Faroun, meaning 'the Treasury of the Pharaoh.' One Bedouin myth says that the pharaoh of the Exodus chased the Israelites here at the time Moses made the Ain Musa spring, for some reason brought his treasure with him, and for some equally unlikely reason left it here in this purpose-built monument. Another legend says that the Israelites ambushed the pharaoh in the Siq and stole his treasure; they hid it here." Jack gave his opinion that the story of the pharaoh's treasure was started by Christian Crusaders rather than the Moslem locals. "The Crusaders were obsessed with finding biblical relics," he said. In fact, Jack doubted that there was any truth in the story of the Crusaders finding the treasure at all. "They probably plundered some jewels and other golden trinkets during their campaigning and made up the story that they discovered them in the Wadi Musa—at a site that was associated with Moses and the Old Testament. Supposed biblical relics could fetch a fortune back home."

As far as I could tell, Jack had no idea that Jebel Musa might have been the Mountain of God; he considered the story of the Ain Musa spring to be merely one of the many miracle tales that link Moses to sites all over the Sinai Wilderness. From my perspective, however, the story was more compelling. I had long ago learned to appreciate the importance of myths and legends associated with ancient sites and was prepared to search for the kernel of truth in the story of the pharaoh's treasure. According to the Bible, the gold for the Ark and other holy vessels Moses instructed the Israelites to make had been "borrowed" from the Egyptians before they left Egypt.

> And the children of Israel did according to the word of Moses; and they borrowed of the Egyptians jewels of silver, and jewels of gold, and raiment: And the Lord gave the people favor in the sight of the Egyptians, so that they lent unto them such things as they required. And they spoiled the Egyptians. (Ex 12:35–36)

Before long, however, the pharaoh decided to go after them:

> And it was told the king of Egypt that the people fled: and the heart of Pharaoh and of his servants was turned against the people, and they said, Why have we done this, that we have let Israel go from serving us? And he made ready his chariot, and took his people with him. (Ex 14:5–6)

Could the legend of the pharaoh's treasure have come about because of some confusion over an original story referring to Temple vessels that had originally been made centuries earlier from the pharaoh's gold?

The Treasury itself was certainly not built by the Egyptian pharaoh, the Israelites, or anyone else as early as the fourteenth century B.C. It did not need an archaeological excavation to reveal that the monument dated from much later times. Its design was clearly influenced by Greek and Roman architecture that did not exist until well over a thousand years after the Exodus seems to have occurred. Nevertheless, it was possible that the Treasury was built at the site of an earlier structure. Perhaps the Edomites had constructed a shrine in the cliff face opposite the Siq when they constructed the Obelisk Terrace and the shrine on the summit of Jebel Madhbah. They might certainly have considered the strange acoustic effect of the wind in the gorge to be a sacred manifestation. If so, then the place where the noise was created—that is, the area around what is now the Treasury—would have been considered holy. The Old Testament book of Numbers referred to what seems to have been the Siq as the Kadesh, which in Hebrew meant a "holy place." And the first time Moses ever arrived at the Mountain of God, during the burning bush episode, he was told that the place was already sacred. Moses hears a voice that tells him: "draw not nigh hither: put off thy shoes from off thy feet, for the place whereon thou standest is holy ground" (Ex 3:5).

As the Edomites had created the impressive religious sanctuaries from the bare rock at the summit of Jebel Madhbah, it seemed quite possible that they might also have created a rock-cut shrine where the Treasury now stands. Nevertheless, even if there was an earlier Edomite shrine at the end of the Siq, the ancient Israelites were unlikely to have secluded their holy relics there for long. According to the Bible, the vessels accompanied the Israelites throughout their wanderings in the Sinai Wilderness. Jeremiah, however, might well have considered such a location a fitting hiding place if he secreted some of these same holy relics at Jebel Madhbah to save them from the Babylonians. Was there any evidence of an early structure at the site?

Jack offered to accompany me to the Treasury and tell me what archaeologists had learned about the monument. Abdul had told me that the Treasury was thought to have been a tomb, but Jack doubted that it was ever used as a burial site. It lacked any of the usual Nabatean, Greek, or Roman inscriptions found in the many other tombs in the Wadi Musa. Neither was there any evidence inside of sarcophagi or niches suitable for interring bodies.

"One thing's for certain," he told me, as we stood looking up at the decorative facade of the structure that is as big as the Taj Mahal. "The Treasury was built to impress. It's the first monument that visitors see when they enter the valley."

Inside, however, the Treasury was something of a disappointment. Although there is a huge entrance hall that must have taken years to cut from the solid rock, it was a cold, bare, cubic hollow with no ornamentation whatsoever. Three smaller chambers led off it, but these too were equally bare.

"It seems to have been built to serve some religious rather than practical function," said Jack as he stooped down and picked up a handful of rocks from the ground in front of the entrance. "This is flood debris. Tons of the stuff has been washed down into the gorge during flash torrents over the centuries." Jack explained that an excavation organized by the Jordanian Ministry of Antiquities in the 1980s revealed that the valley floor at the time the Treasury was made, around two thousand years ago, was much lower than it is today. "The entrance to the monument was ten feet up the cliff side, but there was no evidence of any steps leading up to it. It couldn't have been intended for practical use because entry would have required a ladder. A tax or other administrative building, as some people have suggested, seems out of the question. As it doesn't appear to have been used as a tomb either, some other religious purpose for the Treasury seems the most likely option."

Jack went on to describe how the excavators dug down into the flood debris in front of the Treasury until they reached the level where the valley floor had been at the time of the earliest Edomite occupation of the area, which they determined by radiocarbon dating animal bones found in the rubble. At this stratum, the archaeologists found evidence of a much earlier chamber cut into the rock to a depth of about twenty feet, directly below the Treasury entrance. It was a passageway, about four feet wide and five feet high, leading to a plain chamber measuring approximately ten feet square and seven feet high.

"It may have been an Edomite tomb, as the entrance was partly sealed by purposely placed boulders," said Jack. "However, it appeared to have been robbed centuries ago, as there was nothing inside."

"Do you think this could have been the treasure cave found by the Crusaders?" I asked.

"They could have dug down to it for some reason, but, as I said, I reckon they made the whole thing up."

I needed to find out more about the Crusaders who had occupied the area before I could make up my own mind about the story. Yet even if the Crusaders had found treasures here, were they the Temple vessels hidden by Jeremiah? Could this have been the cave mentioned in the book of Maccabees?

I was not surprised that there had been an Edomite construction opposite the Siq: It fit with my theory concerning the site's sacred associations. Jack said it was thought to be a tomb, but it might just as easily have been a shrine. If it was, then Jeremiah might have considered it an appropriate place to hide the Temple treasures. There were a number of possible scenarios. As their religion appeared to have been closely related to Judaism, there might have been Edomites sympathetic to the Jewish plight who took charge of the Ark and kept it in this cave. Alternatively, the cave might have been long buried with debris by the early sixth century, and its existence might have been forgotten by all but Jeremiah and a few high priests. As such, Jeremiah might have uncovered the site and hidden the treasures secretly as the book of Maccabees asserts. However, this was all wild speculation. I needed to return to Jerusalem and consult the Israel National Library's database to see if I could discover anything more about the supposed Crusaders' treasure.

Back at the library, I discovered that Johannes Burckhardt himself described the Crusaders' find as comprising "treasures of pure gold, precious stones, and a golden chest." The chest could have been the Ark of the Covenant, and the precious stones might even have been the Stones of Fire that were said to have always been kept with it. Equally, they could have been any old chest and jewels. Unfortunately, Jack was right about there being no earlier reference to the legend, so there was no way of knowing what the Crusaders might really have found, if anything. However, I did manage to find out which particular Crusaders had been in the Valley of Edom during the period in question.

By the end of the first millennium A.D., the entire Middle East was under Moslem influence. As this region included the Bible lands, or the Holy Land, as Christians referred to it, the Europeans felt that it was their duty to conquer the area and bring it under Christian control. The wars that followed were known as the Crusades and the warriors who fought on the Christian side were the Crusaders. In the twelfth century, Crusaders from European countries such as France, Germany, and England conquered Jerusalem and set up a Christian kingdom in what is now Israel. In order to protect Christian interests in the region various religious militias were formed, and one of these, the Knights Templar—or Templars for short—briefly occupied the ruined city of Petra in the 1180s to protect the important trading routes that ran through the Shara Mountains. As these Templars had been the only Crusaders to occupy the Valley of Edom, it must have been they who were credited with having made the find.

At this time their commander was an English knight named Ralph de Sudeley, so perhaps the historical records concerning his life might reveal something further regarding the purported treasure. There was nothing else about him in the National Library's database, so it seemed that such records could only be found in England. As this was where I happened to live and needed to return on other business anyway, I decided I would follow up on the de Sudeley lead once I got back home. I did not really expect it to go anywhere. However, I was in for a big surprise.

10
Treasure Trail

The story told to Johannes Burckhardt purported that certain Crusaders had found a golden chest, gemstones, and other items of gold in a cave near the Treasury monument when the Valley of Edom was being abandoned by the Christians in the 1180s. If there was any truth in the story, the man in command of the Knights Templar who garrisoned the valley at the time, Ralph de Sudeley, may have been the person responsible for the find. Even if he was not personally involved in the discovery, he would certainly have profited from it. I needed to find out more about de Sudeley and the Templars under his command.

When the Knights Templar order was founded in France in the early 1100s, its members were French Cistercian monks who vowed to fight for Christianity in the Holy Land. Within fifty years, however, men from other European countries such as Germany and England joined the ranks, and many of these were far from being monks. Most were either professional soldiers or simply adventurers whose motives were a combination of glory and greed. (Rich pickings were to be had from plundering the Moslem population of the Middle East.) Although the Knights Templar order still considered itself to be an army of holy warriors, by the 1180s it was more like an early version of the Foreign Legion: an international militia under French control that made up its numbers with mercenaries. One such mercenary was Ralph de Sudeley. He had come from a relatively wealthy English family, but as a younger son he did not stand to inherit his father's estate. Like many before and after, he chose therefore to make for a soldier, and in 1182 he joined the Jerusalem garrison of the Knights Templar.

At the time, Jerusalem and surrounding regions had been occupied for decades by a combined Christian army of French and Germans, but the entire region was coming under increasing threat from the Moslem Saracens from what is now Syria. De Sudeley did not remain in Jerusalem for long, but was instead posted south to where the Crusaders had built a series of forts to protect the trade routes that ran through the Shara Mountains. One of these was on Jebel Habis, a rocky mesa overlooking the ruined city of Petra, and it was here that Ralph de Sudeley was sent to command a small Templar garrison that controlled the Valley of Edom. But his stay was short. In 1187, the Saracen leader Saladin conquered Jerusalem and two years later forced the Crusaders to abandon the Shara Mountains. In 1189, Ralph de Sudeley returned to England. Most pertinent, he was now, somehow, an extremely wealthy man.

On his arrival home, de Sudeley immediately bought a large estate in an area called Herdewyke (pronounced Herdwick), in the county of Warwickshire in central England. Here he built a lavish manor house, married, and settled down to start a family. One year later, in 1190, the English king Richard I decided to mount a new crusade to retake Jerusalem. To finance the campaign, Richard demanded money and men from his barons, and de Sudeley was able to amply provide both. He not only had the resources to provide plenty of gold for the venture, he even built a barracks on his estate to train new recruits for Richard's army. Having been a Templar, de Sudeley decided to make his training camp a Templar institution—a half-military, half-religious establishment known as a preceptory.

During this period, there was no such thing as a full-time, professional army in England, and in wartime troops were supplied by landlords who raised the required number of men from among their tenants. Most of these were sent into battle with little or no training. The exception, however, could be found in warrior orders such as the Knights Templar. Although they were called knights, only the Templar officers were actually knights in the true sense—men of status who had been honored by the king and trained to fight as heavily armored cavalrymen. The rank and file were lightly armored horse soldiers, about three-quarters of whom were warrior monks and the rest laymen. A Templar preceptory was consequently a strange cross between a military base and a monastery. While they were there, the monks lived a monastic life in one part of the camp, while the laymen lived in traditional barracks in another part of the base. From the records that survive, it is clear that the Herdewyke preceptory was a huge establishment, housing around a thousand men. To feed, shelter, equip, and train such a regiment must have cost a fortune.

De Sudeley was clearly a very rich man. However, when he had set off to join the Crusaders a decade before, he had been a man of modest means. The local *Feet of Fines*, contemporary records of land and property holdings, show that de Sudeley's entire family could not have afforded such an enterprise. So where had he obtained his money? It could have been from plundering the Arabs or charging a levy on the merchants who traveled through the Valley of Edom. However, the *Feet of Fines* preserved in the Warwickshire Records Department suggests that de Sudeley's estate had included expensive holy relics brought back from the Middle East. An entry for the year 1192 included mention of certain *objets sacrés*—sacred artifacts—that were housed in de Sudeley's preceptory chapel. Unfortunately, no specific details are given, other than the fact that pilgrims donated large sums of money to the preceptory when they visited the chapel to see these items. As official documents in the twelfth century were frequently written in French, the term *objets sacrés* was the usual way of describing holy relics returned from the Crusades. If de Sudeley did possess such relics, they would go some way toward accounting for his sudden and mysterious wealth: At the time, holy relics were big business.

Usually, holy relics were the earthly remains of saints—their bones or, in some cases, a mummified appendage. Relics were believed to hold divine power; they could heal sickness, protect against evil, and secure spiritual well-being. In the Middle Ages, between the tenth and fourteenth centuries, relics were priceless and highly sought throughout Christian Europe, and their acquisition became an international obsession. Throughout Europe, relics were displayed in public shrines to be visited by thousands of pilgrims in the hope that they might be helped, cured, or enlightened by their close proximity to the remains. Pilgrims were prepared to pay to view or touch the relics, and vast wealth was donated to the monasteries, abbeys, and cathedrals that contained the bones of the most famous saints. Often a religious center would grow rich and powerful solely from the proceeds of its relics.

An excellent example is Glastonbury Abbey in southwest England. The existing ruins of the abbey date from the late twelfth century and suggest the impressive structure that replaced much older buildings that had been destroyed by fire in 1184. Following the fire, the abbey was desperately in need of funds for rebuilding, and the only sure way to raise the money was to attract large numbers of pilgrims. In 1190, during renovations to the abbey ruins, the monks claimed to have discovered in the foundations the bones of at least three famous saints. The relics were put on display and attracted generous donations from multitudes of worshipers. So wealthy did the abbey become that it was reconstructed as one of the most splendid in the country.

Relics did not only include bodily remains. The most prestigious relics were artifacts thought to have been associated with the Bible. Items associated with Jesus—for instance, splinters from the cross and the famous Turin Shroud in which Christ's crucified body was said to have been wrapped—attracted vast numbers of pilgrims. Equally prized were Old Testament relics, such as a ring said to have belonged to Solomon that was housed at Lucca Cathedral in Italy and a gem claimed to have come from the hilt of King David's sword that was kept in Valencia Cathedral in Spain. Most of these purported relics were donated or sold to the Church by Crusaders returning from the Holy Land, and the most prolific relic hunters were members of the orders of Crusader knights such as the Templars. An excellent example is the so-called sacred accoutrements of Cyprus. The Old Testament refers to the Israelites making dishes, spoons, and bowls of pure gold to be used in the tabernacle (Ex 25:29), and in the late thirteenth century another order of Crusader knights, the Knights Hospitaller, claimed to have found these items near the city of Acre (modern Akka on the coast of northern Israel) and brought them back to Saint Nicholas Cathedral on the island of Cyprus. Here they attracted thousands of pilgrims for two centuries—until the Ottoman Turks captured the cathedral and turned it into a mosque. Judging by the *Feet of Fines* account, it seemed that Ralph de Sudeley had claimed to have found similar relics. Another reference to the items in the Herdewyke chapel describes them as *Vestiges d'ancien Testament*—quite literally, "Old Testament Relics." The question was, Were these the same treasures supposedly discovered in the Valley of Edom?

Unfortunately, neither the *Feet of Fines* nor any other contemporary records that I could discover specified what de Sudeley's holy relics actually were. They could have been vessels from the Jerusalem Temple, splinters from the cross, or anything! However, from the 1600s there did survive record of a local tradition that held that the Herdewyke Templars had hidden some kind of treasure when they were forced to disband in the fourteenth century.

By the early 1300s, there were hundreds of Templar preceptories throughout Europe, and many had become exceptionally wealthy. Although their riches were originally plunder from the Crusades, the Templars had amassed further wealth by leasing land and acting as some of the first bankers in Christian Europe. In the early fourteenth century, fearing their power and influence, the Pope ordered the Templar order to be dissolved. In England, however, King Edward II had fallen out with the Pope and allowed the order to continue, particularly as he enjoyed their financial support. In 1322, however, when they refused to continue financing the king, he ordered the Templars to be arrested and their property seized. Upon Ralph de Sudeley's death, the Herdewyke preceptory had been bequeathed to the Templar order, and they were still in residence at the time of Edward's purge. Accordingly, their possessions were seized by the crown—or, at least, some of them were, if a local legend was to be believed. According to the Warwickshire historian William Dugdale, who wrote in 1656, the Elizabethan explorer Sir Walter Raleigh visited Herdewyke in 1600 and was told a story about the Templars hiding treasure in the area. For some reason or other, Raleigh took it seriously and spent months looking for treasure. He persuaded his wealthy wife (Elizabeth Throckmorton, Maid of Honor to Queen Elizabeth I) to buy the Herdewyke estate and had a gang of men excavate the ruins of the Templar preceptory. However, once again, there were no specific details about the purported treasure.

For some months, my research progressed no further. There was no way of knowing whether the story of the Crusaders' find at the Treasury was anything more than a fanciful tale. Neither could I discover whether the supposed find had any link with the relics apparently housed in the Herdewyke preceptory chapel, nor if the treasure Walter Raleigh had searched for was thought to include these actual relics. Even if these various treasures were one and the same, I still had no idea whether the Ark of the Covenant was believed ever to have been among them. I had just about considered the whole case closed when I discovered something that suddenly and unexpectedly opened up a whole new avenue of research.

I was researching for a British documentary about the legendary hero Robin Hood when I came across reference to a nineteenth-century amateur historian who believed that the fabled outlaw had been a historical figure who was buried in his local churchyard. The historian, one Jacob Cove-Jones, came from the Warwickshire village of Loxley, and a village of the same name is included in some of the early tales of Robin Hood. Deciding the theory was worth pursuing, I began to read up on Cove-Jones's background. Apparently, he was a rich landlord who had a passion for local history and devoted much of his life in the late 1800s and early 1900s to investigating Warwickshire folktales. Although I was looking for information regarding Robin Hood, I was surprised to find that one of the folktales Cove-Jones had investigated concerned the legendary treasure supposedly hidden by the Herdewyke Templars. He had evidently come across the account of Walter Raleigh's search and decided to follow it up himself. As Herdewyke was only a few miles from where he lived, Cove-Jones spent many months investigating the area in search of evidence to substantiate the legend. Eventually, he concluded not only that the treasure was real, but that Templars had left clues to reveal its secret hiding place.

Cove-Jones was convinced that these clues had been left in a series of paintings on the walls of a nearby church—the medieval All Saints Church in the village of Burton Dassett, a couple of miles from Herdewyke. The church had been built by Herdewyke Templars, some of whom managed to survive the purge of 1322 by becoming outlaws when Edward II ordered their arrest and seized their lands and property. Five years later, the Herdewyke Templars helped depose Edward by aiding his queen, Isabella of France, who placed her young son Edward III on the throne as puppet king. Out of gratitude, these Templars were granted amnesty, but their lands were not returned. As their preceptory remained in the possession of their rival order, the Knights Hospitaller, the Templars raised the money to build a new church at Burton Dassett. Now a purely religious order (the Knights Templar had long ceased to be a military organization), the men required the church for their devotions. Sadly, these peaceful Templars did not survive long. In 1350, they and the entire Burton Dassett community were killed off by the Black Death.

The Black Death, or bubonic plague—that fatal disease spread by fleas that lived on rats and human beings—started in Asia and traveled to Europe on trading ships, reaching England in 1348. Over the next three years it claimed more than a million lives—over a third of England's population at the time. Few who caught the Black Death ever survived, and entire towns and villages were completely wiped out by the disease. Burton Dassett, with its estimated eight hundred inhabitants, was no exception. It was at this dire time, Jacob Cove-Jones believed, that the Templars had hidden their holy relics and left clues in the hope that some future generation might find them. I could find nothing that hinted why Cove-Jones thought that the Burton Dassett Church paintings held such clues, but I decided that they were worth seeing for myself.

The Herdewyke estate had encompassed about nine square miles and included both a region of low-lying land now called Temple-Herdewyke, after the Templars who were once there, and the

Burton Dassett Hills that rise to over a thousand feet to the immediate southeast of it. Situated close to the center of England and just a few miles east of William Shakespeare's birthplace of Stratford-upon-Avon, Temple-Herdewyke and the Burton Dassett Hills are now sparsely populated with a couple of tiny villages and a few small farms.

Nothing remains of the medieval barracks or monastic buildings, but remarkably, the preceptory chapel still stands. The country lane that leads up into the Burton Dassett Hills from the northwest runs right past it, and when I first saw the place I could not believe my eyes. It was marked on the map as a ruined chapel, but instead of the ecclesiastical building I expected to see, the place was being used as a cattle shed. Rusty corrugated iron sheeting blocked what had once been the grand entrance, and inside, cows wandered around among bales of hay. Having received permission from the farmer to enter, I looked around at the dirty, damp space, some twenty feet wide and fifty feet long, trying to imagine what it had been like in de Sudeley's day. Once the chapel would have been filled with the chanting of monks and the smell of incense; now it stank of cattle dung and echoed with the mooing of cows. It still retained something of its ecclesiastical past, as the gothic framework of the bricked-up windows had somehow been preserved. Nothing, though, remained of the interior ornamentation except for the stone altar that still stood against the east wall and was now being used as a feeding trough. It was hard to imagine that eight centuries earlier holy relics had been displayed here that attracted pilgrims from all over the country. However, this was not the church that housed the paintings that Jacob Cove-Jones believed held clues to the whereabouts of the Herdewyke treasure. That church was one and a half miles to the southeast, up on the Burton Dassett Hills.

Unlike the ruined chapel at Temple-Herdewyke, the medieval All Saints Church is not only well preserved, it is still in use today. It stands on the hillside at the edge of the tiny hamlet of Burton Dassett, after which the upland is named. To its north are rugged green hills where rabbits run free and sheep noisily graze, and to the south are wooded glades that echo with the song of birds. Judging by the size of the church, it was built for a large congregation. After the Black Death, however, few people resettled the area, and today the church is lucky if it gets more than a dozen worshipers for Sunday prayer.

As I walked around the interior of the church, my footfalls echoing against its cold stone walls, I mulled over Cove-Jones's theory in my mind. If the Herdewyke Templars had possessed holy relics that they had managed to keep from the clutches of Edward II, then it would have made sense for them to hide these at the time of the Black Death. Because the population of inland Britain did not tend to travel much in the Middle Ages, the Black Death took time to reach central counties like Warwickshire. It started at the coastal ports and worked its way inland over a period of a year or so. The few travelers the people of Burton Dassett did encounter must have told them of the terrible disease that was encroaching upon them from all sides. It was quite possible that, knowing their end was nigh, the Templars had hidden their precious possessions in the hope of preserving them intact. Indeed, many monastic communities are known to have done just this. A number of hoards of gold and silver vessels have been found by archaeologists over the years, believed to have been hidden by monks threatened by the plague. If Cove-Jones was right, however, the Herdewyke Templars had done something else: They had left clues for finding the cache. It did not take me long to find the paintings that he believed had held these clues. To either side of the north transept window were ancient, faded depictions of what appeared to be kings.

Luckily, the church had a guidebook that gave a potted history of the building, and from it I learned that the paintings were unique. They were dated to around 1350, the very time of the Black Death, and had been preserved because they were plastered over for centuries. After the Black Death, the church had been abandoned for some years before coming back into use as a Roman Catholic church. During the English Reformation in the fifteenth century, it had been taken over by the Protestant Church of England and had become the Anglican parish church of the district. Preferring plain, rather than decorative, places of worship, the Protestant movement of the time had plastered over the earlier decorations. However, during repairs to the building in 1890, the plaster was removed from the internal walls and the paintings were revealed. Hidden for centuries to either side of the north transept window were crude depictions of two human figures wearing crowns, each surrounded by a series of strange spiral designs unique to medieval Christian art. The meaning of the paintings had baffled scholars, but Cove-Jones immediately became convinced that they were a type of secret code.

I could not discover why Cove-Jones had decided that these murals contained a ciphered message, but it may well have been a logical deduction. The legend recorded by William Dugdale in the seventeenth century said that the Herdewyke Templars had hidden a treasure. Dugdale's account had not referred to holy relics, but Cove-Jones may have put two and two together after learning of the holy relics mentioned in the *Feet of Fines*, and concluded that the legendary treasure and the Templars' relics were one and the same. He may, too, have noted the connection between the arrival of the Black Death and the creation of the enigmatic transept murals in 1350 and speculated that they held the secret to the hidden treasure simply because they were so mysterious and so fortuitously dated. However, there was also the possibility that he had known something the experts had not.

Looking up at the murals, I realized that they appeared to contain Templar symbolism. The pictures to either side of the window were rusty red, faded images, but they were still clear enough for me to make out that the crowned figures they depicted were holding something in their hands. The one on the right was a robed, bearded man examining what appeared to be some type of lidded chalice. The one on the left was also robed and bearded, but he was holding up a severed head.

A severed head was certainly associated with the Knights Templar. When the French king Philip IV ordered the Templars arrested in Paris in 1307, many were put on trial for heresy. During these trials one of the many accusations leveled against them was that they worshiped a severed head. Various witnesses said they had seen the head and that it was called Baphomet, which was taken to be some kind of devil. Under excruciating torture, some Templars confessed to worshiping the demonic head, but historians have found little evidence that the Templars were really involved in heretical practices, and many think that the accusations of devil worship were completely false. Most Templars had been devout, even fanatical Christians, and it is far more likely that their severed head was the relic of some saint, perhaps, some have suggested, the supposed head of Saint John the Baptist. Whatever it really had been, the Templars had become notoriously associated with a severed head, and the window mural depicted someone holding one.

The other figure was holding a chalice, and the Templars were also famous for being associated with a famous cup—the Holy Grail—the cup said to have been used by Jesus at the Last Supper. Although there is no documentary evidence that the Templars themselves claimed to have possessed the Grail, many medieval legends made the claim for them. One German poet, Wolfram von Eschenbach, in his epic story *Parzival* of 1205, actually portrayed the Templars as the guardians of the Grail.

Jacob Cove-Jones could certainly have interpreted the mural images as Templar symbolism. However, I could see nothing that might have given him the idea that they were clues to the whereabouts of a hidden treasure. Perhaps the relics that the Herdewyke Templars possessed had included a saint's head and a sacred chalice, but there appeared to be nothing in the paintings that immediately suggested itself as a code, unless it had something to do with the enigmatic red spiral designs that were painted above and below each figure.

Later that day I visited the county museum in the nearby town of Warwick to find out if there had been any recent research into the murals. From what I could discover, no one seemed to have paid much attention to them in years. As for Jacob Cove-Jones's theory, it appeared to have been totally dismissed by academics. However, one of the museum's staff who was familiar with the legend of the Herdewyke treasure suggested that I speak to one of Cove-Jones's descendants, a Mr. David Baylis, a local historian. As Mr. Baylis lived nearby, I visited him that evening only to find out that he had little faith in his ancestor's theories either. Nonetheless, he was very helpful and told me as much as he knew about Jacob Cove-Jones's work.

Evidently, Cove-Jones not only claimed to have solved the mystery of the murals, he also swore that he had found some of the Templars' treasure. Unfortunately, however, he produced only one artifact as proof, one that Mr. Baylis still had in his possession. It was a four-inch-high sculpture of a human hand, made from lead and inlaid with a circular piece of black jet on the palm. Over the jet there was a spiral design made from silver, similar to the spirals depicted in the church murals. The artifact was apparently discovered in a small compartment, secreted behind the foundation stones of a medieval holy well that stands next to Burton Dassett Church. At first the county museum took an interest in the discovery and dated it to the fourteenth century, but its purpose remained an enigma as no similar artifact had been found anywhere else in England. Eventually, when Cove-Jones refused to explain how the murals had led him to the find, the museum began to question the discovery and ultimately accused him perpetrating of a hoax. They apparently came to the conclusion that he had acquired the lead hand on the antiquities market, although the charge was never proved.

"Following the museum's lead, the Burton Dassett Church authorities wanted nothing to do with the lead hand either, and that's how the artifact remained in my family's possession," said Mr. Baylis. "By all accounts, Jacob did not take the slur on his reputation well, and when he later claimed to have found more hidden relics, he refused to show them to anyone."

"You doubt he really found these relics?" I said.

Mr. Baylis smiled. "I think it was all part of a scheme he concocted to get his own back on his critics."

Mr. Baylis explained that Cove-Jones had announced that he had found more Templar relics: three gemstones and something else that he described only as "a discovery of immense importance." Instead of showing them to anyone, he decided to hide them in new locations and left a series of his own clues to lead to their whereabouts. Mr. Baylis believed that his ancestor had hoped to infuriate the museum and stir up general interest in his work, but did not believe for one minute that he had really found the items as he claimed. Nevertheless, he did think that Cove-Jones had hidden something, as he had gone to a great deal of expense and trouble to create his clues.

Jacob Cove-Jones's clues were certainly fascinating and included a paper he had written about the legendary treasure, a copy of which was still in Mr. Baylis's possession. Although the paper failed to explain how or where he discovered the stones or the other mysterious item, it did describe the clues leading to where he had rehidden them—apparently, in four separate locations somewhere in the local area. The clues were in two parts: the first in the form of three Bible verses, and the second in a coded picture in the form of a stained-glass window that Cove-Jones had commissioned a local artist friend called Bertram Lamplugh to make according to his instructions. When completed in 1907, the window was donated to and installed in the parish church in the nearby village of Langley.

"Jacob died later that year and the secret went with him to his grave," said Mr. Baylis. "Some of my ancestors took him seriously and tried to solve the conundrum, but as far as I know no one succeeded."

While Mr. Baylis did not believe that the supposed relics had anything to do with the Templars' treasure, he did think that correctly decoding Cove-Jones's clues would lead to three gemstones and to something else he had hidden. But Mr. Baylis clearly didn't want me to get my hopes up too high.

"He probably just bought the stones from a jeweler and whatever else he hid from an antique shop or something, and hoped that if anyone found them that they would be accepted as genuine relics."

"These three gemstones he claimed to have found. What kind of stones were they?" I asked.

"One was onyx, one jasper, and the other was beryl," he said, flicking through Cove-Jones's writings.

Mr. Baylis had just about convinced me that the Jacob Cove-

Jones lead was a dead end with no genuine connection to the Templars' treasure and certainly nothing to do with my research into the lost Ark. However, he had suddenly said something that grabbed my attention.

"The stones were onyx, jasper, and beryl?" I said.

"Yes, does that mean something?"

"I'm not sure," I said, not wanting to commit myself without further thought.

Mr. Baylis made me a photocopy of Cove-Jones's cryptic Bible references, and I left with the promise that I would keep him informed if I found out anything new.

Until now, there had been nothing concerning the mystery of the Herdewyke treasure to specifically link it with the Crusaders' purported find in the Valley of Edom. The *Feet of Fines* had not named the relics in the Herdewyke preceptory; William Dugdale's account of Raleigh's search had not stated what the legendary treasure was supposed to have been; and there was no reliable evidence that Cove-Jones had found anything at all. However, the types of gemstones that Cove-Jones had claimed to have found did tie up with the biblical story of the Ark of the Covenant.

The story related to Johannes Burckhardt had referred to the Crusaders finding "precious stones" with a "golden chest" in a cave at the foot of Jebel Madhbah. I had already considered the possibility that these might have been the Stones of Fire. Apparently the Ark's power could only be controlled with the Stones of Fire, which were always kept with the Ark. They had originally been set in the high priest's breastplate, which was described in detail in the book of Exodus as a square design made from twined golden linen and inlaid with twelve precious stones set in four rows. According to the Exodus account, the three stones in the bottom row were "a beryl, and an onyx, and a jasper"—the very same types of gems Jacob Cove-Jones claimed to have found. It may just have been a coincidence, but it seemed strange that Cove-Jones should just so happen to have chosen these particular stones if he had made the story up. If Cove-Jones was being honest, and the Templar murals had led him to find an onyx, jasper, and beryl stone, then his find would be the closest thing yet to link the Crusader find to the Temple treasures hidden by Jeremiah. The book of Maccabees said that the Ark had been hidden in a cave at the Mountain of God, a mountain that seemed to be Jebel Madhbah; the Templars commanded by Ralph de Sudeley had supposedly found a golden chest and precious stones in a cave at Jebel Madhbah; Ralph de Sudeley had what were said to be Old Testament relics in his chapel; and Cove-Jones claimed to have found some of these relics, including three gemstones that matched three of the Stones of Fire.

Of course, the entire thing could have been a wild-goose chase. Jacob Cove-Jones might have been lying through his teeth. I wanted to take a look at the stained-glass window in Langley Church, but before I did, I decided to check out something that might indicate whether Cove-Jones had invented his supposed discoveries. He had claimed to have found the lead hand in a secret compartment in the old holy well that stood next to Burton Dassett Church. Examining the structure might reveal whether Cove-Jones was lying or telling the truth about this discovery. If he had genuinely discovered the lead hand, then he may also have been telling the truth about the other relics he claimed to have found. I really hoped he was; I could not help wondering what his "discovery of immense importance" might have been. Could it have been the Ark itself?

11

Divine Fire

$\mathfrak{I}$n medieval times, certain natural springs were considered sacred, as their waters were believed to have curative properties. Often, the Church would consecrate such a spring to a particular saint and build a little shrine over it, making it a holy well. The well where Jacob Cove-Jones claimed to have found the lead hand was one such place. Situated about forty feet due north of Burton Dassett Church, it is now covered by a seventeenth-century, plain, rectangular stone building, about ten feet long, seven feet wide, and five feet high. A flight of steps leads down from a low opening at the front into a shallow pool, some three feet below ground level. This lower part is much older than the rest of the structure and dates back to around the time All Saints Church was built. It was supposedly somewhere here that Jacob Cove-Jones made his discovery. Unfortunately, the lower well structure was in such bad condition that it was impossible to tell if there had ever been a concealed compartment here as Cove-Jones claimed.

I may not have been able to find evidence from the well to help determine the truth or otherwise of Cove-Jones's discovery, but I was not inclined to dismiss his claim on the same grounds as his contemporaries. Although they had initially dated the lead hand to the same period as the well's original construction, the experts eventually decided that Cove-Jones had acquired it on the antiquities market and made up the story of finding it in the well. The local museum, it seems, had ultimately decided that the purported discovery was a hoax, purely because Cove-Jones had refused to explain how the church murals had led him to find it. Although this was understandable, it seemed to me that the man could have had other grounds for secrecy: He might have been playing safe. Cove-Jones may well have feared that if he revealed what he had discovered from the murals in the church, others would hijack his research and look for the treasures themselves. His motive may not have been deceit, as the local museum believed, but self-interest. He may simply have been waiting until he discovered more before he disclosed the full details of what he had found. If this was the true scenario, then it had resulted in the most unfortunate state of affairs. Cove-Jones's reaction to having been branded a fraud led him not only to keep his discoveries to himself but to go to considerable lengths to hide what he had found once more.

Another reason that the museum and others refused to take Cove-Jones seriously was the elaborate treasure trail he devised. If he had really found the other items he claimed, then why not show them to the world? Why hide them again and concoct an inane trail of clues? Mr. Baylis had thought the whole scheme was Cove-Jones's way of annoying his contemporary historians. However, there was another possibility. It was something of a fad during the late nineteenth century for wealthy collectors of ancient relics to hide one or more of their prized possessions at the end of a trail of ciphered messages as a kind of personal epitaph, set for future generations to decode. Indeed, I had followed one such trail myself, which led to a small onyx cup that the Victorian owner had believed was the original Holy Grail. In fact, the clues Cove-Jones had devised were very similar.

Of course, the museum authorities could have been right about Cove-Jones. There was no way of knowing for certain one way or the other. Nevertheless, if he had hoaxed the discovery, why choose a lead hand as the artifact in the well? It was an unusual object no one seemed to be able to identify. Cove-Jones was a rich man, so if he *had* decided to buy an artifact on the antiquities market, as the museum believed, why not choose something more spectacular and appropriate like an ancient silver bowl or a golden chalice?

Whatever the hand was, it could not have been one of the items in the Herdewyke chapel in Ralph de Sudeley's time, which—according to Cove-Jones's theory—were the treasures the mural clues alluded to. Mr. Baylis had assured me that the hand was around 650 years old, as his mother had it valued in the 1980s. Art experts who examined it at the time said that its method of manufacture was unquestionably of mid-fourteenth-century style.

Obviously, Cove-Jones may have had all sorts of motives that I could not even guess at, but it seemed to me that there was no evidence on which to completely dismiss his claims as the experts had done. Nevertheless, if Cove-Jones had found the lead hand at the well by deciphering the church murals, what did it mean? While the artifact could not have been one of the supposed relics that had been in the Herdewyke preceptory chapel, it did appear to tie in with the paintings in the church. Above and below the two figures holding the chalice and the severed head were red spiral designs, very similar to the silver spiral on the hand's palm. If the find was genuine, then obviously this symbolism had to have meant something to the Herdewyke Templars.

When I first saw the spirals in the church, I was sure they reminded me of something. It was only after I got the photographs I had taken in the Valley of Edom back from the printers that I realized what it was. On a ledge halfway up the steps that led up Jebel Madhbah, there was an alcove carved into the cliff face that contained a carved block of stone, believed to be an Edomite altar. I had taken a picture of the alcove, which showed that beside the altar stone there was a design etched into the rock—a pattern of two interlinked spirals. On seeing the photograph, I asked various historians and archaeologists if they could tell me what the spirals meant, but they could offer no explanation. If the pictograph was contemporary with the altar, then it may have been Edomite religious symbolism that had some connection with their sacred mountain. If so, then this would be a further link between Jebel Madhbah and the Herdewyke Templars. Unfortunately, there was no way of telling how old the spirals at Jebel Madhbah actually were; they may even have been graffiti made by a modern tourist. All the same, the spirals had me intrigued. It was when I asked a gentleman I met in Burton Dassett Church whether he had any idea what the spirals in the murals represented that an entirely new perspective opened up for my research into the secrets of the lost Ark.

I had returned to the church and was busy taking photographs of the murals when a voice from behind me made me jump.

"They're some of the oldest church decorations in the country."

I turned to find myself looking at a short, bearded, gray-haired man around sixty years of age. "Err, yes. It's okay if I take photographs?" I said, surprised that I was no longer alone in the building. The place echoed like crazy, yet I had not heard him approach.

"Feel free," he said with a smile. I gathered he must be the churchwarden as he began lighting the altar candles while leaving me alone to continue taking pictures.

"Have you any idea what the murals mean?" I asked him when I had finished.

He told me pretty much what I already knew about them having mystified the experts, until I asked him what he thought the spirals represented.

"It's just my own little theory, but I think they might have something to do with the apparitions at the well," he said, beckoning me to follow him outside.

We stood by the well as he told me how there had been miraculous visions of saints and angels reported here during the Middle Ages. "People still see strange things here, although they no longer consider them miracles," he said.

I listened with growing interest as he told me of one such occurrence that had been reported by a previous vicar. One night, the vicar was leaving his house on the other side of the road when he noticed a red glow coming from inside the well building. He was about to investigate when he had the shock of his life. A ball of fiery red light, which he described as around a foot in diameter, emerged from the well and floated across the road, a few feet above the ground. When it reached the gate at the bottom of his drive, it gave off a loud crack and something resembling a miniature bolt of lightning shot from it and set fire to the wooden gatepost. As the vicar watched in astonishment, the mysterious ball of light shrank to the size of a tennis ball and shot into the air, spiraling upward into the night sky to disappear from view.

"I know of many people who say they've seen this strange light," said the warden. "What it is—who knows? But I reckon it was this same apparition that people in olden times took to be angels or saints."

The man had me more fascinated than he could have known. What he was describing sounded just like the strange balls of light reported at Jebel Madhbah.

"You said you thought these apparitions had something to do with the murals?" I said.

"Yes. Those who have seen the light often describe it as disappearing into the air with a spiraling motion. You know, like when you play with sparklers as a child. The fast-moving point of light leaves a circular afterimage in the eye. I think the people who painted the spirals around the murals were trying to represent what they had seen. Of course, *they* took it to be a miracle."

I was about to ask the man if he had seen the light himself, but he said he had to attend to something in the church and wandered back inside. For some time, I examined the well structure more closely and went across the road to look at the gatepost that had apparently been set ablaze by the strange light. The gate, however, seemed to have been replaced fairly recently. After about ten minutes, I went back to the church, hoping to question the warden further about the light, but he was no longer inside. I walked around the graveyard for a while, hoping to find him, but he must have finished his duties and left. He had certainly left me confounded. My research into the Ark of the Covenant had led me to a place where a phenomenon just like the one at Jebel Madhbah had been reported. Was this just an extraordinary coincidence? I had to find out more about the strange light at the well. Amazingly, when I began researching at the public library in the county town of Warwick, I discovered that similar strange lights had been seen all over the Burton Dassett Hills.

I found dozens of newspaper clippings reporting all kinds of mysterious luminosities: spheres, columns, and pinpricks of light, usually red or orange, but sometimes blue. They had been reported on the hills, in the woodlands, and even in the Temple Herdewyke area. The phenomena seemed to come in waves, cresting for several days following heavy rainfall, before subsiding again, sometimes for years. Because of the hundreds of reports, scientists from Oxford University investigated the occurrences in the 1990s and concluded that they were electromagnetic phenomena caused by the rock strata and subterranean streams. The Burton Dassett Hills are capped by carnelian granite, and a minor geological fault line runs through the entire area. It seemed that the rocks here produce the same enigmatic geoplasma found at Jebel Madhbah and thought to be created by a combination of seismic activity and fast-flowing water, although they occur more frequently in the Burton Dassett Hills as the rainfall is much higher.

The reports of the strange lights seen at Jebel Madhbah had sounded very similar to the Old Testament accounts of the "glory of the Lord'" and the "devouring fire" that appeared on Mount Sinai. Many of the witness reports of the lights around the Burton Dassett Hills also sounded uncannily similar to biblical accounts of the divine manifestations on the Mountain of God.

One man I interviewed personally was Warwickshire schoolteacher Simon Bowen. He had witnessed a remarkable phenomenon while he was riding home on his motorbike along the deserted stretch of country lane that runs beside the cowshed that had been the Templar chapel. Suddenly and inexplicably, his engine cut out and the headlights died. Searching for a flashlight in his saddlebag, he noticed that it was getting eerily light. The whole area was bathed in a red glow coming from a clump of bushes beside the road. At first he thought that the bushes were on fire, but suddenly a sphere of bright red light, some five feet in diameter, rose above them. It hovered motionless for a few seconds before shrinking to a pinprick of light that shot into the sky, spiraling upward into the darkness. I couldn't help recalling Moses's first encounter with the presence of the Lord at the Mountain of God:

> And the angel of the Lord appeared unto him in a flame of fire out of the midst of a bush: and he looked, and, behold, the bush burned with fire, and the bush was not consumed. (Ex 3:2)

A bush that burned without being consumed! This is precisely what Simon Bowen had thought he was seeing.

Of course, Mr. Bowen had not thought he was seeing an angel, but many witnesses to the Burton Dassett lights over the years *had* interpreted the phenomenon in a religious context. For instance, an orb of blue light seen by inhabitants of the village of Farnborough, to the southeastern end of the Burton Dassett Hills, in the fifteenth century was thought to be a vision of the Virgin Mary; something described as a floating flame seen over a nearby lake during the First World War was taken to be an angel; and as recently as 1986 a shining iridescent sphere that appeared outside a Pentecostal church just to the north of the hills was considered a visitation by the Holy Spirit.

Clearly, the same phenomenon that occurred at Jebel Madhbah was occurring in the Burton Dassett Hills. Only a few locations in the world have the right combination of geology, seismic activity, and precipitation to create geoplasma. Surely, it was more than coincidence that such a rare phenomenon should occur in two places that were linked with Ralph de Sudeley and his Templars. Jebel Madhbah may originally have been considered sacred because the strange lights had been seen there—phenomena that were thought to be a manifestation of God. It was quite possible that the Templars stationed in the Valley of Edom had seen such lights themselves and also took them to be some kind of divine appearance. Had Ralph de Sudeley and his Templars decided to build their preceptory at the foot of the Burton Dassett Hills because similar phenomena were known to have occurred here?

In fact, de Sudeley's Templars may actually have considered Jebel Madhbah to have been the Mountain of God and believed such strange lights to have been the "glory of the Lord" described in the Old Testament. The Templars stationed in the Valley of Edom certainly knew the area had biblical associations because contemporary Crusader maps refer to the region as *Le Vaux Moise*—"the

Valley of Moses." Furthermore, the Bedouin Ain Musa shrine was there at the time the Templars arrived, meaning that the Templars must have known that this was where Moses was thought to have created the miraculous spring. As such, it was quite possible that they had worked out that Jebel Madhbah was the Mountain of God. If they were familiar with the Bible (and as many of them were monks, they must have been), then they would have known that Moses created this spring at "the rock in Horeb." As Horeb was one of the Old Testament names for the Mountain of God, it would not have taken much imagination for them to conclude that the Ain Musa shrine was at the foot of what must have been this same holy mountain. Once the Saracens forced the Templars to abandon the Valley of Edom, then another place where "the glory of the Lord" was thought to manifest would be the perfect location to set up a new preceptory. Moreover, if de Sudeley's Templars had found what they considered to be biblical relics at the foot of Jebel Madhbah, then a chapel at the foot of the Burton Dassett Hills would be the ideal sacred place to house them. To them, the Burton Dassett Hills may have been the new Mountain of God.

As I continued to investigate the strange lights around the Burton Dassett Hills, I began to suspect that I was on to something far more significant. It seemed that these peculiar phenomena might actually hold the key to solving one of the greatest mysteries concerning the Ark of the Covenant—what it might really have been.

According to the Old Testament, the glory of the Lord appeared many times on and around the Mountain of God, but once the Israelites left the area, the same glory of the Lord continued to appear to them. Now, however, it came from the Ark. For instance, Leviticus 9:23 describes how, after the Ark was placed in the inner sanctum of the tabernacle, God's presence manifested:

> And Moses and Aaron went into the tabernacle of the congregation, and came out, and blessed the people: and the glory of the Lord appeared unto all the people.

When the Ark was consulted in the tabernacle, not only the glory of the Lord but a miraculous cloud sometimes appeared. For example, the book of Numbers says that the Israelites "looked toward the tabernacle of the congregation: and, behold, the cloud covered it, and the glory of the Lord appeared" (Nm 16:42). This cloud is even said to have hung over the Ark when it was being moved:

> The ark of the covenant of the Lord went before them in the three
> days' journey, to search out a resting place for them. And the cloud
> of the Lord was upon them by day. (Nm 10:33–34)

It seems that at night the manifestation was seen as fire and by day it was seen as a cloud. Exodus 13:21 describes the appearance of the Lord in this way: "And the Lord went before them by day in a pillar of a cloud, to lead them the way; and by night in a pillar of fire."

The Burton Dassett lights were reported during hours of darkness, but an equally strange phenomenon has been seen in broad daylight. It has been described as a "small cloud that floats just above the ground," "a column of mist," and "a dancing ball of smoke." In fact, one witness I managed to interview myself gave a description that sounded as if it had come right out of the Old Testament.

The lake near the village of Farnborough, where the floating flame was seen during the First World War, has been the site of dozens of reports of both strange lights and a mysterious column of mist. Gary Selby, an angler from the city of Oxford, was quietly fishing with two friends one summer's day in 1999 when the ducks on the lake suddenly took flight. Wondering what had disturbed them, the three men looked across the water to find themselves confronted by a bizarre spectacle. What Gary described as a human-sized column of dark gray mist descended from the sky to hang motionless above the middle of the lake. It remained there for a while, then drifted back and forth, about ten feet in each direction, before spinning like a tiny tornado and disappearing into the air.

According to the book of Exodus, Moses saw something very similar when God manifested from the Ark in the tabernacle: "And it came to pass, as Moses entered into the tabernacle, the cloudy pillar descended, and stood at the door of the tabernacle" (Ex 33:9).

Both the strange mist and the fiery balls and columns of light have been reported many times over the Farnborough lake, and like the biblical descriptions of the glory of the Lord, they may well be the same phenomenon visible differently in daylight and darkness. Experts have explained the phenomena as something called marsh gas: vapors released from rotting vegetation that can sometimes spontaneously ignite. However, it is difficult to see how marsh gas, at the mercy of the wind's direction, could move in two different directions. It seemed more likely that the strange mist was somehow related to the daytime appearance of geoplasma; only in darkness would it be seen to glow.

As we saw earlier, it is quite possible that the biblical accounts of the glory of the Lord seen on Mount Sinai were actually descriptions of geoplasmic phenomena and that the same divine fire was somehow produced by the Ark of the Covenant. It has been suggested that geoplasma might prove to be an alternative source of energy—to fuel industry, supply electricity, and even provide a means of interstellar travel. At present, scientific research into the phenomenon is in its infancy, and its power is far from being harnessed. However, if the glory of the Lord was in reality geoplasma, then Moses seems to have known exactly how to harness it. I realized that I was engaged in wild speculation, but I could not help wondering if the Ark of the Covenant was actually some kind of geoplasmic device.

The team of scientists from Oxford University who had investigated the Burton Dassett lights had conducted similar experiments to those carried out by the US Bureau of Mines in 1981, compressing carnelian granite and arenite sandstone cores to produce low-level geoplasma. I managed to speak with Dr. James Mellor, one of the team responsible for the experiments, and asked him if it would be possible to make a device to artificially reproduce the phenomenon on a larger scale.

"It would require a gigantic machine to compress the amount of rock required," he told me over the phone. "It would be completely impractical. It may be possible to artificially produce earthlights [the popular term that the Oxford team used for geoplasma] without the need for a compressor by electron bombardment and a strong enough magnetic field. However, the only way to test that theory at present is with a particle accelerator, but there are not many of these in the world."

"Do you think it might be possible in the future to make a portable device to produce geoplasma?" I asked.

Dr. Mellor told me that it might, if solar energy could be harnessed by making photoelectric silicon cells to convert sunlight into enough electricity. Unfortunately, he explained, we have yet to discover how to maximize the conversion of solar into electric energy.

"If it could be done, what would a geoplasmic generator look like?" I asked.

"I have no idea," he said, "but it would need to have a carnelian granite or arenite sandstone core and be insulated by thick polycarbonate or a dense metal like lead or gold."

Although these details may have disappointed a scientist, I was thrilled. Dr. Mellor could have been describing the Ark of the Covenant. It had a gold-plated casing and it did surround slabs of arenite sandstone. The Bible tells us what was in the Ark when it was opened in the Jerusalem Temple: "There was nothing in the ark save the two tablets of stone, which Moses put there at Horeb" (1 Kgs 8:9). These two stone tablets, on which God is said to have inscribed the Ten Commandments, were apparently cut from the bare rock on top of Mount Sinai. (According to Exodus, Moses broke the first two tablets and God told him to cut a second set himself from the bare rock on the summit of Mount Sinai.)

> And he [God] gave unto Moses, when he had made an end of communing with him upon mount Sinai, two tables [tablets] of testimony, tables of stone, written with the finger of God. (Ex 31:18)

The summit of Jebel Madhbah is composed of arenite sandstone, which, like the carnelian granite of the Burton Dassett Hills, is one of the few rocks known to produce geoplasma. The importance of the sacred tablets may not only have been that they carried God's commandments, but also that they were made from a certain type of stone. Of course, there was no biblical description of anything that might have contained photoelectric silicon cells, but a crucial part of the Ark goes undescribed—the mysterious mercy seat.

Was it possible that the ancient Israelites had somehow stumbled upon what is at present only at the cutting edge of theoretical physics and created a geoplasmic generator of some fashion? Whatever it really was, if the Bible is to be believed, the Ark of the Covenant produced something that was remarkably similar to the Burton Dassett Hills and Jebel Madhbah phenomena. Moreover, it could be extremely dangerous, just as was the light reported by the Burton Dassett vicar that discharged what appeared to be electrical energy and set fire to his gatepost. One Old Testament passage describes something very similar coming from the Ark: "And there came a fire out from before the Lord, and consumed upon the altar the burnt offerings" (Lv 9:24).

The Burton Dassett Hills phenomenon can be far more destructive, as it was in 1931 when a flaming ball of light crashed into a windmill, setting it on fire and burning it to the ground. The miller and his wife narrowly escaped with their lives. When the glory of the Lord appeared to the ancient Israelites, some of them were not so lucky: "And the fire of the Lord burnt among them, and consumed them that were in the uttermost parts of the camp" (Nm 11:1). Yet whatever this divine fire was, the Israelites were apparently able to control it. The next verse of this story describes how Moses stopped the devastation: "And the people cried unto Moses; and when Moses prayed unto the Lord, the fire was quenched" (Nm 11:2).

Repeatedly, the Ark was not only used to communicate with God but also deployed as a fearsome weapon. According to the Old Testament, God instructed the Israelites to found a Hebrew kingdom in Canaan, a land already occupied by dozens of different hostile peoples who vastly outnumbered them. To overcome such overwhelming odds, the awesome power of the Ark was used to smash chariots, bring down city walls and defeat entire armies, until only one enemy remained: the mighty Philistines. In a series of decisive battles, which finally enable the Israelites to establish their kingdom of Israel, the Ark is used to level the opposition. According to the first book of Samuel, the Philistines are at first victorious until the Ark of the Covenant is deployed:

> And when the people were come into the camp, the elders of Israel said . . . Let us fetch the ark of the covenant of the Lord out of Shiloh unto us, that, when it cometh amongst us, it may save us out of the hand of our enemies. (1 Sm 6:2–3)

Most pertinent for our purposes, the divine fire that emanated from the Ark was no random occurrence but was deliberately summoned by the Israelites. Moses, for instance, called the power of God from the Ark to destroy his enemies:

> And it came to pass, when the ark set forward, that Moses said, Rise up, Lord, and let thine enemies be scattered; and let them that hate thee flee before thee. (Nm 10:35)

It seems, then, that the ancient Israelites had not only created something that acted very much like a geoplasmic generator, they had also used it like a futuristic weapon of mass destruction.

However, there was no way of knowing what the Ark of the Covenant really was unless it could be found. I may have had no proof that de Sudeley and his Templars had actually found the Ark at Jebel Madhbah, but there was reasonable evidence that they had found a golden chest that they believed was a biblical relic. This same relic could well have been among the relics housed in the Herdewyke chapel. Jacob Cove-Jones claimed to have found (and re-secreted) some of these same relics, which included "a discovery of immense importance." It was just possible that this was the same golden chest. He had evidently left clues to his own cache in the stained-glass window in the church in the Warwickshire village of Langley. I had to see the window for myself.

12

The Epiphany Code

When I visited Langley Church, I was accompanied by Graham and Jodi Russell, a married couple from the United States. Graham, a singer-songwriter from the hit band Air Supply, and I had met some years earlier when we worked together on a historical stage musical. We had since become good friends, and both Graham and Jodi shared my fascination with historical mysteries. I had told them of my research into the Ark and that a stained-glass window in Langley Church supposedly held clues to the whereabouts of the three gemstones and some other mysterious artifact Jacob Cove-Jones claimed to have hidden. I had to admit that I had no idea if the gems really were three of the Stones of Fire that had once been set into the biblical Breastplate of Judgment, or whether the "discovery of immense importance" was actually the Ark of the Covenant, but I told them that Mr. Baylis had been certain that his ancestor had really hidden some artifacts, and they were probably still there to be found.

Langley is a leafy Warwickshire village a few miles north of Stratford-upon-Avon—a tiny place without a single store or bar. Most houses in the area were fairly new, and one of the only old buildings in the village was the church itself, which turned out to be a small one-room chapel that had been built at the end of the nineteenth century. We immediately found what we had come to see. In the middle of the south wall was the stained-glass window Mr. Baylis had mentioned. As in most churches in England, there was a guidebook that gave the history of the building, and this confirmed that the window had been designed by Jacob Cove-Jones's artist friend Bertram Lamplugh in 1907 and donated to the church. It was a small window about three and a half feet high and two feet wide— much smaller than I thought it would be. In fact, it was nothing like I expected. I had assumed the window would have illustrated a scene from the Old Testament, perhaps including the Ark or the sacred breastplate. Instead, it depicted the Nativity scene from the New Testament, showing the three wise men offering their gifts to the baby Jesus. According to the guidebook, it was called the Epiphany Window, as Epiphany is the name for the day on which the three wise men are traditionally thought to have visited the Christ Child. Epiphany is still celebrated by many Christians on the twelfth day after Christmas, January 6. However, none of this seemed to link with the Ark of the Covenant or the Stones of Fire.

"Do you think Cove-Jones's relics might have been to do with Jesus rather than the Old Testament?" asked Jodi, as we examined the window. "Maybe they were the wise men's gifts."

According to the New Testament account given in the gospel of Saint Matthew, a strange new star appeared in the sky at the time of Jesus's birth. Somewhere to the far east of Judea, three wise men believed that the star was a sign from God to reveal the birthplace of the Messiah. They set out and traveled in the direction of the star until they reached Bethlehem. There they discovered the stable in which Jesus was born, and each offered the child a gift: One had brought gold, one had brought frankincense (religious incense), and the other had brought myrrh (a precious aromatic oil). The stained-glass window did indeed depict the wise men with these presents. However, it did not seem that they had anything to do with what Jacob Cove-Jones claimed to have found.

"If Cove-Jones's finds had been relics that had once been housed in the Herdewyke chapel, as he claimed, then they were Old Testament relics. At least this is how they were described in the *Feet of Fines*," I said. "The Old Testament was written over five hundred years before Jesus was born."

"Do you think the window really does contain a code?" said Graham Russell.

"Mr. Baylis thinks it does," I said. "Cove-Jones paid for it to be made, and it would have been a simple matter for him to have instructed his artist friend to incorporate a few coded images into the work without anyone knowing."

"If it does, don't you think somebody's already solved it by now? It's been here for almost a century," said Jodi.

"Mr. Baylis doesn't think so," I said. "A few of Cove-Jones's descendants tried to solve the conundrum but gave up without success. As far as I know, very few people these days have even heard of Jacob Cove-Jones, let alone know anything about the supposed clues in the window."

"Perhaps there's a clue in the name of the window," suggested Graham. "What does the word *epiphany* mean?"

I had no idea, but the guidebook said that it came from the Greek word *epiphaneia*, meaning "appearance," referring to the miraculous star that appeared in the sky to lead the wise men to Bethlehem. The stained-glass window certainly showed the star at the top of scene, and next to it a cock was crowing. According to early Christian tradition, a cock perching above the stable where Christ was born crowed at midnight to reveal to the wise men exactly where the baby Jesus was to be found. Perhaps, as the star and the cock had led the wise men to Jesus, Cove-Jones chose this imagery to lead seekers to where he had hidden his supposed relics.

Besides the window, the only other clues to the whereabouts of the relics were apparently contained in the three Bible passages Cove-Jones had written down. I took out the photocopy that Mr. Baylis had made and read them out to the Russells. Although these passages made no mention of the Ark of the Covenant, they did refer to the three gemstones Cove-Jones claimed to have hidden. One concerned the onyx stone, one the beryl, and the other the jasper. Was it possible that each passage somehow related to the hiding place of one of the stones? Cove-Jones had apparently hidden each of his artifacts in a different location in the local area; maybe these would lead to three of them.

"Mr. Baylis thought that the three Bible passages would only make sense when coupled with the window imagery," I said.

"And there are three wise men. Maybe they each hold a clue to lead to one of the gemstones, too," said Jodi.

Indeed, two of the wise men were quite literally holding something—their individual gifts of gold and myrrh. Upon the caskets that contained the gifts was an image. On one, there was what appeared to be a bridge; and on the other, there was a church surrounded by a wall and a large gate. The third figure's gift was obscured. Instead, he was looking toward another strange image on the cloak of one of his companions: a waterwheel leaning against a tree with a crown around it and a single capital letter *B* underneath. These were certainly incongruous images that seemed to have no place in the Nativity scene. Other distinctive images that immediately seized our attention were a capital letter *M*, toward which the figure holding the casket with the image of the church on it was looking, and a dove perched on a hay dispenser that was looking toward the waterwheel.

"I think you're right," I said in answer to Jodi's question. "Each of the passages not only refers to one of the stones, two of them mention the gifts the wise men gave to Jesus. Perhaps if we couple together the appropriate wise man with the right passage, we will have three complete sets of clues, one for each location."

It seemed logical. As one of the passages mentioned gold and another referred to myrrh, two of the wise men's gifts, it was clear which passage pertained to which wise man. It was not immediately clear, however, which gift each man held. Luckily, however, the church guidebook was able to help. According to early Christian tradition, the three wise men were named Melchior, Balthazar, and Gaspar: Melchior brought the gold, Balthazar brought the myrrh, and Gaspar brought the frankincense. The guidebook told us which figure was which in the stained-glass window.

If we were right, then the passage mentioning myrrh would couple with the imagery associated with the Balthazar figure—the one looking toward the image of the waterwheel. As this passage referred to beryl, then, together with the Balthazar imagery, it might lead us to the hiding place of the beryl gem. The passage mentioning gold would tie up with the imagery associated with the Gaspar figure—the one who held the casket with the bridge image on it. As this passage referred to onyx, then taken together with the Gaspar imagery, it might lead us to the hiding place of the onyx gem. Although the third passage did not mention frankincense, it would have to link with the imagery associated with the Melchior figure—the one with the casket with the church and gate image on it—as he was the only one left. Accordingly, the final biblical passage that referred to jasper, together with the Melchior imagery, might lead to the hiding place of the jasper gem. One problem, however, remained: If these were indeed clues, how could they lead us to Cove-Jones's hidden relics?

"Perhaps Cove-Jones found hiding places in the local area with landmarks that linked with these images and the biblical verses in some way," said Graham after a while.

Graham's suggestion seemed logical, so we spent some days studying maps of the area and reading up on the history of Warwickshire to determine which prominent landmarks were actually there when the window was installed in 1907. Eventually, we did find something that appeared to link with one of the images. The Balthazar figure had been looking toward the image of the waterwheel, and there was an old mill not far from Langley Church that still had a working waterwheel. In fact, we found a book with a photograph of the waterwheel that had been taken just the year before the window was made, proving that it had been there in Cove-Jones's day. Although there were a number of old mills still standing in the Warwickshire countryside, this particular mill was situated on a road called Crowntree Lane. In the window image, the waterwheel was leaning against a tree with a crown around it. Surely this was too much of a coincidence.

Dating from the Middle Ages, the mill had been a working watermill for centuries, until it was converted into a restaurant and bar in the 1970s. Now called the Saxon Mill, it stands about two miles west of the county town of Warwick. Outside, it was unaltered from Jacob Cove-Jones's time, and the waterwheel still survived in working order. When Graham, Jodi, and I first arrived it was getting dark, but as it was warm evening, we ordered drinks and sat on the

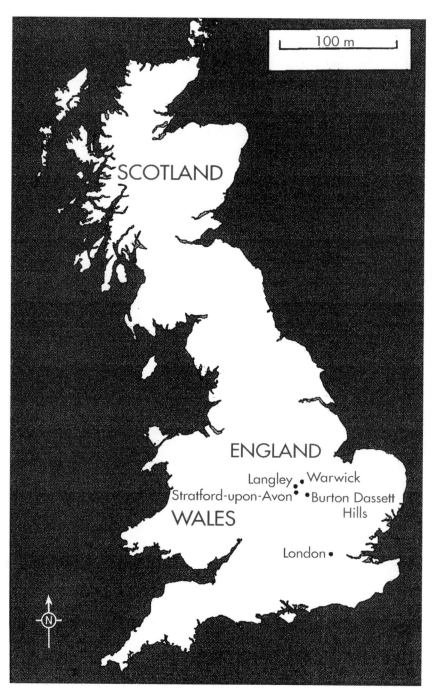

England and the main sites in the search for the Stones of Fire

floodlit patio outside. Looking out across the river that ran beside the building, we reread the biblical passage that Cove-Jones had left as a clue to find what we had reasoned was the beryl stone. It was chapter 2, verses 12, 13, and 14, of the Old Testament book Song of Solomon:

> His eyes are as the eyes of doves by the rivers of waters, washed with milk and fitly set. His cheeks are as a bed of spices, as sweet as flowers: his lips like lilies, dropping sweet smelling myrrh. His hands are as gold rings set with the beryl.

The scene before us only helped confirm that we were in the right location. A weir beside the mill constantly churned the water so that the surface of the river was snow white with froth and foam for at least a hundred feet downstream. The words from the passage, "waters, washed with milk," could not have been more apt. But, try as we might, we could not work out where to search. We had thoroughly examined the waterwheel itself, but nothing anywhere near it struck a familiar chord. However, one clue we had yet to consider from the Epiphany Window was the capital letter *B,* which had been just below the waterwheel image, and Jodi suggested we look out for a prominent letter *B.* Perhaps it was inscribed on something. We searched the Saxon Mill from top to bottom but found nothing.

It was getting late, the bar was closing, and we were about to abandon the search for the day when my attention was suddenly seized by a dove that fluttered noisily from the eaves of the restaurant and flew over the bridge that led across the weir to the other side of the river. It not only reminded me of the dove in the stained-glass window that had been looking in the direction of the waterwheel, but also of the first line of the biblical passage: "His eyes are as the eyes of doves by the rivers of waters." Perhaps the dove reference was important. Maybe there was a dovecote (a structure specially built for doves and pigeons to nest in) in the darkness over the other side of the river and it was here that Cove-Jones had hidden the stone.

It was still bright enough to see by the floodlights shining from the Saxon Mill, so we crossed the bridge to the other side. As

Graham Russell and I searched in the dark woods beyond to see if we could find a dovecote that the dove might have flown to, Jodi examined an old wall that separated the path from the rushing waters of the weir. Immediately, something caught her eye. One of the top stones of the wall was carved with a letter *B,* about four inches high. Kneeling down to examine it closely, she noticed that below the stone was a narrow crevice, just wide enough to fit her arm into. Doing so, she felt inside, almost up to her elbow, where her hand discovered a sharp rise, leading to a narrow shelf. Upon it she felt something round and smooth. Pulling it out, she called to us.

We arrived to find Jodi sitting on the wall with a look of astonishment on her face. In her hand was a small stone, shaped like half of an egg, about three quarters of an inch long, and artificially cut and polished, such as one that might fit in a ring.

"I can't believe it," she said. "It was right up in that crevice."

As Graham bent down and felt whether anything else was there, I examined the stone. It was a rich grainy-brown gem. We had brought a book with us that was illustrated with photographs of all types of gemstones, just in case we did find something. When I got it from the car, we found that the stone Jodi had discovered matched perfectly with a picture of a beryl gem—exactly what we thought we had been looking for.

Next day we had the stone examined by a jeweler, who told us that the gem was indeed made from beryl. To our amazement, we seemed to have cracked one of the Cove-Jones codes. It seemed most unlikely that anyone else had decided to put just such a gem in the crevice in the wall, and underneath a stone marked with the letter *B.* It must have been Jacob Cove-Jones who hid it there almost a hundred years before. When we checked, we found that the wall was contemporary with the mill, and so would certainly have been there in Cove-Jones's time. It also seemed to us that it was a shrewd hiding place. It was in a location that was unlikely to change for many years. The mill, the weir, and the wall had been there for hundreds of years and would probably remain for as long again. No one would even have noticed the crevice, let alone push an arm up inside to feel around, unless they were specifically looking for something.

Mr. Baylis seemed to have been right about his ancestor having hidden the stones as he claimed. The question in my mind was whether this beryl stone really was one of the Old Testament relics that were once housed in the Herdewyke chapel. Or was it, as Mr. Baylis believed, any old gem that Cove-Jones happened to have bought? Unfortunately, there was no way to date the stone itself, as only organic remains can be radiocarbon dated. The best the jeweler could do was to examine it under a microscope to determine that it had not been cut and shaped by modern machinery. It had, he told us, been made by hand, but this didn't really prove much: There were plenty of jewelers in Cove-Jones's time who could have cut and polished the stone by hand.

"How come we managed to find it in a few days, when Cove-Jones's ancestors searched for years?" asked Jodi, after we left the jewelers.

Personally, I did not think that there was anything strange in that, as the last people we knew of who had searched for the stones had done so during the early years of the twentieth century, when the maps and reference books that had been so essential to our search were rare or nonexistent. Nonetheless, something that I could not quite put my finger on did seem odd about the way we found the stone. I decided to put it out of my mind. We had found one of the stones and were impatient to see if we could find the others.

As the window imagery associated with the Balthazar figure had led to a waterwheel, it seemed logical that the landmarks where the remaining two stones were hidden had to be a bridge and a church, as these were the images on the caskets held by the two other wise men. The problem with either of these landmarks, however, was that unlike waterwheels, there were hundreds of old churches and bridges in Warwickshire. Eventually, however, it was the bridge that proved easiest to identify.

The image on Gaspar's casket showed an unusually designed bridge, which appeared to be reinforced with girders. On it were the Latin words *Venite Adoremus*, which are the first words of the Christmas carol "O Come All Ye Faithful" and fit the Nativity scene. However, there is nothing to do with a bridge in the story of

Jesus's birth, let alone a bridge with reinforcing girders, an engineering development that did not occur until the Industrial Revolution of the late eighteenth century. What was this doing in a scene depicting Jesus's birth two thousand years ago? Such an incongruous image must have been as important as the waterwheel had been.

Researching in the Warwick library, we discovered that there were in fact only a couple of dozen bridges with such girders surviving from Cove-Jones's day in the county of Warwickshire, and the nearest one to Langley Church was about three miles south of the village. It was an aqueduct, known as Bearley Aqueduct, which carried the Stratford-upon-Avon Canal over a river and a country road. Having been built in 1814, it had been there when Jacob Cove-Jones was alive. Cove-Jones's biblical passage that alluded to gold (Gaspar's gift to Jesus) and included a reference to the onyx stone seemed to tie up well with the Bearley Aqueduct. It was Genesis 2:10–12:

> The name of the first is Pison: that is it which compasseth the whole land of Havilah, where there is gold. And the gold of that land is good: there is bdellium and the onyx stone.

According to the Bible, Havilah was a land beside the Garden of Eden which was rich in bdellium, an expensive aromatic gum, and where gold and pure onyx stone could be found. Pison was a place in Havilah from where four rivers were said to have flowed in different directions. The Bearley Aqueduct carried the canal over a river, creating a site from which, for all intents and purposes, waterways did lead off in four different directions. In fact, it was the only place for miles around where this actually happened.

When the three of us arrived at the Bearley Aqueduct, it was a glorious summer's day and the yellow flowers that carpeted the surrounding fields shone golden in the midday sunshine. The aqueduct bridge was supported by towering red-brick pylons that stood on either side of the road, and beside one of them there was a steep path that led up to the canal. As Graham Russell wandered up the path onto the aqueduct, Jodi and I searched the roadside and riverbanks to see if we could find anything in which an onyx gemstone might be hidden.

At first we had no idea what we were looking for, until Jodi suggested that we might find another letter inscribed on something. As the clues to the beryl stone had been associated with the first wise man, Balthazar, and the letter *B* had been involved, perhaps we should expect to find a letter *G*, for Gaspar. In fact, there was a capital letter *G* in the stained-glass window's border above the figure's head. We searched the area but found nothing upon which anything could be inscribed. Up on the aqueduct, Graham was having no luck either. It was only as an idle thought that I decided to examine the pylons that supported the bridge. Obviously, they had been here in Jacob Cove-Jones's day, but as they were ordinary cemented house bricks, I didn't think for one minute that anything would be hidden here. However, I was in for a surprise. After a few minutes searching the brickwork of the pylon between the river and the road, I did find one that was inscribed with the letter *G*. In fact, the brick looked as though it had replaced an earlier one, as it was slightly darker and smaller than the other bricks. Calling to the others, I began to scrape away at the cement with my penknife. After a few minutes, I had made a gap large enough to reveal that there was indeed a narrow recess behind the cement. Inside, something caught the light. I managed to get my finger inside and felt a smooth surface, and when I removed it we could see that it was another stone, the same size and shape as the first, though colored smoky green. We had hoped to find an onyx stone, and when we compared it with the photographs of onyx in the gemstone book, it matched. Indeed, when we later had it checked by the jeweler, he confirmed that onyx was exactly what it was. I was as amazed as Jodi had been when she found the beryl stone! The gem could not in a million years have got there by accident. It had to be the second of Cove-Jones's stones.

For some time we sat on the banks of the river beneath the aqueduct, discussing our discoveries. I had to admit that Jacob Cove-Jones had been a clever man. Both hiding places were ideal for something that might need to remain hidden for years. The aqueduct had stood for almost a century at the time the stained-glass window was installed, and it would probably remain for another hundred years. As with the hiding place for the beryl stone, no one was likely to interfere with the brickwork of the aqueduct unless they were specifically looking for something. Furthermore, both stones had been in places to which anyone would have access if they solved the clues. A road ran right beside the pylon, and a public footpath led over the bridge and beside the weir wall at the Saxon Mill. Cove-Jones must have had a remarkable imagination, not to mention patience, to have found Bible passages that not only mentioned each of the stones by name and made reference to the wise men's gifts, but could also be used cryptically to describe the hiding places he chose. This, together with the expense and effort that went into making the window in Langley Church, made me seriously question whether Cove-Jones had contrived the treasure hunt simply to taunt the museum authorities, as Mr. Baylis thought. I was beginning to believe that Jacob Cove-Jones really had found the artifacts as he claimed by solving clues in the murals in the Burton Dassett Church. If he had, then it would mean that the Herdewyke Templars must have hidden them and they were probably among the relics that had been housed in their preceptory chapel. As we drove away through the Warwickshire countryside that afternoon, I looked down at the two gemstones in my hand. Could they really have been two of the Stones of Fire that the ancient Israelites had set in the Breastplate of Judgment—two of the ancient gems by which Moses and his successors were said to have controlled the awesome power of the Ark?

There was still one gem left to find—the jasper stone. Cove-Jones's biblical passage relating to this gem's hiding place was Revelation 21:11–13:

> Having the glory of God: and her light was like unto a stone most precious, even like a jasper stone, clear as crystal; And had a wall great and high, and had twelve gates, and at the gates twelve angels. On the east three gates; on the north three gates; on the south three gates; and on the west three gates.

The final wise man in the Epiphany Window, Melchior, was holding a casket fashioned in the shape of a church with a wall around it and a prominent gate. Written on the casket were the Latin words *Benedicte Omnia*. As this phrase simply meant to give praise and was consistent with the Nativity theme, we doubted that it was relevant to our search. However, the image of the church and gate certainly did seem relevant. The Bible passage referred to a wall with twelve gates, so we reasoned that we must be looking for a church surrounded by twelve gates. There could not have been many churches in Warwickshire with so many gates, so we initially thought it would be easy to locate the one Cove-Jones was alluding to. However, despite reading dozens of books, surfing the Internet, and scouring maps, we could find no such place. Ultimately, we decided that there was only one thing we could do and that was to drive around the county to visit every church in turn. This would have taken years. Almost 1,500 Anglican churches dotted the region in Cove-Jones's time, in addition to hundreds of Roman Catholic churches and goodness knows how many Baptist and Methodist chapels. Nevertheless, we decided to drive the country lanes of Warwickshire, in an ever widening area from Langley Church, in the hope that we might see something that seemed to link with the window imagery or the biblical passage.

"I can't help thinking that the star's important," said Graham as we drove on past farms, barns, and cottages. Graham had a point; it was a prominent image and at the very top of the Epiphany Window.

"It's possible," I said. "A star was what guided the wise men to find the baby Jesus."

"Perhaps we have to go in the direction of a particular star," suggested Jodi. "What was the star the wise men followed?"

"I don't think anyone knows. Even if they do, the positions of the stars change all the time," I said.

"What about a star on a church?" said Graham.

Most old churches have a weathervane on top of their steeples, and it was possible that one was decorated with a star, so we drove around for some time in the hope of seeing one but without success. No one we stopped and asked knew of any such church. We were about to give up when Graham halted the car at a crossroads to give way to another vehicle. Suddenly, the sound of a cock crowing on a fence right outside the open car window made us jump. Jodi and I laughed at the incident, but Graham pulled the car up at the side of the road and got out a local guidebook from the glove compartment.

"What is it?" I asked.

"That cock crowing reminded me that there was a cock in the Epiphany Window, next to the star," he said. "Perhaps we're looking for a cock and not a star. Maybe there's a pub in the area called the Cock," he said.

Graham could have been on to something. Many old English country pubs have names associated with animals, such as the Bull, the Ram's Head, or the Black Horse. There could well have been one called the Cock, the Cockrell, or something similar. However, as Graham and I looked through the guidebook, Jodi suddenly let out a gasp of excitement.

"Oh my God," she said. "Look!"

Right outside the car window there was a signboard painted with the name of one of the roads that arrived at the crossroads—Star Lane.

Could this be the star we were looking for? The Saxon Mill had been on Crowntree Lane and the image of the tree with the crown around it had related to that. Might Star Lane lead us to a church with twelve gates?

Following the lane for about a mile, we arrived at a main road, and there on the hill before us was a church in a village called Claverdon. When we saw the name of the church—Saint Michael and All Angels—we knew we must be on to something. The biblical passage had referred to twelve angels that guarded the twelve gates. Once we were inside, we were left with no doubt that we had found the place we were looking for. An elderly lady who was attending to the flowers told us that the sixteenth-century church had indeed been surrounded by twelve gates until the 1950s, when a few of them were removed. They had apparently led off in various directions: to the vicarage, the graveyard, and the roads and pathways that converged on this central village spot. Moreover, she told us that the gates were once each named after twelve different angels. The biblical passage had read: "at the gates twelve angels."

The passage had made reference to both gates and a wall, and in the Epiphany Window, Melchior's casket design showed a gate set in a church wall. The beryl stone had been hidden in a wall, its location indicated with the letter *B*. The onyx stone had been hidden in a wall, its location indicated with the letter *G*. Melchior had been depicted kneeling before the Virgin Mary and the baby Jesus, but he was looking past them, toward a capital letter *M* set into the window's border design. There could be little doubt that we were looking for a wall beside a gate, with a brick or stone with the letter *M* inscribed upon it. We all set off in different directions to examine the gates that still survived. But before I had managed to examine two of them, I heard Graham's voice calling from the other side of the churchyard. He had found what we were looking for. Hidden behind long grass at the bottom of a low wall, just to the side of one of the gates in the corner of the graveyard, a brick was inscribed with a letter *M*. The stone directly beneath it was a darker color than the rest, and when we removed it we found a narrow recess behind. Inside was a third gem, exactly the same shape and size as the others. However, this one was variegated with shades of red. Next day when we had it examined, the jeweler again confirmed what we expected—it was indeed a jasper stone.

Once more, it seemed, Cove-Jones had chosen a clever hiding place. It was an ideal location to hide something that might need to remain hidden for many years. The church had survived for centuries and would probably continue to do so for many more. Again, the gate where the stone was found was on unrestricted land, as a public footpath ran through it. Finally, it was highly unlikely that anyone would examine the brickwork unless they were specifically looking for something.

The evening after we found the last of the three stones, we retuned to the Saxon Mill and sat on the patio beside the river, discussing what we had discovered so far.

We had definitely found the stones hidden by Jacob Cove-Jones in 1907, but were they really three of the biblical Stones of Fire? Cove-Jones claimed to have found them by deciphering the fourteenth-century murals in the Burton Dassett Church. I could have been wrong, but it seemed to me most unlikely that he would have gone to all the trouble of hiding the stones, working out an elaborate series of clues, and paying to have the stained-glass window made and installed in Langley Church had he not believed they were genuine. The Herdewyke Templars must have left the murals in Burton Dassett Church because of the date they were painted, and the same Templars are recorded to have had what were believed to be Old Testament relics. These same Templars had occupied the Valley of Edom at the very time Crusaders apparently found "precious stones" and a "golden chest" at Jebel Madhbah, and Jebel Madhbah seems to have been where Jeremiah had hidden the Ark and perhaps the Stones of Fire. It was indeed possible the gems we had each found could have been three of these same stones.

"If these are three of the Stones of Fire, then they're supposed to possess extraordinary properties," I said.

"Well, nothing extraordinary has happened yet," said Jodi, examining the ordinary-looking gemstones in her hand.

"I don't know," said Graham, staring out over the foaming waters beside the mill. "Perhaps it has."

Jodi and I exchanged puzzled glances.

"It seems strange that we found all three stones so quickly when Cove-Jones's family didn't even find *one*," said Graham.

"Yes, but we had maps, books, and the Internet that they wouldn't have had," I said.

"You don't see what I'm getting at," said Graham. "I don't think we would have succeeded without some very strange coincidences. If the cock hadn't crowed when it did, we would never have seen the sign for Star Lane. We might never have found the church otherwise. I don't know what the cock in the window actually means, but it wasn't one of Cove-Jones's clues to lead to the jasper stone. Cove-Jones may have been a clever man, but he couldn't make a cock crow precisely on time a hundred years after his death."

"Just a coincidence," I said.

"You think so. What about the dove?" asked Graham.

I realized what Graham was saying, and suddenly knew why I had thought there was something strange about the way we had found the first stone. There was a dove in the Epiphany Window, and doves were mentioned in the biblical passage, but both were extraneous to the clues. When we were searching around the Saxon Mill, we would never have thought of looking on the other side of the river had we not been erroneously searching for a dovecote. There had been no dovecote there. Had it not been for the dove that flew across the weir, we might never have crossed to the other side and found the stone's hiding place. Cove-Jones could not have trained a dove to sit in the rafters of the mill for a hundred years waiting to fly out at the right moment.

"The cock—a coincidence perhaps," said Graham. "But another bird helping us to find another of the stones—I'm not so sure."

13

Extraordinary Encounter

When Graham and Jodi returned to the States, I spent much time examining the Epiphany Window, trying to work out how it might lead to the hiding place of Jacob Cove-Jones's fourth and final artifact—the mysterious "discovery of immense importance" he had supposedly made. Cove-Jones had hidden three stones, and the window's three wise men had each held clues to one of them. There were also the three biblical passages that had held part of the code. As there did not appear to be such a biblical passage to help find the fourth artifact, I could only assume that the window itself contained all the clues that were necessary. In fact, the more I thought about it, the more I realized that two of the stones could have been found without the biblical passages. The mill on Crowntree Lane could have been found from the window imagery alone, as could the aqueduct. All of the letters inscribed on the bricks were also revealed in the stained-glass window. I could not quite work out how the window alone could have pointed to the church with the twelve gates, but there were a number of images in the window that we had not yet considered. It was possible that we had overlooked other clues to the whereabouts of the three stones. Perhaps Cove-Jones intended the window to contain all the clues and the Bible passages were just a backup. However, if the window alone could reveal the hiding place of Cove-Jones's fourth artifact, I had to decide which part of its imagery was relevant.

The fourth artifact—the "discovery of immense importance"—

180

must have been the most important of the four artifacts, and as such the code to lead to it might be the subject matter of the window itself. Why had Cove-Jones chosen the Nativity scene for the stained-glass window? There had been three wise men and three stones, but if the number three was important he could have chosen a whole variety of Christian themes that involved it: the Trinity or Jesus and the two thieves at the Crucifixion, for instance. I could not help feeling that the theme of the three wise men following a star to find Jesus was somehow significant. We had already followed Star Lane to find Claverdon Church, but the same imagery could have been used twice. The wise men had followed a star to find Jesus. Perhaps by following a star I might be led to the fourth relic. However, what star should I follow?

Besides the cock, there was one other image right next to the star in the window. I had noticed it before but had not paid too much attention to it, as the church guidebook had said that it was a pelican, a Christian symbol for the Virgin Mary. (Pelicans feed their young with entire fish they keep in their large bills, so the bird came to represent the Virgin Mary caring for the infant Christ.) As this imagery was quite consistent with the Nativity scene, we didn't consider it again. However, Graham Russell had got me thinking about birds after he suggested that fate may have helped us to find the stones. I had to admit that the incidents with the dove and the cock certainly appeared strange, but eventually I had put them down as coincidences. The idea that the ancient Israelites may somehow have been able to manipulate geoplasma was weird enough, let alone the notion of meaningful coincidence—or synchronicity, as the Swiss psychologist Carl Jung called it in the 1950s. Nevertheless, I had birds on the mind, so when I saw the pelican image again, I studied it more carefully. It was only when I did that I realized that the guidebook had got it wrong. It wasn't a pelican but a phoenix.

The phoenix is a bird from Greek mythology. According to the legend, each year this exotic creature made its nest of spices, and when the sun's rays set it alight it was burned to cinders. A few days later, however, the phoenix was reborn, rising majestically from the ashes. There could be no doubt that the bird next to the star was a phoenix, as it was depicted with its head back and its wings outstretched, burning in flames. In fact, its hooked beak made it appear more like a bird of prey, which is exactly how the phoenix was portrayed in ancient myth. Such pagan symbolism clearly had no place in the Nativity scene, so like the images on the wise men's caskets, it may have been another of Cove-Jones's clues. Above the phoenix was a capital letter *B* and below it a capital letter *M*, each with crowns above them. We had already determined that these letters were the initials of two of the wise men's names. However, why they had crowns above them, and why they were on either side of the phoenix image, I had no idea. The phoenix might have been meant to represent a particular star. In fact, there is a Phoenix constellation of eleven stars. However, these southern stars are not visible from England, so I deemed it unlikely that any of these could have been incorporated into Cove-Jones's clues.

Moreover, if Cove-Jones had used a star to indicate a hiding place, I would not only need to work out which one, but also need to know where and when it was meant to be observed. The positions of the stars change all the time, not only in relation to the rotation of the earth but also throughout the course of the year as the earth orbits the sun. If Cove-Jones had hidden his discovery somewhere that was, for instance, indicated by a star rising above it, then I would need to know the precise time and day of the year to look for it. Furthermore, I would need to know where to observe the star from, as it would appear to rise over different locations depending on my viewing site. As far as I could see, Cove-Jones had left no clues in the window to account for any of this.

Unable to figure out anything new from the Epiphany Window, I decided to concentrate on the artifacts we had already found. Could these gemstones really have been three of the Stones of Fire?

The first thing I needed to do was to have the stones examined by a geologist. Although the jeweler assured us that the stones were handcrafted, this did not prove when they had been cut and polished. A geologist, however, could at least tell me where the stones originated. As Dr. Mellor had been very helpful when I questioned him concerning the artificial creation of geoplasma, I decided to contact him again. As a geologist who has been involved for many years in the field of geophysics (the scientific study of the physical properties of the earth), he was the ideal person to examine the stones. He knew that I had been investigating the Burton Dassett lights but had no idea what I was looking for, and I told him nothing about their discovery. However, I did say that they might have been medieval relics and that I needed to find out from where in the world they had come.

It turned out that this was fairly easy to determine, as Dr. Mellor had access to a comprehensive database of gems from all over the world. Different types of gems are unique to certain geographical locations, and the banding and specific texture of a given stone can be used to determine where it was mined. It did not take Dr. Mellor long to tell me that our beryl stone came from Egypt, the jasper from Arabia, and the onyx from the area around the Dead Sea. This was good news for Jacob Cove-Jones. If he had picked up any old jasper, onyx, and beryl gems from a jeweler, the chances were that they would have come from the main mines where these stones had been obtained during the nineteenth century, which were in the Americas and the Far East—two areas of the world from which the ancient Israelites or the Herdewyke Templars could not have obtained them. Although Dr. Mellor's conclusion did tend to support Jacob Cove-Jones's claims, it did not prove that they were genuine Old Testament relics. The Herdewyke Templars could have picked them up anywhere in the Middle East, as they would have been relatively common gems possessed by the medieval Arab population.

The next thing I asked Dr. Mellor was if he could scientifically test the stones to see if they possessed peculiar properties. If they were three of the Stones of Fire, then they were supposed to have been able to control the power of the Ark—or at least manipulate geoplasma somehow, if my speculations were in any way founded. These tests I had to pay for, but I considered it worth the expense. Over the next few weeks, the stones were subjected to various tests that were way over my head, such as magnetometer and spectrometer readings, and were examined under ultraviolet light. There seemed to be nothing unusual about them. However, a few days after the stones were returned, a puzzled Dr. Mellor called me to say that he had discovered something strange. While in the laboratory, the onyx stone was left for a while on top of an envelope containing photographic paper. When the paper was later developed, there was an inexplicable fogged, oval gray image of the stone on every one of them. Dr. Mellor was mystified. Only radioactivity should be able to produce such an effect, he told me, yet Geiger counter tests on the stones had produced negative results; they were not radioactive.

The mysterious incident had me hoping we were on to something, but when Dr. Mellor borrowed the stones to try to reproduce the effect, nothing happened. I tried it myself by leaving all three stones on top of an envelope of photographic paper for days but without results. When I told Graham and Jodi about the fogged image, Graham suggested that if the stones really did have some strange properties, then, like the geoplasma produced by rocks, they might only activate under certain conditions. It was possible, I conceded, but there was no way of proving it. What I was left with was yet another tantalizing mystery.

This is how things remained for some months until I saw a news item on British television about a strange light that had been seen at night over the Burton Dassett Hills. Although the report referred to it as a UFO, it was actually a large red ball of light that had been reported by a dozen or so witnesses from the nearby village of Fenny Compton. In fact, when I followed up the story it turned out that there had been a number of other reports of a similar red sphere of light from various locations in the Burton Dassett Hills over a period of a few weeks. I was not surprised to discover that for some time before the lights began to appear there had been torrential rain in the area. It seemed that for the first time in years, the Burton Dassett lights were back.

When Graham and Jodi heard about it, they caught the next plane to England in the hope of seeing the phenomenon themselves. However, although we spent a good few nights in the area of the Burton Dassett Hills, we saw nothing. Then one evening when we were sitting in a local pub discussing the matter, Jodi suggested that we use the stones.

"How do you mean?" I asked.

"If the stones really are the Stones of Fire, and if the Bible is right, then they controlled the power of the Ark," she said. "If this power is the same energy that makes the strange lights appear, then wouldn't the stones be able to influence it? Even make them appear?"

"There are a lot of ifs," I said with a smile.

"It's worth a try," said Graham. "Why don't we take the stones to a place where the lights are already being seen?"

"Yes," said Jodi. "It may be geoplasma, or whatever you call it, that activated the onyx stone in the laboratory and made it fog the paper."

I hadn't thought about it before, but Jodi had a point. The laboratory did conduct tests into geoplasma with their rock-crushing machines. Perhaps the close proximity of the stone to such a test had influenced it in some way.

Although it wasn't very scientific, I agreed that we might as well give it a try. What did we have to lose?

As far as I knew, there had been about a dozen separate reports of the strange lights recently, and three of these had been at the lake outside the village of Farnborough where Gary Selby and his friends had seen the column of mist in 1999 and others had reported seeing a pillar of flame. One of the recent witnesses had even produced what was claimed to be a photograph of the phenomenon. According to Carol Lane, a student from Warwick University, she was photographing reflections of the evening sun upon the water when she suddenly noticed a sphere of red light by the opposite bank. It only remained there for a few brief seconds, and before she had time to photograph it, it disappeared. When her pictures came back from the printers, however, she was shocked to see that the light did appear in one of the frames. Just to the edge of the picture, a ball of red light could clearly be seen hovering over the water. Carol said she was mystified, as she was sure it had not been visible when she had taken any of the photographs. Graham, Jodi, and I had been to the Farnborough lake twice already—on one occasion we stayed all night—but we saw nothing. However, it was an isolated place and seemed to be the best location to try out Jodi's idea. I did not for one moment think that anything would actually happen.

It was just after dark when we arrived at the secluded lake, and by flashlight we followed the path leading along the water's edge. A low mist hugged the surface of the long, narrow lake as we followed its bank into the thick woodland that surrounded its far end. There were no houses or main roads anywhere nearby, and the only sound to be heard was the occasional squawk of a night bird somewhere deep in the trees. I was expecting to spend another long night sitting on the bank in the darkness, bored stiff. But suddenly Graham, who was leading the way, halted and turned off his flashlight.

"What is it?" I asked, catching up with him.

"Turn off your flashlight; there's something there," he said, pointing across the lake to the opposite bank, about forty feet away.

It took my eyes some time to adjust to the dark, but when they did I could clearly see a point of red light, which seemed to be hanging in the air just above the bank.

"It's a cigarette," said Jodi.

I assumed that she was right and that someone was standing on the water's edge in the darkness, doing what we were doing and hoping to see the strange light.

"Hello!" I shouted.

No one answered. In fact, the lake was eerily quiet. For a minute or so we remained still, staring at the pinprick of light that remained completely motionless. All of a sudden it vanished.

"I don't think it's a cigarette," I whispered. If it was, then whoever was holding it had remained perfectly still.

After a few moments waiting in the silence and darkness, we trained our flashlight beams on the opposite bank where the light had been, but besides the overhanging branches of half-fallen trees, we could see nothing. However, when we again switched off the flashlights the light reappeared.

"I can't hear anyone. Perhaps they—" Jodi's voice cut off mid-sentence as the light winked off and immediately reappeared in a different location, about ten feet further along the bank. A few seconds later it moved again, about five feet higher in the air. A number of

The shrine of Ain Musa, where Bedouin tradition holds that Moses created the miraculous spring when the Israelites arrived at the Mountain of God.
(Photograph: Andrew Collins)

View into the Valley of Edom through the narrow gorge to the southeast, where the cliffs of Jebel Madhbah rise high above the Treasury. A strange effect of the wind creates a bizarre sound in this gorge that may have been the "trumpet exceeding loud" that the ancient Israelites heard when they camped at the foot of Mount Sinai.
(Photograph: Jane Taylor)

The summit of Jebel Madhbah. Is this the true Mountain of God?
(Photograph: Andrew Collins)

Obelisk Terrace below the summit of Jebel Madhbah. This may have been the "nether part of the mountain" where the Israelite elders are said to have encountered God.
(Photograph: Andrew Collins)

The shrine on the summit of Jebel Madhbah. This is where Moses may have obtained the Ten Commandments and was inspired to make the Ark.
(Photograph: Andrew Collins)

View of the Treasury from within the Siq. The cave where Jeremiah may have hidden the Ark was found buried below the entrance.
(Photograph: Jane Taylor)

Jodi and Graham Russell at the holy well in Burton Dassett.

All Saints Church in Burton Dassett built by the Templars just before the Black Death in 1350.

The mysterious murals either side of the window in Burton Dassett Church. Did they hold clues to the lost treasure of the Knights Templar? *(Photographs: David Moore)*

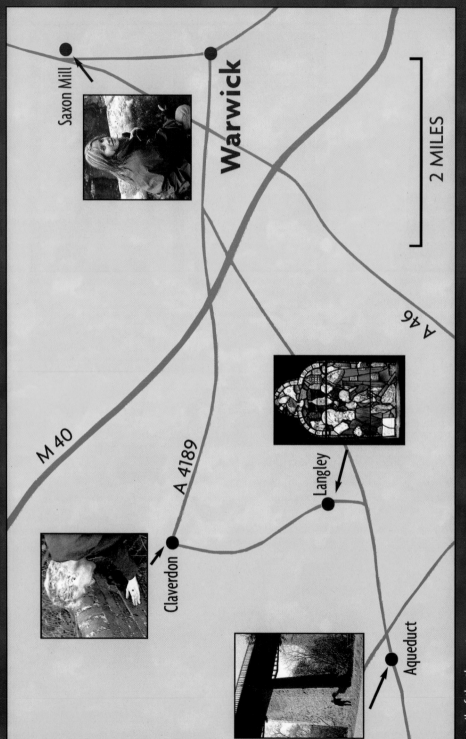

The trail of the three stones.

The tiny church in the village of Langley where Jacob Cove-Jones left his secret code

The Epiphany Window in Langley Church which held the clues to lead to the hiding places of the lost relics.

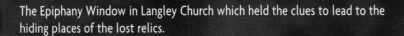

The Epiphany Window (detail), showing the crown tree and the waterwheel with the capital letter B beneath.

Jodi Russell shows the hiding place where she discovered the beryl stone.

The bridge over the weir at the Saxon Mill. The wall on the other side of the river is where the beryl stone was found. *(Photograph: Scott Masterson)*

The Epiphany Window (detail), showing the third wise man's casket with the church and gate design.

Saint Michael and All Angels Church in Claverdon.

The wall beside the gate where the jasper stone was hidden.

The Epiphany Window (detail), showing the bridge design on the second wise man's casket.

Graham Phillips stands by the aqueduct pylon where the onyx stone was found.

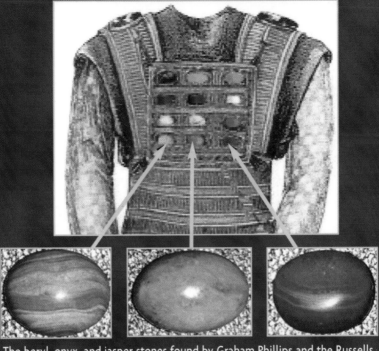

The beryl, onyx, and jasper stones found by Graham Phillips and the Russells. These may have been the gems that were set into the bottom row of the Breastplate of Judgment.

Carol Lane's photograph of the Farnborough Lake showing the strange red light over the water by the opposite bank. *(Photograph: Carol Lane)*

The cock and star from the Epiphany Window with the phoenix and letters above and below it.

Close-up of the phoenix from the Epiphany Window.

Graham and Jodi Russell work
out the final secret of the
Epiphany code.

The Beacon on the Burton
Dassett Hills where the old
windmill once stood.

Napton Hill on the horizon, as
seen from the top of the
Phoenix Hills.

Jodi Russell examines the water fountain at Church Green.

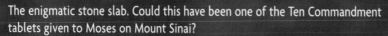
The enigmatic stone slab. Could this have been one of the Ten Commandment tablets given to Moses on Mount Sinai?

Graham Phillips examines the bank where the enigmatic stone slab was found.

(Photograph: Kerri Morton)

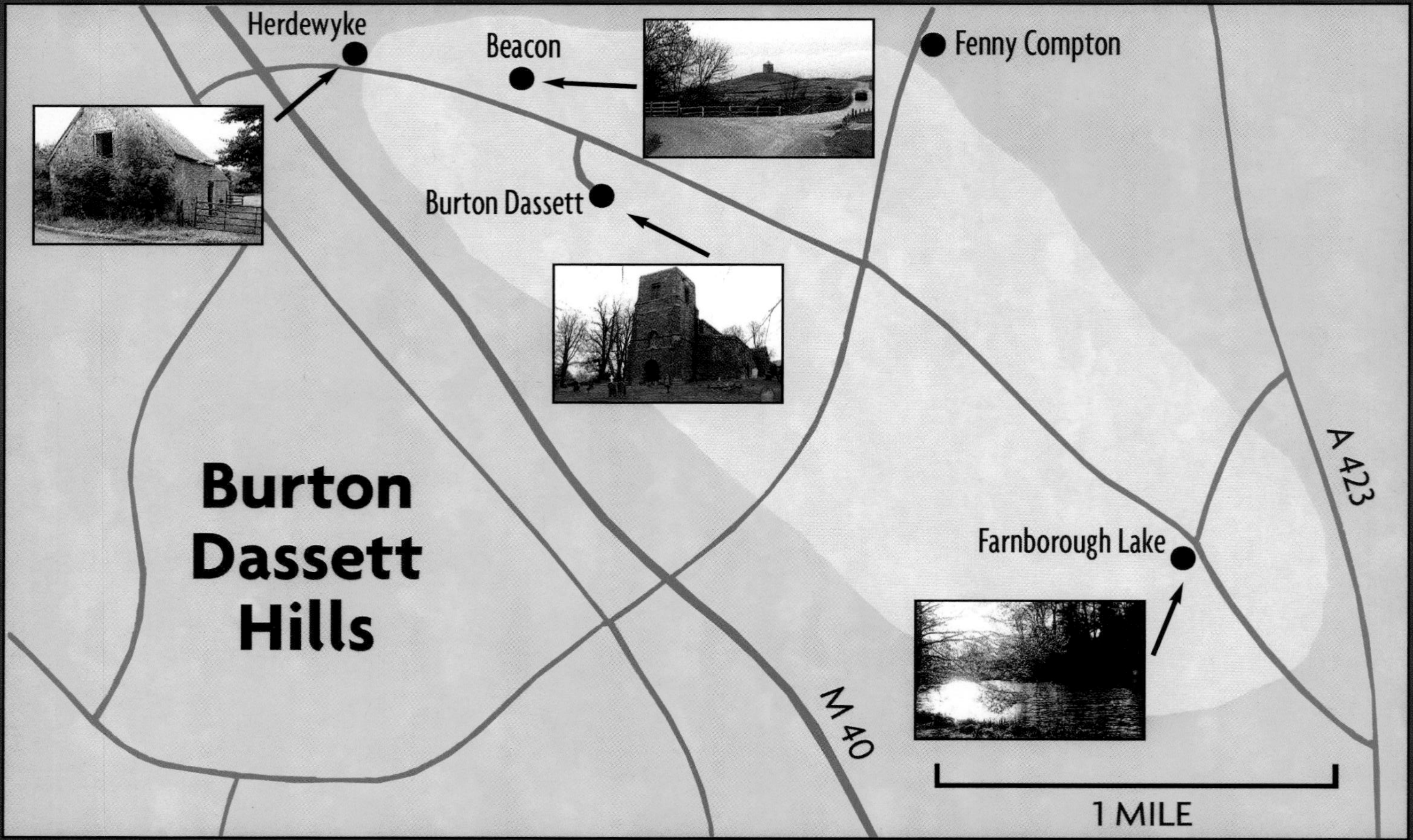

The Burton Dassett Hills.

A 423

1 MILE

Fenny Compton

Farnborough Lake

M 40

Beacon

Burton Dassett

Herdewyke

Burton Dassett Hills

times it blinked on and off, constantly changing position, before vanishing again.

For a good few minutes nothing happened, and we again swept the opposite bank with our flashlight beams, but there was no sign of anyone.

"It must be someone messing about," I said.

"How?" said Graham. "The light was jumping all over the place."

"Fireflies?" suggested Jodi.

"Not in England," I said.

All of a sudden, there came a loud cracking sound from the woods on the opposite bank. It sounded as if someone had broken a branch, and I was just about to say so when it happened once more. A few seconds later the noise came again, followed immediately by another crack, and another, until it sounded like someone rapidly banging rocks together.

As I tried to shine my flashlight further into the trees to see what was causing the din, I suddenly realized that the beam was growing dimmer. I bashed the flashlight on my hand, but it continued to die. Looking across to Graham and Jodi, I saw that their beams were fading too. A few seconds later we were plunged into darkness.

By now the cracking noises were coming so quickly that they sounded like a machine gun being fired. I was about to suggest we get the hell out of there when the red light reappeared. This time, however, it was the size of a soccer ball. I had heard plenty of eyewitness accounts of the strange lights but had never really imagined what it would actually look like. I couldn't believe my eyes. The orb of bright red light was just hanging motionless, about five feet in the air above the opposite bank. The eerie crimson glow it gave off clearly illuminated the surrounding trees and cast a ghostly image on the surface of the lake. As the three of us stared in awed fascination, the weird sound suddenly ceased and was replaced by a high-pitched whining noise that remained me of a child's humming top, but much louder. At first I thought the light was getting bigger, until I realized that it was beginning to move toward us. We all stood rooted to the spot as it hovered across the water and stopped about three feet in front of us. The bizarre orb was so close that we could have reached out and touched it, and there was the strangest tingling sensation all over our bodies, like being in a strong field of static electricity. Vividly recalling what had happened to the vicar's gatepost, I was about to suggest we run for it, but at that moment, the light began moving away, back across the lake, shrinking down to the size of a tennis ball. Suddenly, there was a piercing hissing sound and it shot into the air, spiraling upward into the darkness until it disappeared over the trees on the opposite bank.

For what seemed like an eternity, we all stood there without saying a word, the afterimage of the flaming red light still in our eyes. All at once, our flashlights blinked back on, making us jump.

Jodi wanted to stay there, in the hope that the light might come back, but I don't mind admitting I was a nervous wreck. I had expected at any second to be hit with a bolt of plasma. I couldn't help remembering that such a phenomenon had completely destroyed a windmill. Graham looked physically shaken too, so we got out of there as quickly as we could.

We were all stunned by the encounter. Although I had heard many firsthand accounts of such lights, I was totally unprepared for what we saw. I had expected the phenomenon to appear like an insubstantial, weightless ball of transparent, glowing mist. Instead, it had looked like a solid crystal globe, brightly illuminated from within by a tumbling core of fire. It seemed incredible that it was able to defy gravity and stay in the air, let alone move around. If this was the same phenomenon that the Israelites had called the glory of the Lord, I could completely understand why they had considered it divine. The incredible sphere of fiery luminescence appeared almost to have intelligence. The way it came over and hovered in the air, right before our eyes, made it seem like it was actually probing us.

Had we witnessed the phenomenon by chance alone or was it really connected with the stones as Jodi believed? The light, or a similar phenomenon, had occurred at the lake at least three times that I knew of over the previous few weeks, and it had been our third vigil there, so the odds of our seeing something had been in our favor. On the other hand, there was the behavior of the light itself—it had moved directly to within a few feet of us, as if attracted by something. What made me finally decide that our encounter may really have had something to do with the stones was what happened to us the next day. When the light appeared, we each had had one of the stones in our hands. In fact, they were the stones we had individually found. I had been holding the onyx stone, Graham the jasper, and Jodi the beryl. Next morning all three of us had a red, prickly rash on the palms of the hands in which we had held the stones. It may have been because we were tightly squeezing the stones when the light appeared. However, I could not see how that would produce a uniform rash all over our palms. I wanted to have a doctor examine it, but I had to wait a day for an appointment. Within twenty-four hours the rash had disappeared—as it had with Graham and Jodi.

Whether the light really had appeared because we had the stones, or whether it was somehow attracted in our direction because of them, there was no way of knowing. We visited the lake on a number of consecutive nights but nothing happened, nor did anything occur when we went to other sites where the strange lights had been reported. All the same, this didn't really prove anything one way or the other. As far as I could discover, no one else reported seeing the lights again for many months.

The extraordinary encounter had, however, got me thinking along new lines. Seeing the ball of light spiraling upward into the air when it vanished had reminded me of what the Burton Dassett churchwarden had said about the murals. He had told me that he thought the peculiar spiral designs around the two figures depicted in the pictures represented the strange lights. Because I had been totally absorbed in the search for the artifacts Jacob Cove-Jones had hidden, it had completely slipped my mind. If these spirals really did represent the lights, then perhaps they were the clues that Cove-Jones had solved. If Cove-Jones was to be believed—and I, for one, no longer doubted his word—then he had only found three gemstones. I speculated that if these were three of the biblical Stones of Fire, there could be nine more, still where they were hidden by the Templars. I needed to examine the murals again.

Graham and Jodi had gone back to the States, so I returned to Burton Dassett alone. When I entered the church, I was pleased to see that the warden was there once more, tending to flowers around the altar.

"Back again," he said with a smile. I was surprised he remembered me.

"Yes, I'm glad you're here," I said. "I wanted to ask you about the murals."

He stopped what he was doing and joined me beneath the window where the pictures were. "How can I help?" he asked.

"You said you thought the spirals represented the apparitions at the well," I said. "You know about similar things being seen all over the hills?"

"Strange, aren't they," he said.

"Have you any idea why the people who made the murals may have wanted to depict these lights?" I asked.

"In olden times the lights were taken to be angels and saints," he said. "That's why they put the murals round this window. Look!" He pointed through the window to the bare green hills that rose above the church. "There have been many such apparitions seen up there. Perhaps they saw them from here in the church, from where we're standing right now. I think that's why the window was considered particularly holy."

"Is that why the church is called All Saints Church—because they thought they saw saints?" I asked.

"Probably," he said. "But the apparitions were here long before Christianity came to this country. That part of the Burton Dassett Hills is now called the Beacon Hills, and most people think it was named after the beacon—a great bonfire—that used to be lit up there to celebrate the twelfth night of Christmas, the medieval New Year. However, the hill was associated with fire long before that, and it had nothing to do with bonfires. Old maps refer to the area as the Phoenix Hills, which is what the Romans called it. The phoenix was a firebird—what better name to call the apparitions?"

Once again, the warden had captivated me more than he could have known. Could the Phoenix Hills have been what was alluded to by the phoenix in the Epiphany Window? When the warden went back to his flowers, I went to the car to retrieve a photograph I had with me of the window in Langley Church. I wanted him to take a look at it; perhaps he might be able to identify some of the symbolism. However, when I returned, he had gone. He seemed to have a habit of disappearing. Hoping to see him again, I stayed for some time, mulling over the possible link between the phoenix and the hills. If I was right about Cove-Jones using a star to indicate where his fourth artifact was hidden, then the highest point on the Phoenix Hills might be the location from where the star was meant to be seen. I looked at the photograph in my hand and examined the phoenix image next to the star, hoping to get some inspiration about which star it might have been and what particular time of the year it should be viewed. The warden had mentioned a bonfire being traditionally lit on top of the hills on the twelfth night of Christmas—perhaps this was significant.

Suddenly, it came to me. I couldn't believe I hadn't realized it before. The answer had been the stained-glass window itself. It was the Epiphany Window, and Epiphany was the twelfth day of Christmas on January 6. Jacob Cove-Jones may have left a clue alluding to a particular day after all. Staring at the photograph, I realized that he also appeared to be indicating a particular moment on January 6—midnight. Right next to the star was the other principal image at the top of the scene—the cock. It was the cock that was said to have crowed at midnight to reveal to the wise man where the baby Jesus was. Interpreted correctly, the window provided a precise moment in the year when Cove-Jones could always count on a star being a specific location. Like the star that shone over Bethlehem to lead the wise men to Jesus, perhaps Cove-Jones had selected a certain star that shone above his "discovery of great importance" on midnight every January 6. All I had to do was figure out which star.

It was some weeks before it all came together. I was typing up the interviews I had taped while I was in Israel and was in the middle of what Dr. Griver had told me when we were driving out into the Judean Wilderness. His words coming from the tape recorder suddenly made me stop. I just had to play them back:

According to the Apocrypha, when Lucifer was cast out of heaven, he was replaced by two chief angels, Michael and Gabriel, who became known as the "kings of heaven" . . . Michael and Gabriel were even represented in the sky by two permanent lights: the two tail stars of the constellation Ursa Major—the Big Dipper—the stars we now call Benetnasch and Mizar. The ancient Hebrew names for these stars were Reysh, meaning the head, as Michael was the head, or supreme of all the angels, and the other was called Kos, meaning the cup, as Gabriel was said to hold the cup of man's salvation.

Not only was Dr. Griver talking about two sacred stars, he said they were thought to represent Michael and Gabriel—one associated with a head, the other with a cup. Michael and Gabriel! These had to be the two figures in the Burton Dassett Church murals—one was holding a head and the other a chalice. They may not have been depicted with wings, but surely these were the two archangels. The churchwarden had even said that people had once thought the strange lights were angels. Moreover, Dr. Griver was saying that these two angels were called "the kings of heaven," and in the murals the two figures were depicted wearing crowns.

I rushed to the closet to get out a box of photographs and rummaged through them until I found the blowup of the phoenix from the Epiphany Window. In the Burton Dassett Church murals, the figures had been on either side of the window that looked out onto the Phoenix Hills. If they were Michael and Gabriel, then they represented the two tail stars of the Big Dipper. At either side of the phoenix in the Epiphany Window there were the letters *B* and *M*! These may have been the initials of two of the wise men, but I was now certain that Jacob Cove-Jones had used them here to represent something else entirely. *B* and *M*—Benetnasch and Mizar—the names of the same two stars. The letters even had crowns above them, and Michael and Gabriel were called the kings of heaven. It was too coincidental. This must have been how Cove-Jones had found his relics. He must have worked out from the murals that the Templars had hidden their treasures in a place somehow indicated by these stars at midnight on January 6—the medieval New Year, when the beacon was lit on top of the hills. He seemed to be using the same clues in the Epiphany Window, which had to mean that whatever Cove-Jones's fourth relic was, it was still in the same place that the Templars had hidden it. Either Cove-Jones had returned it to where he found it, or he had left it where it was.

I was sure I now knew exactly what to do. It was not one star but two stars that would somehow lead the way. I knew where to go—to the top of the Phoenix Hills. I knew when to go—midnight on January 6. And I knew what to look for—Benetnasch and Mizar, the tail stars of the Big Dipper. Surely they had to show me where Cove-Jones's "discovery of immense importance" was waiting to be found.

14
Written in Stone

Strangely enough it was the end of December when I finally worked out the code—only a few days before Epiphany. Graham and Jodi had already arranged to come to England to spend the New Year, so when they arrived they listened with fascination as I told them my theory.

We didn't actually have to wait until January 6 to find out where the two stars would be at midnight on that day. We were able to download some computer software that could work out the positions of the heavenly bodies at any second of any day, as seen from any place in the world. This gave us a rough idea where the stars were with relation to the highest point on the Burton Dassett Hills, but we decided to wait until the appointed day to verify this with our own eyes. Not only did Graham and Jodi have an intervening appointment in London, it had been raining torrentially—nonstop for days—and the sky was completely overcast. In fact, only on the evening of Epiphany Day did the weather finally break.

During the afternoon of January 6, we made our way up to the highest point on the Burton Dassett Hills in driving, freezing rain. The wind was blowing so hard over the bleak hilltop that it was difficult to stand. Although the fertile plain of Warwickshire stretched out below us in all directions, much of the horizon was obscured by mist and cloud. However, when we returned an hour before midnight, the rain had stopped and the clouds had cleared. The shape of the landscape could even be made out in the bright moonlight, and

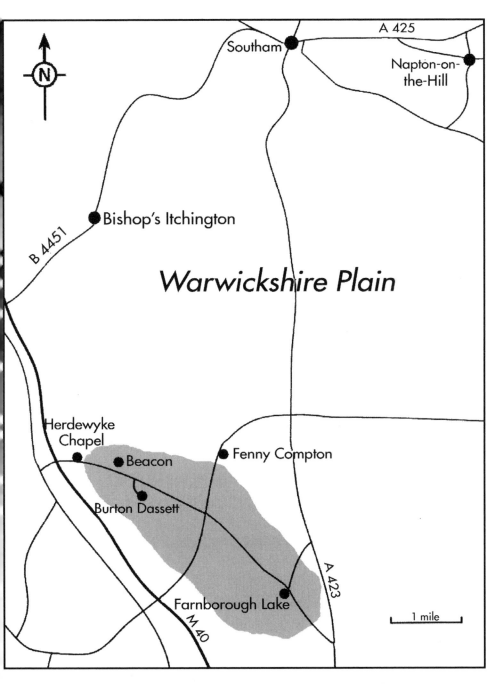

The Burton Dassett Hills and the Warwickshire Plain

we could see for miles in all directions. The lights of towns could be seen on the far horizons: to the north, the town of Warwick where we had done most of our research; to the west, Stratford-upon-Avon close by Langley Church; and to the south, the university city of Oxford where the stones had been analyzed. To the east, however, there was darkness, except for the twinkling lights of a few small villages and farmsteads. It was here, in the sky above, that the Big Dipper hung in that blackness of space. As the minutes ticked by, the constellation moved slowly as the earth continued to rotate. Finally, the moment of midnight arrived.

The two tail stars of the Big Dipper were almost exactly to either side of a hill that stood out in the moonlight as a stark silhouette on the far horizon. By flashlight we got a bearing on the map and found what the place was called—Napton Hill.

Napton Hill was about fourteen miles away, and as we drove through the night along winding country roads in its direction, we wondered what we might find there.

"The hill is pretty big," observed Jodi, as she looked at the map in the back of the car. "There's an entire village called Napton-on-the-Hill on top of it. What do you think we should be searching for?"

"It must have something to do with the archangels Michael and Gabriel," said Graham.

Jodi and I agreed that it was a possibility. The stars had been thought to represent these two angels and the Burton Dassett Church murals had depicted them on either side of the window. The two stars had flanked Napton Hill in the same way.

"Weren't they the two angels depicted on the Ark?" said Jodi.

"Yes, they were solid gold effigies, either side of the mercy seat," I said.

"I think, as these two angels were the final clue to lead us here, that the final relic must be the Ark," said Graham.

A steep road leading upward from the Warwickshire plain finally took us up to the village of Napton-on-the-Hill and to the church that stood at the highest point. I had hoped that the church would be dedicated to the two archangels, as this might confirm that it was here we should look. However, the signboard said that it was called the Saint Lawrence Church. As Saint Lawrence was a third-century Spanish monk who was renowned for helping the sick, I could not see how he could be linked with our search.

The church was locked and for some time we wandered around the graveyard, reading the headstones in the hope of finding something familiar. However, after about ten minutes, Jodi thought we ought to leave.

"Look!" she said, pointing down into the darkness at the bottom of the hill. "A police car!" There was a flashing blue light that appeared to be moving slowly in our direction.

Graham and I agreed that it was not a good idea to be sneaking around a church in the middle of the night. The police were obviously patrolling, and we would have some explaining to do if we were found in the graveyard. We decided to leave and return when it got light.

Next day we returned to the church to find it open. Inside was a guidebook that further made us doubt we were in the right location. Built from ochre-colored, mottled stone, the church was old, but it was not built until the late 1300s. If I was right about Jacob Cove-Jones leaving his "discovery of immense importance" where it was found, then whatever we were looking for must have been here when the murals in Burton Dassett Church were painted—some fifty years before the Saint Lawrence Church was built. However, the guidebook did tell us that construction of an earlier church had been attempted at the bottom of the hill, just outside the village in an area still called Church Green. Interestingly, there was a legend that the church was moved to the top of the hill because "spirits" kept interfering with the building work on the original church.

"Do you think these spirits could have been geoplasma?" suggested Graham.

"Unlikely," I said. "The only place anywhere in the county that has the right kind of rocks to produce geoplasma is the Burton Dassett Hills, almost fifteen miles away."

"Yes, but if you're right, the Ark can make geoplasma on its own," said Graham.

He had a point. If it really could produce geoplasma somehow, then the phenomenon could occur anywhere, as it may have done after the Israelites left the Mountain of God. In fact, if this was true, then it meant that geoplasma itself might lead us to the Ark.

"If it is the Ark we're looking for and it's buried somewhere in this area, then I suppose it's possible that strange lights have been seen in the location where it's hidden," I said.

"And if the 'spirits' that interfered with the building of the original church were geoplasma, then the church may have been being erected over the spot where the Ark was," said Graham. "Perhaps the construction somehow activated it."

"It's certainly possible that they were building the church on a previously sacred site. Many early churches were built around or near holy wells, like Burton Dassett Church," I said. "If the spot was already considered sacred, the Templars may have considered it a fitting place for their relics."

"Maybe that's why there were spirals around the murals," suggested Jodi. "If they did represent the lights, then the final clue would be to find the place where such lights were seen at Napton Hill."

We left the church and drove down through the village to arrive at the Church Green. It was a country road, lined with a few farmhouses and modern buildings. Unfortunately, the guidebook didn't specifically say where the original church had been. After we had driven up and down the road about a dozen times, we decided to ask a farmer who was tending to a couple of horses in a field. He knew about the original church, but told us that its precise location had been long forgotten. We came right out and asked him if he knew of anyone seeing strange lights in the area. He seemed rather puzzled at our question, but assured us that he had never heard of such a thing. We thanked him and were just walking away when an idea occurred to me.

"Do you know if there's an old well in the area?" I asked. If the original church had been built around or near a holy well, as many churches were, then it might still be here.

"Not a well," he said. "But there's the old water fountain."

"The water fountain?" I said.

"Yes, beside the road over there." He pointed down the lane, in the direction of the village. He explained that the fountain had been a Roman Catholic shrine before the Reformation, when the Protestant Church took over in England. In those days, it was an old building erected over a natural spring that was thought to have curative properties. This structure had crumbled away until it was replaced by a water fountain around a hundred years ago. It was still there but it hadn't worked for years.

A few minutes later we found the simple red brick structure that stood, half overgrown, on the grassy verge beside the road. It was a rectangular structure, about three feet high, four feet wide, and a foot thick, with an arched niche in which a tap for the spring water had obviously once been set.

"If this was a Catholic well shrine, then this may have been where or near where they had tried to build the original church," I said.

"You know something, this site falls directly between where the two stars were," said Jodi, looking at the map.

That morning we had drawn two straight lines on the map, joining the summit of the Burton Dassett Hills with the points on the horizon over which the two stars had been. Wondering where we might need to look, we had also drawn a third line directly between the two. Jodi was right, the center line did run smack through where we now were. I looked up to Napton Hill, just to the northeast of us, and turned around to look back at the Burton Dassett Hills on the far horizon in the other direction. If Cove-Jones's "discovery of immense importance" was anywhere, this water fountain was a good bet. It was at the bottom of Napton Hill, along a direct central bearing obtained from the two stars.

The problem was what to do next. If anything *was* buried here, we couldn't just go digging up the area. In Jacob Cove-Jones's day, the area may have been uninhabited, but now there were modern homes all around. The verge was obviously owned by the local county authority, but I doubted very much that they would grant us permission to excavate since doing so would probably entail digging up half the road. Besides which fact, what reason would we give? We thought the Ark of the Covenant was buried here? They'd lock us up.

However, we decided we would visit the county council offices (the English equivalent of city hall) to find out who actually owned the field on the other side of the hedge, behind the shrine. As in Burton Dassett, the original church might have been built beside the well, rather than around it, and it would be worth investigating the land here if we could. However, when we examined the deeds and landholdings of the district we were greatly disappointed. We discovered that in the 1950s the entire area around the shrine had been dug up, not only to widen the road for modern vehicles but to put in water, gas, and electricity mains for the new houses that were being built. In fact there was a specific mention of the water fountain being unplumbed, removed, and later replaced. If there had been something buried anywhere around it, the chances were the workmen at the time had already found it.

"Surely if they had discovered a huge gold box the size of the Ark, everyone would have known about it," said Jodi, as Graham and I became despondent.

"Not if the workmen decided to keep it to themselves," I said. "The gold alone would be worth a fortune. They could have melted it down and sold it off for scrap without anyone knowing."

"It may not be the Ark we're looking for," said Graham. "It could be anything."

We decided to go back and ask the locals if they had heard of anything of interest ever being dug up in the area. That evening we visited a local pub called the Crown, which was about half a mile up the road from the water fountain. Here we chatted with a villager who knew all about the history of the village, but he wasn't much help. He did know of various historical artifacts that had been found in the village, but none of these seemed to have anything to do with what we might be looking for. However, when we asked him about the 1950s development of the Church Green area, he told us of an elderly man who had actually lived in one of the few cottages that stood there at the time. His name was Alfred Carter and he was now in his eighties. We visited Mr. Carter at his home the next day, but he was understandably reluctant to let us into his house. On the doorstep, however, he did tell us something that was extremely interesting. I asked him if he knew if the workmen who had dug up the Church Green area in the 1950s had found any historical artifacts. Mr. Carter said he hadn't heard of such a thing. However, he told us that if they had dug something up, it was probably in the rubble from the excavations that was used to dam up a stream in a nearby field. Unfortunately, he couldn't remember which field it was.

Could Jacob Cove-Jones's "discovery of immense importance" be lying amid a pile of overgrown rubble somewhere in the area of Napton Hill?

That lunchtime we again sat in the Crown pub, this time carefully examining a large-scale map of the area, marking the streams in the district. Mr. Carter had remembered that the rubble had been used to dam a stream, but there were dozens of them in the area.

"It will take us forever to walk along every single stream to find a dam," said Graham.

"We could ask the local farmers if they have dams on their land," I said. There happened to be a farmer in the pub, so I asked him if he had any on his. He said that he did, but when I questioned him further, he told me something that made the whole thing appear hopeless. Small farmland dams, he told me, were usually temporary structures, built during periods of flooding. They were being made and pulled down again all the time. I realized now that the 1950s rubble could have been anywhere in the thousands of acres of farmland around Napton Hill. It could have been used to fill a hole, as part of another dam, or even as the foundations of a new barn. Even if the rubble had not been used for anything else, the dam had probably been pulled down long ago and the rubble was just lining the stream bank, overgrown with fifty years of vegetation. I decided we might as well give up.

"Even if the workmen in the 1950s didn't find what we're looking for, it could be anywhere," I told Graham and Jodi grimly.

"What about asking around the area to see if anyone has seen any strange lights," suggested Graham. "I know the farmer hadn't heard of anything like that around Church Green, but now we know the artifact or artifacts could be anywhere, strange light might have been seen somewhere else."

I doubted that would do us much good. The possibility of geo-plasma guiding us to Cove-Jones's discovery relied on its being the Ark. And that was only *if* the Ark really could produce geoplasma and *if* it still worked.

"If the Ark was Cove-Jones's 'discovery of immense importance,' then it will not be among a pile of rubble," I said. "It was four feet long, two and a half feet high, and two and a half feet wide. The workmen couldn't possibly have missed it."

"What if it was only part of the Ark?" said Jodi. "Perhaps whatever the mercy seat was? If the Ark was a geoplasmic device, then the mercy seat might have been what made it work."

After some discussion, I agreed that it might be worth asking around to see if anyone did know of any strange lights in the area. However, twenty-four hours later we were back in the same pub and back where we started. We had questioned dozens of people without one reporting having heard of a strange floating light being seen within miles of Napton Hill. There were a number of interesting ghost stories, such as the "blue lady" that was said to haunt a local wood and even some UFO sightings, but nothing that sounded like geoplasma. As Graham and I were standing at the bar trying to work out what to do next, Jodi had been examining the map that she had spread out on a table.

"Hold on! This can't be right," she suddenly said.

We went over to the table to see what she had found.

"Remember when we visited the Saint Lawrence Church the other night and saw the police car at the bottom of the hill? Well, there is no road anywhere in that area."

I looked at the map. Jodi was right. The area in which we had seen the flashing blue light was open fields interspersed with a few tiny woods.

"Maybe the police were driving across the fields to investigate cattle rustling or something," I suggested.

"Maybe it wasn't the police at all," said Jodi. An idea had suddenly occurred to her. "Where would you estimate the light was?" she said, indicating to the map.

"About here, I guess," I said, pointing to an area of woodland to the southwest of Napton Hill.

"That's where the blue lady is said to haunt," she said. Jodi explained that what we had thought was the light of a police car might actually have been what people had called the blue lady—and she may really have been geoplasma. Witnesses to the lights in the Burton Dassett Hills had taken them for angels, saints, and even ghosts.

"The blue lady! It's certainly a strange name for a ghost," said Graham.

"Don't you think it's strange that we should have seen a blue flashing light in the area of the same woods?" said Jodi

"But it's still more likely to be a police vehicle searching for poachers or something," I said.

"With their warning light flashing?" said Jodi.

I had to admit she was right. Besides—now that she mentioned it—I didn't remember the light being accompanied by headlights. If a police vehicle had its warning light on, wouldn't it also have its headlights on too?

"It would be a coincidence, though—us just happening to arrive here for the very first time when a geoplasmic phenomenon occurs," I said.

"So were the dove and the cock, but they helped us find the stones," said Jodi.

Could this wood really be where the pile of rubble ended up?

We left the pub and spent the rest of the afternoon searching the wood. A tiny stream ran right through the middle of it, and we looked for evidence of a dam having ever been here. The problem was that the entire wood was so overgrown that it was impossible to tell what was in the undergrowth. Days of torrential rainfall had also turned the area into a swamp, making many parts of the wood completely inaccessible. We were covered from head to foot in mud by the time darkness began to fall.

"We'll have to give up for the day," I said, exhausted. "It's getting too dark to see a thing."

"Maybe darkness is just what we want," said Jodi.

"Sorry?" I said, having no idea what she was on about.

"We can use the stones." Jodi suggested that if the stones were responsible for making the light appear over the lake, then they might be able to make the light appear here. And if the light was somehow related to whatever we were looking for, then wherever it appeared was where the artifact was buried.

It was worth a try. I didn't really expect that it would work. In fact, I doubted that the blue lady or the blue light that we had seen had any connection with geoplasma. Although some witnesses had described geoplasmic phenomena as blue, most witnesses reported earthlights as fiery red.

Having collected the stones from the car, we each held the one we had found and made our way back to the wood. As we walked along the muddy path that ran along the edge of it, the only sound on that calm winter's night was the noise of the little stream babbling away in the blackness within the trees. We had only been there for a few minutes when it began.

Somewhere at the heart of the copse there was a flare of blue light, as if someone had set off a flashbulb. A few seconds later, it came again, but this time—as I was looking right toward it—I could make out that it seemed to be a circular source of light, visible for just a second. It was difficult to determine how big it was, as there was no way of telling its distance.

"Come on," shouted Jodi, as she climbed over the fence and began to push her way through the undergrowth among the trees. Graham immediately followed, but I hesitated. I could not help remembering the verse from the book of Numbers: "And the fire of the Lord burnt among them, and consumed them." All the same, I jumped over the fence and followed.

Somewhere before us in the trees, the light was now flashing regularly, getting faster and faster until it became a shimmering orb. We, however, were getting slower and slower, repeatedly falling into the mud and getting entangled in brambles and thornbushes. Somehow, we eventually made it to a small clearing and got our first proper view of the light.

The shining blue sphere, about the size of a tennis ball, seemed to be hanging like a bizarre Christmas decoration in the bushes that grew along the edge of the stream. Jodi stopped suddenly, and Graham and I almost piled into her.

Just as I was about to ask the others what we should do next, the orb blazed brilliant white and shot silently into the air, spiraling upward before disappearing into the darkness.

This astonishing light had me more dumbfounded than the one we had seen at the lake. I had thought that the appearance of the first one was probably coincidence, but a second light—it had to be something more. I shone my flashlight into the palm of my hand and looked at the onyx stone. I wanted to say something but could not think of any appropriate words. Jodi, however, was shouting for us to follow her to where the light had been.

Graham and I began to tear back the undergrowth as Jodi jumped down to the side of the stream and began to shine her flashlight up and down the banks. She had only been there for a few moments when she called out, "I've found something!"

We clambered down to find her pulling away at something sticking out from the bank. After a few tugs it came free from the hardened earth. It appeared to be a flat slab of stone about an inch thick, a foot and a half long, and a foot wide.

"There are symbols or something carved into it," said Jodi, holding up the stone. By the light of the flashlight, I could see that one end appeared to be broken, while the other was rounded at the corners. Most of it was covered in silt, but at the top were clearly carved symbols that were filled with dirt. After we washed it down in the stream, some of the sediment came away, and we could clearly see that the whole of one side was deliberately carved with what could have been foreign lettering.

"It was half-sticking out the bank," said Jodi. "I could see that there was something carved on it."

For some time, Jodi and I searched the surrounding area to see if we could find anything else, while Graham dug with a stick around the hole where the slab had been to see if he could find any more of it. Eventually, when we found nothing else, we decided to come back when it was light and thoroughly examine the area.

Back in Graham and Jodi's hotel room later that night, we were able to properly clean up what we had found. It turned out that there were what appeared to be thirteen separate symbols on it, cut into the stone to a depth of about a quarter of an inch. The slab had clearly been broken off from a longer piece, as the one end was irregular and jagged. The other end, however, was smoother and had been deliberately rounded at the corners. While it was impossible to know which way up they should be viewed, the characters appeared to be arranged in three separate horizontal lines. The bottom line—when the slab was viewed with the rounded end uppermost—included a cross, something that looked a bit like the Greek letter *pi*, a capital Y shape, something similar to a lowercase *i*, and a lowercase *t* tipped over to the left. The middle line presented a check mark shape; a left-slanting squiggle with a dash above it; something that looked like an upright feather; an irregular, left-slanting shape; and a dot. And the top line was composed of an inverted, reversed, left-slanting lowercase *t*; an upside-down capital Y shape; and a backward check mark with a dot and a line attached to it. None of us recognized the symbols as any form of lettering we knew. I was familiar with a number of ancient alphabets, but these characters did not seem to belong to any I had seen. All we could tell was that the slab appeared to have been carved a long time ago. Green and white algae of some sort grew over it, and the symbols were worn. We knew we would have to have the slab examined by experts, but first we needed to find out if anything else was buried in the copse.

The next day we discovered who owned the land and asked him if we could go into the wood to search for an old pile of rubble that had been dumped there in the 1950s. We told him that the rubble had come from the Church Green and might contain artifacts that were linked with the Catholic shrine that had once stood where the water fountain now was. He had no objection. In fact, as the land was too swampy to be used for anything, he didn't even mind us digging in the wood if we so chose. Yet a whole day searching the area where we had found the slab yielded us nothing. At the end of the day, I decided to show the owner of the land what we had found the night before and asked if he could identify it. He had no idea what it was, but as it was of no interest to him, and seemed to be of no value, he said we could keep it.

If Jodi was right, then the strange light had led us to find this slab. I was about as bewildered as I could hope to be and had no idea whether she was right or wrong. We had to find out what the artifact was! Graham and Jodi decided to extend their stay and together we took the slab to the British Museum in London, which boasts England's best facilities for identifying ancient artifacts. However, the examination was inconclusive.

There are basically two scientific methods to directly date archaeological discoveries. First, there is radiocarbon dating. Organic matter, either animal or vegetable, contains a (harmless) slightly radioactive component called carbon 14. Once the living organism has died, the radioactivity gradually fades away until after some 60,000 years it is no longer detectable by current techniques. By chemically analyzing the amount of carbon 14 in organic matter—such as bones, ivory, or wood—discoveries can be dated. However, the slab was not organic, so radiocarbon dating was not an option. Unfortunately, the second method was equally inappropriate. Thermoluminescence is the process in which a mineral emits light while it is being heated. Pottery and ceramics can be dated in this way because the light emitted from such objects changes over time. However, as the process can only determine how long ago an artifact was fired—in other words, baked in a kiln—it was no use to us. Our slab was merely shaped and cut rock. We hoped that someone at the museum could identify the symbols. However, they could not be matched with any known alphabet or symbol system on their massive database.

If Jodi was right and the geoplasma, or whatever we had seen, had been created by what we had been looking for, then I couldn't see how this slab could possibly be it—at least not on its own. We had to find out if there was anything else buried where we had found the slab, and the only way to do this was with a full geophysics survey. Although this would be expensive, we decided it had to be done and hired a geophysics team from London. The team had sophisticated scientific equipment that could detect almost anything that was buried in the ground. They were usually employed by the petrochemical industry to look for signs of oil-bearing rock, but they had been also been used by archaeologists.

Over three days the team scanned a large area around where we had found the slab. First, they used a proton magnetometer, which measured any magnetic anomalies beneath the surface and would have detected metal artifacts. But apart from locating rusty old pieces of farming equipment, nothing was found. Second, they used a resistivity meter, a double-pronged device that sends a current through the ground and measures any change in electrical resistance. It can detect different types of materials beneath the surface, such as rocks, stones, or any underground rubble. This produced some interesting results when it found a lot of irregular bricks around the area where the slab had been. These were later identified as cobblestones from an old road, which suggested that it may have been the pile of rubble that Mr. Cater had told us of. (When the old road at Church Green was resurfaced, the previous road surface would have been among the discarded rubble.) On the third day the team tried the most advanced equipment of all, ground-scanning radar that could produce a three-dimensional image of what lies deep below the ground. However, apart from more cobblestones, more bits of farm equipment, and lumps of rock, there was nothing in the area at all.

If there were any other artifacts in the area, then there was one last possibility: They were in the surrounding fields. It would have been far too expensive to hire the geophysics team to scan the entire area—it would have taken weeks. However, we did manage to persuade a metal-detecting club to sweep the wood and the area all around. This would at least determine if there were any gold or silver artifacts in the area. Unfortunately, despite dozens of metal detectors sweeping every inch of a quarter of a mile radius from where we had found the slab, nothing of interest was found.

It seemed that the only man-made artifact that could possibly be linked with our search was the enigmatic stone slab. However, it couldn't be dated and its symbols couldn't be identified. What on earth was it?

We had witnessed what must surely have been geoplasma. Yet the area had no rocks that are connected with the phenomenon. The slab appeared to be sandstone, but even if it turned out to be arenite sandstone—one of the rocks thought to produce geoplasma—I could not imagine how such a small quantity could create what we had seen. In a laboratory, subjected to massive pressure in a rock-crushing chamber, perhaps! But even then, the phenomenon would be on a tiny scale.

"You said you thought that the ancient Israelites had been able to produce geoplasma somehow without a rock crusher. And on a massive scale," said Jodi, once the metal detector team had found nothing.

"The 'glory of the Lord' described in the Bible does sound very like geoplasma," I said.

"And the same phenomenon was created by the Ark?"

"Yes, it seems so."

"What was kept in the Ark?" she said.

"A few relics at one time, but mainly the stone tablets inscribed with the Ten Commandments."

I realized what Jodi was getting at, but I could not bring myself to believe that our stone slab was actually one of these same tablets. "Even if it was, such a small amount of rock could not produce geoplasma," I said.

"But you think the Ark may have been some kind of geoplasmic device?"

"Yes, but we know for certain that the Ark was nowhere in the area or the metal detectors would have found it."

"What if the stone tablets themselves were what created 'the glory of the Lord'?" she said.

"How?"

"I've no idea, but something made that light appear," said Jodi.

I had to admit that even if my theory about the ancient Israelites creating geoplasma was right, then neither I nor any scientist I had spoken to had any idea how they might have managed it.

"I suppose that there could be something special about the rock itself," I said.

We had already sent a fragment of the slab to Dr. Mellor so that he could identify what kind of was rock it was and where it came from. However, he had been on vacation for a few weeks and had not yet given us the results. When he did, they seemed at first to be disappointing. Unfortunately, unlike tracing a gemstone, it had been impossible to tell where exactly in the world the rock was from. It was, however, made from arenite sandstone—the type of sandstone associated with geoplasma. Nevertheless, there was nothing unusual about it. It had been subjected to the same tests as the three stones, but without any positive results. It was just an ordinary piece of arenite sandstone.

However, the fact that it was arenite sandstone might be significant. The summit of Jebel Madhbah is made from arenite sandstone. This fact may not prove that the slab actually came from there, as there are many other places in the world where the rock is found. Nonetheless, it does show that the slab *could* have been one of the tablets containing the Ten Commandments, as it was on top of the Mountain of God that Moses is said to have made them according to God's instructions.

When Graham and Jodi finally returned to the United States, I sat down and tried to think everything through. If we had deciphered the Epiphany Window clues correctly and I was right about the Burton Dassett Church murals, then it seemed that the water fountain at the bottom of Napton Hill was where Jacob Cove-Jones's "discovery of immense importance" had been. We had got the geophysics team and the metal detectors to scan all around that area as well, but there was nothing found there either. We had no proof that the inscribed slab was among the pile of rubble removed from the fountain area, although the cobblestones found in the copse indicated it might have been. Nevertheless, we had been led to find the slab by a truly astonishing phenomenon. Graham believed that fate may have lent a hand in helping us in our search, and Jodi was sure the three stones had created the phenomena we had seen. I, however, had no idea what to think.

Many times after the stones and the slab were discovered we tried to make geoplasma—or whatever it was—reappear. But despite taking them to places where strange lights have been reported, despite taking the slab back to where we found it, the phenomenon never occurred again.

All the same, my quest to solve the secrets of the lost Ark did lead me on a completely unexpected adventure. I may not have discovered the Ark of the Covenant, but I was sure I had solved a number of crucial mysteries surrounding it. I was sure that I had discovered where it was hidden after it left the Jerusalem Temple and that I had found the long-forgotten location of the Mountain of God. It is also possible that Graham, Jodi, and I had found three of the Stones of Fire. Most significant, I was certain that the phenomenon that the Old Testament asserts the Ark of the Covenant could manifest was in reality geoplasma. I could not prove that the Herdewyke Templars really did find the Ark of the Covenant or that it was ever hidden in the center of England. However, the order did possess relics claimed to date from the time of the Old Testament, and the inscribed slab may have been one of these. If it was found in the cave at the foot of Jebel Madhbah, then it could, just possibly, have been one of the tablets that were inscribed with the Ten Commandments.

The slab appears to have been broken in two, so there may be another piece still to be found. Sadly, no one has been able to identify its symbols. The Hebrew alphabet, as we know it today, did not develop until about 1000 B.C. Around this time the Israelites began to trade extensively and exchange cultural ideas with their neighbors the Phoenicians, from what is now Lebanon, and it is from the Phoenician alphabet that the Hebrew alphabet developed. However, the characters on the stone slab are neither early Hebrew nor Phoenician. They *could* be some yet earlier form of Israelite writing, as the story of the Ten Commandments is set around 1360 B.C., some three and a half centuries before the Hebrew alphabet developed. As we have no clues to go on one way or the other, the slab we found is now stored away in a bank vault near Graham and Jodi's home in the United States. Here I assume it will stay, like the Ark in Spielberg's movie, until it can be better understood. If it is what Jacob Cove-Jones called a "discovery of immense importance," it will have to be deciphered before we know just how immense it really is. At present there are plans to have the stone slab scientifically examined at Brigham Young University in Utah, while David Deissmann is arranging for various linguists to examine the inscription at the Hebrew University in Israel. What the results will be, we will have to wait and see.

Whatever the artifacts we had found really were, I had to admit that the entire investigation into the Ark of the Covenant had been truly amazing. And there was one last strange incident that occurred. Graham Russell had said repeatedly that fate had intervened in our search. I had dismissed the idea as coincidence. But something happened a few weeks after we discovered the stone tablet that made me wonder. I returned to Burton Dassett Church in the hope of meeting the warden again to thank him for his help. However, not only was he nowhere to be found, but when I asked around the area, no one seemed to know who he was. In fact, the vicar told me that no one matching his description was a churchwarden at All Saints Church. To be honest, the old man had never told me who he was. I had just assumed that he was a churchwarden as he had been lighting candles and tending the flowers. Search as I might, I never saw the old man again and never discovered his identity. Whoever the man was, he clearly did not visit the church regularly, yet both times I had been there he was there to help. In fact, without him my research might never have gone as far as it did, and I doubt that we would ever have found the enigmatic stone slab—whatever it is. Graham may or may not have been right about fate giving us a helping hand. If it did, I cannot explain how or why. What I can say is that there was something strange about the man I had taken to be a churchwarden. The first time I had met him he had somehow entered the church and snuck up behind me without my hearing a thing. Not only did the sound of footsteps on the stone floor of the building echo like crazy, but the church door creaked like hell.

As I stood in the church once more, looking up at the enigmatic murals to either side of window, I hoped that the man would return to aid me again. I could not help wondering if the Ark of the Covenant might still be hidden somewhere around the Burton Dassett Hills.

Chronology of Key Events

The matter of dating biblical events is a difficult and controversial one. The dating used here is based on a general academic consensus. Primarily, such dates have been arrived at based on one crucial datable event mentioned in the Old Testament. The Bible refers to the besieging of Jerusalem by the Assyrians during the reign of the Judean king Hezekiah. The Assyrian king Sennacherib's own identical account of the same siege survives on a stone that is now in the British Museum. As the inscription has a precise Assyrian date that corresponds to 701 B.C. according to our modern calendar, this is a precisely datable Old Testament event. Earlier dates can be approximately estimated based on the length of the reigns of previous Hebrew kings as given in the Old Testament.

B.C.

1385–1360   Reign of Egyptian pharaoh Amonhotep III. Rebuilding of Avaris.

1360   Eruption of Thera. Plagues of the Exodus. Israelites leave Egypt.

1360–1343   Reign of Akhenaten. The Aten is installed as chief deity.

1360–1320   Israelites in the Sinai Wilderness. The Ark of the Covenant is made.

1320	Conquest of Jericho.
1300	Conquest of Hazor.
1287–1220	Reign of Ramesses II.
995–967	David unifies the tribes of Israel. City of Jerusalem captured from the Jebusites and made the capital of the kingdom of Israel. The Ark brought to Jerusalem.
967–925	Solomon king of Israel and the building of the first Jerusalem Temple. The Ark is installed in the Temple.
932	Tribe of Judah splits from Israel and founds an independent kingdom with its capital at Jerusalem.
914	Sheshonq I of Egypt besieges Jerusalem. Temple riches plundered.
650	Oldest known form of coinage used by the Lydians.
640–609	Josiah is king of Judah.
622	Last biblical reference to the Ark being in the Jerusalem Temple.
597	Babylonians invade Jerusalem. Temple is plundered and its treasures taken to Babylon. The Ark is hidden by Jeremiah.
539	Babylonian empire conquered by the Persians. Persian king Cyrus II allows the Jews to return to Jerusalem.
525	The Jerusalem Temple is rebuilt.
333	Alexander the Great annexes Judah.
169	Antiochus IV plunders second Jerusalem temple.
167	Revolt led by Judas Maccabaeus.
130	Qumran monastery built.
63	Romans annex Judah.
37	Herod installed as king of Judea.
19	Work begins on Herod's temple.
4	Death of Herod.

A.D.

6	Direct Roman rule in Judea.
26	Pontius Pilate made procurator of Judea.
30	Jesus preaches in Palestine.
66	Jewish revolt.
70	Romans sack Jerusalem and destroy the third Temple.
78–94	Flavius Josephus writes his histories of the Jews.
1187	The Saracen leader Saladin conquers Jerusalem.
1189	The Crusaders abandon the Valley of Edom. A golden chest, precious stones, and other treasures purported to have been discovered at Jebel Madhbah.
1190	Herdewyke preceptory founded by Ralph de Sudeley.
1192	Biblical relics recorded in the Herdewyke preceptory.
1307	Knights Templar arrested in Paris.
1322	Templars arrested in England.
1327	Herdewyke Templars granted amnesty by Queen Isabella.
1350	Murals painted in Burton Dassett Church. The Black Death wipes out the village of Burton Dassett.
1600	Sir Walter Raleigh searches for the Herdewyke treasure.
1656	William Dugdale records the legend of the Herdewyke treasure.
1812	Johannes Burckhardt visits Petra.
1890	Murals discovered in Burton Dassett Church.
1907	Epiphany Window installed in Langley Church.

Select Bibliography

All biblical quotations used in this book are from the King James I English translation. The bibliography that follows includes the books the author used in his research for this work as well as suggested further reading.

Ackroyd, P. R., and C. F. Evans, eds. *The Cambridge History of the Bible.* Cambridge: University Press, 1963–70.

Aharoni, Y., M. Avi-Yohan, A. F. Rainey, and Z. Safrai. *The Macmillan Bible Atlas.* New York: Hungry Minds, 1993.

Albright, W. F. *The Archaeology of Palestine.* New York: Penguin, 1949.

———.*Yahweh and the Gods of Canaan.* Winona Lake: Eisenbrauns, 1990.

Aldred, C. *Akhenaten, Pharaoh of Egypt.* London: Thames & Hudson, 1968.

———. *Akhenaten, King of Egypt.* London: Thames & Hudson, 1986.

Anati, E. *Palestine Before the Hebrews.* London: Jonathan Cape, 1963.

Anderson, G. W. *The History of the Religion of Israel.* Oxford: Oxford University Press, 1966.

Avi-Yonah, M., ed. *Encyclopaedia of Archaeological Excavations in the Holy Land.* Oxford: Oxford University Press, 1977.

Bacon, E., ed. *The Great Archaeologists.* London: Bobbs-Merrill, 1976.

Bahat, D. *The Illustrated Atlas of Jerusalem.* New York: Simon & Schuster, 1990.

Baikie, J. *Egyptian Antiquities in the Nile Valley.* London: Methuen, 1932.

———. *The Amarna Age.* London: Methuen, 1926.

Baines, J., and J. Malek *Atlas of Ancient Egypt.* New York: Checkmark Books, 2000.

Barnett, R. *Illustrations of Old Testament History.* London: British Museum Press, 1977.

Barrett, C. K. *The New Testament Background: Selected Documents.* London: Harper Collins, 1989.

Bartlett, J. *The Bible: Faith and Evidence.* London: British Museum Press, 1990.

Ben-Dov, M. *In the Shadow of the Temple: The Discovery of Ancient Jerusalem.* New York: Harper and Row, 1982.

Biran, A. *Biblical Dan.* Jerusalem: Israel Exploration Society, 1994.

Brammel, E., and C. Moule. *Jesus and the Politics of His Day.* Cambridge: Cambridge University Press, 1984.

Brandon, S. *Creation Legends of the Ancient Near East.* London: Hodder & Stoughton, 1963.

Breasted, J. H. *Ancient Records of Egypt.* Chicago: University of Illinois Press, 2001.

Brotherstone, G. *World Archaeoastronomy.* Cambridge: Cambridge University Press, 1989.

Brown, F. *Hebrew and the English Lexicon of the Old Testament.* Oxford: Oxford University Press, 1906.

Bryant, A. E. *Natural Disasters.* Cambridge: Cambridge University Press, 1991.

Buber, M. *Moses.* Oxford: Oxford University Press, 1946.

Burckhardt, J. L. *Travels in Syria and the Holy Land.* London: The Association for Promoting the Discovery of the Interior Parts of Africa, 1822.

Casson, L., and E. L. Hettich. *Excavations at Nessana.* Princeton: Princeton University Press, 1950.

Cassuto, U. *A Commentary on the Book of Exodus.* Jerusalem: Magnes Press, 1961.

Castledon, R. *Minoans: Life in Bronze Age Crete.* London: Routledge, 1993.

Cerny, J. *Hieratic Inscriptions from the Tomb of Tutankhamun*. Oxford: Aris & Phillips, 1965.

Chester, D. *Volcanoes and Society*. London: Routledge, 1993.

Childs, B. *Myth and Reality in the Old Testament*. Napierville: A. R. Allenson, 1960.

Clark, R. *Myth and Symbol in Ancient Egypt*. London: Thames & Hudson, 1991.

Clayton, P. *Chronicle of the Pharaohs*. London: Thames & Hudson, 1994.

Comay, J. *Who's Who in the Old Testament*. London: Routledge, 1993.

Comrie, B., ed. *The Major Languages of South Asia, The Middle East and Africa*. London: Routledge, 1990.

Daiches, D. *Moses, Man in the Wilderness*. London: Weidenfeld and Nicolson, 1975.

Davidson, R., and A. R. C. Leaney. *The Penguin Guide to Modern Theology*. Harmondsworth: Penguin, 1970.

Davies, G. I., ed. *Ancient Hebrew Inscriptions, Corpus and Concordance*. Cambridge: Cambridge University Press, 1991.

Davies, P. *In Search of Ancient Israel*. Sheffield: Sheffield Academic Press, 1995.

Dawson, W. R., and E. Uphill. *Who Was Who in Egyptology*. London: Egypt Exploration Society, 1972.

Dothan, T. *The Philistines and Their Material Culture*. London: Israel Exploration Society, 1982.

Doumas, C. *Thera, Pompeii of the Ancient Aegean*. London: Thames & Hudson, 1983.

Driver, G. *Canaanite Myths and Legends*. Edinburgh: T. & T. Clark, 1978.

Emery, W. B. *Archaic Egypt*. Harmondsworth: Penguin, 1961.

Eusebius. *The History of the Church from Christ to Constantine*. Trans. G. Williamson. Harmondsworth: Penguin, 1965.

Evenari, M., L. Shanan, and N. Tadmore. *The Negev: Challenge of a Desert*. Cambridge, Mass.: Harvard University Press, 1982.

Fox, R. L. *Pagans and Christians*. San Francisco: Harper & Row, 1986.

Freedman, D., ed. *The Anchor Bible Dictionary*. New York: Doubleday, 1998.

Gardiner, A. *Egyptian Grammar.* Oxford: Griffith Institute, 1957.

———. *Egypt of the Pharaohs.* Oxford: Griffith Institute, 1961.

Goldstein, M. *Jesus in the Jewish Tradition.* New York: Macmillan, 1950.

Grabbe, L. *Judaism from Cyrus to Hadrian.* Minneapolis: Fortress Press, 1992.

Grant, M., trans. *Annals of Imperial Rome.* Harmondsworth: Penguin, 1956.

Graves, R. *The Greek Myths.* Harmondsworth: Penguin, 1960.

Greenberg, M. *The Hab/piru.* New Haven: American Oriental Society, 1955.

Harker, R. *Digging up the Bible Lands.* London: Bodley Head, 1972.

Harris, R. *Exploring the World of the Bible Lands.* London: Thames & Hudson, 1995.

Hawkes, J. *Man and the Sun.* London: Cresset Press, 1962.

Hershel, S., ed. *Understanding the Dead Sea Scrolls.* New York: Doubleday, 1992.

Herzog, C., and M. Gichon. *Battles of the Bible.* London: Weidenfeld & Nicolson, 1978.

Heschel, A. *The Prophets.* New York: Harper & Row, 1962.

Hornung, E. *Conceptions of God in Ancient Egypt.* London: Routledge, 1983.

Hutchison, R. W. *Prehistoric Crete.* Harmondsworth: Penguin, 1962.

Ions, V. *Egyptian Mythology.* London: Hamlyn, 1982.

James, E. O. *The Ancient Gods.* London: Weidenfield & Nicholson, 1960.

Jones, A. *The Herods of Judea.* Oxford: Clarendon, 1967.

Josephus, Flavius. *Jewish Antiquities.* Trans. L. Feldman. Cambridge, Mass.: Harvard University Press, 1981.

———. *The Jewish War.* Trans. G. Williamson. Harmondsworth: Penguin, 1981.

Keller, W. *The Bible as History.* London: Hodder & Stoughton, 1956.

Kemp, B. J. *Ancient Egypt: Anatomy of a Civilisation.* London: Routledge, 1989.

Kennedy, A. *Petra, Its History and Monuments.* London: Country Life, 1925.

Kenyon, K. M. *Archaeology in the Holy Land*. London: Ernest Benn, 1965.

──────. *Digging Up Jericho*. London: Ernest Benn, 1957.

Kopp, C. *The Holy Places of the Gospels*. New York: Herder & Herder, 1963.

Levy, U. *The Lost Civilisation of Petra*. Edinburgh: Floris, 1999.

Lichtheim, M. *Ancient Egyptian Literature*. Berkeley: University of California Press, 1980.

Maccoby, H. *Revolution in Judea: Jesus and the Jewish Resistance*. London: Ocean Books, 1973.

Magnusson, M. *BC: The Archaeology of the Bible Lands*. London: Simon & Schuster, 1977.

May, H. G., ed. *Oxford Bible Atlas*. Oxford: Oxford University Press, 1974.

Mazar, A. *Archaeology of the Land of the Bible, 10,000–586 BCE*. New York: Doubleday, 1990.

Metzger, B., and M. Coogan, eds. *The Oxford Companion to the Bible*. Oxford: Oxford University Press, 1993.

Meyers, E. *The Oxford Encyclopedia of Archaeology in the Near East*. Oxford: Oxford University Press, 1996.

Millard, A. *Discoveries from the Time of Jesus*. Oxford: Lion, 1990.

Moorey, P. R. S. *Biblical Lands*. London: Phaidon, 1975.

Moule, C. *The Birth of the New Testament*. London: Adam & Charles Black, 1962.

Murray, M. *Petra, the Rock City of Edom*. London: Blackie, 1939.

Negev, A., ed. *Archaeological Encyclopaedia of the Holy Land*. London: Oxford University Press, 1973.

Nims, C. F. *Thebes of the Pharaohs*. London: Elek Books, 1965.

Noth, M. *The History of Israel*. London: A. & C. Black, 1960.

Page, D. L. *The Santorini Volcano and the Desolation of Minoan Crete*. London: The Society for the Promotion of Hellenistic Studies, 1970.

Pattie, T. S. *Manuscripts of the Bible*. London: Hutchinson, 1979.

Peet, T. E. *The City of Akhenaten*. London: Egypt Exploration Society, 1951.

Playton, N. *Zakros: The Discovery of a Lost Palace of Ancient Crete*. New York: Charles Scribner's Sons, 1971.

Posener, G. *A Dictionary of Egyptian Civilisation*. London: Methuen, 1962.

Pritchard, J. B. *Ancient Near Eastern Texts Relating to the Old Testament*. Princeton: Princeton University Press, 1969.

Redford, D. B. *A Study of the Biblical Story of Joseph*. Leiden: VTS, 1970.

———. *Egypt, Canaan, and Israel in Ancient Times*. Princeton: Princeton University Press, 1992.

Renfrew, A. C. *Archaeology and Language*. London: Cape, 1987.

Rogerson, J. *Chronicle of the Old Testament Kings*. London: Thames & Hudson, 1999.

Romer, J. *Valley of the Kings*. London: O'Mara Books, 1981.

Rowley, H. H. *From Joseph to Joshua*. London: Oxford University Press, 1950.

Rubin, R. *The Negev as a Settled Land*. Jerusalem: The Israel Exploration Society, 1990.

Scholem, G. *The Messianic Idea in Judaism*. New York: Schocken, 1971.

Shanks, H. *Understanding the Dead Sea Scrolls*. New York: Random House, 1992.

Sherwin-White, A. N. *Roman Society and Roman Law in the New Testament*. Oxford: Clarendon Press, 1963.

Simkin, T., and R. S. Fiske. *Krakatau 1883: The Volcanic Eruption and Its Effects*. Washington, D.C.: Smithsonian Institution Press, 1983.

Smith, G. A. *The Historical Geography of the Holy Land*. London: Hodder & Stoughton, 1915.

Smith, R. W., and D. B. Redford. *The Akhenaten Temple Project*. Toronto: University of Toronto Press, 1988.

Spencer, A. J. *Early Egypt: The Rise of Civilisation in the Nile Valley*. London: British Museum Press, 1993.

Strong, J. *The New Strong's Exhaustive Concordance of the Bible*. Nashville: Nelson, 1990.

Tacitus. *The Annals of Imperial Rome*. Trans. M. Grant. Harmondsworth: Penguin, 1956.

Taylor, J. *Petra*. London: Aurum Press, 1993.

Thomas, D. W., ed. *Documents from Old Testament Times*. London: Thomas Nelson & Sons, 1958.

Unterman, A. *A Dictionary of Jewish Lore and Legend*. London: Thames & Hudson, 1991.

VanderKam, J. *The Dead Sea Scrolls Today*. London: Oxford University Press, 1994.

Vermes, G. *The Dead Sea Scrolls in English*. Harmondsworth: Penguin, 1962.

Waddell, W. G., trans. *Manetho*. Cambridge, Mass.: Harvard University Press, 1940.

Wilkinson, A. *Pharaonic Egypt: The Bible and Christianity*. Jerusalem: Magnes Press, 1985.

Wilkinson, J. *Jerusalem as Jesus Knew It: Archaeology as Evidence*. London: Thames & Hudson, 1982.

Williams, D., ed. *New Concise Bible Dictionary*. Leicester: IVP, 1989.

Williamson, G., trans. *The History of the Church from Christ to Constantine*. Harmondsworth: Penguin, 1965.

Wilson, I. *The Exodus Enigma*. London: Weidenfeld & Nicolson, 1985.

Wiseman, D., ed. *Peoples of the Old Testament*. Oxford: Clarendon Press, 1973.

Yadin, Y. *Hazor: Great Citadel of the Bible*. London: Weidenfeld & Nicolson, 1975.

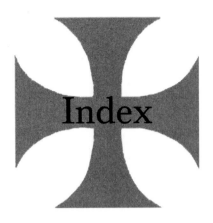

Index

BOOKS OF RELATED INTEREST

Atlantis and the Ten Plagues of Egypt
The Secret History Hidden in the Valley of the Kings
by Graham Phillips

The Chalice of Magdalene
The Search for the Cup That Held the Blood of Christ
by Graham Phillips

The Templars
Knights of God
by Edward Burman

The Templars and the Assassins
The Militia of Heaven
by James Wasserman

Art and Symbols of the Occult
Images of Power and Wisdom
by James Wasserman

The Mystery of the Copper Scroll of Qumran
The Essene Record of the Treasure of Akhenaten
by Robert Feather

Montségur and the Mystery of the Cathars
by Jean Markale

The Church of Mary Magdalene
The Sacred Feminine and the Treasure of Rennes-le-Château
by Jean Markale

Inner Traditions • Bear & Company
P.O. Box 388
Rochester, VT 05767
1-800-246-8648
www.InnerTraditions.com

Or contact your local bookseller